The Clash of *Ijtihad*

Fundamentalist

The Developme

Contem

The Clash of *Ijtihad*
Fundamentalist *versus* Liberal Muslims

The Development of Islamic Thinking in Contemporary Indonesia

Editor

HISANORI KATO

Religion, Politics and Society Series, No. 3

2011

(Dr.) Vladimir Ionesov

> Samara International Society for Cultural Studies, Moscow State University of Service in Samara, Russia

(Dr.) Dennis Walker

> Monash Asia Institute, Melbourne, Australia

(Prof.) Brikha Nasoraia

> Visiting Professor in Arabic Literature, Emirates University, United Arab Emirates

(Rev. Prof.) George E. Tinker

> Professor of American Indian Cultures and Religious Traditions, Iliff School of Theology, USA

Series Editors

Rev. Raul Fernández-Calienes, Ph.D., St Thomas University, Miami, Florida, USA

Em. Prof. Garry W. Trompf, Ph.D., University of Sydney, Australia

Series Titles

1. *The World of Religions: Essays on Historical and Contemporary Issues*, edited by Garry W. Trompf and Gildas Hamel, 2001
2. *Root of David: The Symbolic Origins of Rastafari*, by Matthew Charet
3. *The Clash of Ijtihad – Fundamentalist versus Liberal Muslims: The Development of Islamic Thinking in Contemporary Indonesia*, edited by Hisanori Kato

Correspondence in the first instance to be directed to:

Garry W. Trompf, Emeritus Professor in the History of Ideas, Department of Studies in Religion, University of Sydney, NSW 2006; or trompf.editorial@arts.usyd.edu.au

The Clash of Ijtihad – Fundamentalist versus Liberal Muslims
Muslims

The Development of Islamic Thinking in Contemporary Indonesia

Religion, Politics and Society Series, No. 3

Contents

Foreword — *Garry W. Trompf* ix

Introduction
Social Demand and the "Clash of *Ijtihad:*"
A Constructionist Approach to Current
Islamic Movements in Indonesia
— *Hisanori Kato* xi

1. Debates on Islam and Secularism in Indonesia
— *Luthfi Assyaukanie* 1

2. Islam, Humanity, and the Equality for Women
— *Lily Zakiyah Munir* 19

3. The Need for Historical Perspectives
in Understanding Islam
— *Abdurrahman Wahid* 35

4. The Concept of *Jihad* and *Mujahid of Peace*
— *Zakiyuddin Baidhawy* 40

5. The Position of Women in Islam:
Criticism on the Compilation of Islamic Law
in Indonesia
— *Siti Musdah Mulia* 58

6. Homosexuality in Islam: Coming out of the Dark
— *Soffa Ihsan* 91

7. What is Right in Islam?
    Ideas of Abu Bakar Ba'asyir
            – An interview with *Abu Bakar Ba'asyir*   109

8. Caliphate, *Sharia* and the Future of *Umat*
            – *M. Ismail Yusanto*   118

9. Ethnic Identity, Nationalism, and Islam
            – *Eka Jaya*   144

10. Life From Muslim Women's Point of View
            – *Qothrun Nadaa*   156

11. Islam as Life's Solution
            – *Cecep Firdaus*   164

12. Islam and *Pancasila*: The Message of a Former Judge
            – *Bismar Siregar*   182

13. Progress of the Country with Justice and Prosperity
            – *Zulkieflimansyah* and *Yon Machmudi*   187

14. The Role of Islam in Politics: Struggling for
    Political Peace, Justice, and Mercy of Islam
            – *Andi M. Ramly*   195

15. Islamic Politics and Political Islam:
    A Standoff between Islam and the State
            – *Andi M. Fatwa*   204

On the Affiliations of the Indonesian Authors **213**

I have been asking myself, who has spent more time researching the complex relationships between religion, politics and society in Indonesia than the Japanese scholar Dr Hisanori Kato? A man committed to the peaceful co-existence between religious groups in Southeast Asia (for he has also written extensively on conflict in the Philippines), Dr Kato has patiently made contact after contact to assemble an extraordinary collection of Indonesian thinkers who all help explain the colour, tensions and complexity of Indonesian Islam. From a former President to active politicians, from stalwart defenders of *sharia* law to liberals against the very idea of Indonesia becoming an Islamic state like Malaysia, from jurists to radical journalists, defenders of women's rights to Muslim revivalists (even one supposedly abetting terrorist acts), Dr Kato has arranged them all in a gallery of variant 'interpreters.' We are thereby privileged to contemplate key issues preoccupying Indonesian Muslim thinkers today: the positions of political parties, the responses to modernity, the competition between political and religious pressures, the challenges presented by cultural plurality, gender or sexual difference, and especially the conflict between modes and methods of interpreting Islam (*ijtihad*). The panorama is indeed striking when set before us in full view, and readers will be truly grateful for Dr Kato's labour of personal engagement to bring such a diversity of 'players' together in the one spectacle.

This is the first of two books by Dr Kato on Indonesia. A second work will follow on the development of religious organizations during the Suharto years and the time of the New Order government. In a shortened version, this has already been published in Indonesian, but the full version is worth seeing the light of day, arising as it does from his doctoral dissertation in Studies in Religion at the University of Sydney. As my former student at Sydney, Dr Kato has done my own Australian university proud for taking his training in the sociology of religion to the people of Southeast Asia, allowing voices, sets of opinions and ideological platforms to be aired in their own terms while at the same time revealing the points of conflict and complementariness. To my mind, he has been doing something quite unique as a researcher, attending as he does to the issue of mutual understanding, not just the amassing and analyzing of data. And all this is unusual work for a Japanese scholar, to step quite outside his cultural framework, study for the highest degree in another country, and then immerse himself in the languages and cultural patterns of Southeast Asia. He used to remind me, admittedly, that the Japanese, in their retreat at the end of the Second World War, ensured the declaration of Indonesia's independence, a point which I, with my Dutch ancestral connections, was supposed to take very seriously! But Dr Kato has always used his knowledge of detail and background to point beyond conflict towards the means of peace through dialogue and shared understanding; with our 'cards laid bare on the table' as it were, we find it harder to project false positions on to 'the other,' and more readily face up to honest difference or possible *rapprochement*.

I heartily recommend this collection to its readers.

Garry W. Trompf
University of Sydney

Introduction
Social Demand and the "Clash of Ijtihad"

A Constructionist Approach to Currrent Islamic Movements in Indonesia
— *Hisanori Kato*

R acial and cultural diversity is a distinctive feature of Indonesia. At the same time, the country's diversity has the potential to be the cause of socio-religious fractures in the Republic of Indonesia. It is, therefore, understandable that Indonesia has adopted *Bhinneka Tunggal Ika*, or Unity in Diversity, as its state motto – with a view to maintaining its coherence as a nation.

Yet, it is a well known fact that Indonesia has experienced various conflicts originating in differences of race and religion among its citizens. Although mutual respect and understanding, regardless of one's race and religion, undoubtedly exist among Indonesians, we have to admit that Indonesia is vulnerable to frictions that could lead the country into disunity.

Islam, the majority religion in Indonesia, is by no means a single entity. Scholars have already indicated several different strands within *umat* Indonesia, such as *santri* versus *abangan*, and traditionalist versus modernist.[1] After the end of the New Order

---

[1] See, for example, C. Geertz, *The Religion of Java*, Chicago, 1976.

period, however, a conspicuous antipathy in the Islamic community has started to emerge, namely, the disagreement between so-called fundamentalist and liberal Muslims. One of the founders of the liberal movement *Jaringan Liberal Islam* (Network of Liberal Islam), Ulil Abshar-Abdalla received death-threats when he published an article expressing "liberal views" in 2002.[2] More recently, a state-sponsored council for religious scholars known as MUI (*Majelis Ulama Indonesia*) issued eleven theoretically rigid *fatwas*, including the disapproval of liberalism in Islam in July 2005. These *fatwas* immediately invited opposition from liberals.

It seems that interpretation of Islam by fundamentalists and liberals patently clashes as they exercise their *ijtihad* or human reasoning. Muslims themselves often develop religious debates on specific matters, such as the interpretation of *jihad*, since, in sharp contrast to Catholicism, there is no single religious authority which determines official beliefs within Islam. These religious disagreements, if not feuds, could be a cause of frictions within the *umat* (or 'Congregation') of Islam. Each *ijtihad* is based on "the correct interpretation of scriptures" that contain the truth of their faith as they respectively insist. Why fundamentalists and liberals clash, in most in-house theological explanation, is usually put down to the alleged fact that the "other side" wrongly interprets Islam. The sociology of religion, however, can offer a different explanation of discord among Muslims. Since we understand that religion and society have been deeply intertwined throughout history, it is worth analysing the societal conditions, including the changes within a given society, in order to obtain a clearer picture of the complex interactions within the Islamic community in Indonesia.

Social Change and Religion

It is probably true that, after China, Indonesia has experienced the most rapid and drastic changes in the world over the last decade. Since the fall of Suharto, the Indonesian political system,

---

[2] His article was published in the daily newspaper *KOMPAS* (18 November, 2002).

at least on its surface, has been democratized insofar as it has introduced a multi-party election system and direct presidential election. Citizens of Indonesia express their political opinions more freely today than during the New Order period. Hardliners in the Islamic community were among the beneficiaries of these democratic changes. After having been suppressed for more than 30 years, so-called fundamentalists have begun to establish a base for propaganda activities. These include the formation of *Front Pembela Islam* (FPI) in 1998 and *Majelis Mujahidin Indonesia* (MMI) in 2000.

As with any other part of the world, historical progress or social change in Indonesia takes place not only in the sphere of politics but also in the fields of culture and society at large. As Western capital pours into Indonesia, this highly populous Muslim country seems to be growing increasingly modernized, indeed Westernized. Western-style shopping malls have mushroomed in Jakarta and in other urban cities throughout the archipelago; American pop culture dominates the lives of Indonesian teenagers; Indonesians have access to dozens of television programmes from all over the world via satellite. Modern technology enables Indonesian to have an online lifestyle, including using more sophisticated bank cards for cash withdrawals, shopping, and utilities payments. With more Westerners residing in the country, restaurants and cafes aimed at foreigners have also become lucrative businesses, with the result that more Indonesians mingle with Westerners and are exposed to Western ways of life and thinking. As Richard Robinson explains, economic development has accompanied the emergence of a middle class in Indonesia:

> The wealth generated by such industrial growth is symbolically manifest in the canyons of skyscrapers that now constitute the major arteries of Jakarta; Jakan Sudirman and Jalan Rasuna Said. That this wealth spreads beyond the corporate world and increasingly embraces a growing middle class is to be seen in a range of indicators.[3]

---

[3] R. Robinson, "The Middle Class and the Bourgeoisie in Indonesia", in *The New Rich in Asia* (eds. R. Robinson and D. S.G. Goodman), New York, 1996, p. 79.

The material advances in Indonesia are among the most significant social changes that Indonesians have ever experienced.

The patterns of societal change vary. However, it seems useful to accept Ernst Gellner's thesis regarding the relationship between social change and religious orientation. He explains that social transformation in modern times is characterized by changes in societal orientation, namely, the transformation "from closed, stable and culturally diversified communities to standardized, mobile, anonymous mass societies."[4] This paradigm of social change is fairly similar to what has taken place in Indonesia. When society becomes "standardized, mobile, and anonymous", Muslims, according to Gellner, tend to be more religiously observant, whereas Westerners are more inclined to become nationalistic.[5] Geller's theory accounts for the emergence of fundamentalist groups in Indonesia in the post-Suharto era since Indonesian society has been transformed in the same way as Geller describes.

We can also assume that there exists a group of people who have been excluded from the broader path of social development. The lower middle class, who have less access to "development," tend to search for ways to express their dissatisfaction either through "ultra-nationalism" or "reactionary religious groups."[6] It is plausible that this "excluded" group is inclined to be more politically vocal as Muslims.

However, the primary cause of fundamentalism's prominence is still unclear. The reason for the emergence of liberal movement is also undisclosed. We should remember two crucial points for understanding both liberal and fundamentalist movements in Indonesia. First, the terminology relating to Islamic movements needs to be understood more precisely. This issue will be discussed in the next section. Second, it is necessary to analyse the

---

[4] E. Gellner, *Nationalism*, London, 1997, p. 83.

[5] *Ibid.*

[6] R. Robinson, loc. cit., p. 88.

characteristics of social change and the socio-cultural background of Indonesia.

Although various functions of religion have been identified by religious sociologists in the past, it seems inappropriate to determine a fixed and single role of religion in a society. Religion is, in a sense, a versatile organism, which means that religious orientation is influenced and affected by it surroundings.[7] This requires careful observation of a given society. In other words, we would fail to comprehend the cause and the meaning of religious phenomena correctly if we failed to attend to each society's uniqueness.

My assumption is that any religious phenomenon is reflective of social circumstances and changes; religion as such is a complex organism that can take several directions. Several scholars have already suggested that fundamentalism is influenced by socio-political developments. Abdullahi Ahmed An-Na'im believes that fundamentalist movements should be viewed as "an indigenous spontaneous response to profound social, political and economic crisis" and these movements are "both products and agents of social change in Islamic societies and communities."[8] This view is echoed by L.K. Choudhary who insists that Islamic fundamentalism is the response to adverse economic circumstances in Islamic communities.[9] James Beckford offers a more precise explanation of his constructionist approach to religious phenomena: "The meanings attributed to religion, are in part, a product of social interaction and ne ons and whole societies."[10] Following these principles of sociology, the hypothesis is that social content – community composition, political situation, influences from the outside world, and history – is a key determinant of the direction taken by religion.

---

[7] H. Kato, *Agama dan Peradaban*, Jakarta, 2002, p. 306.

[8] An-Na'im, "Islamic Fundamentalism and Social Change," in *The Freedom to Do God's Will* (ed. G Harr), New York, 2003, p. 25.

[9] Choudhary, "Challenges of Islamic Fundamentalism: Problems and Possibilities," *India Quarterly* 57, 3 (2001): 6.

[10] Beckford, *Social Theory and Religion*, Cambridge, 2003, p. 197.

Semantic Pitfalls in Naming Islamic Movements

Overwhelmed by Western or Christian civilization, Islam has, unfortunately, a negative connotation in the world today. This is particularly visible in the Western media, especially CNN and Fox News. Terms such as fundamentalism and radicalism are frequently used when referring to violent acts by "Muslims." It is misleading. Although a particular act may have been carried out by someone claiming to be Muslim, the perpetrator only happens to be a Muslim. In addition, militarism and fundamentalism are two different characteristics. The former denotes a willingness to use force to achieve religious or political goals, while the latter refers to a religious attitude of strict adherence to original scriptures with less flexibility towards "new-fashioned" interpretations of the faith. Radicalism originally meant first; it comes from the Latin word for root, *radix*. In this respect, fundamentalists and radicals, at least semantically, share a common frame of reference, and they differentiate themselves from militants. Terrorism only ever sides with militarism, accordingly, while fundamentalism and/or radicalism does not necessarily amount to supporting of terrorism.

Another important element in a society is religious conservatism, which is often confused with fundamentalism. Journalists and even some scholars often fail to understand the difference between the two groups. In Indonesia, conservatism is more manifest among the masses, who are not necessarily as religiously strict as fundamentalists. They tend to pursue goals of personal welfare. However, the masses are inclined to emphasize superficial religious sentiment in their lives. The lifestyle of these people seems religious in that they like to wear religious clothes; they like to participate in rituals, including prayers; they like to use religious terminology; they even emphasize their religion when protesting governmental policies. For example, if there is a political demonstration organized by a fundamentalist group to protest against a governmental policy of, say, increasing taxes, a number of Muslims, including housewives who wear *jilbab*, will participate in the rallies. However, this does not necessarily mean that all participants in the demonstration are as pious as fundamentalists who are able to read *al-Quran* in Arabic and strictly observe their religious duties without exception. The primary concern of the masses is the price of rice rather than the religious crisis that is taking place outside the country. And yet they still choose to adopt a religious perspective when expressing their worldly wishes and opinions; in the name of religion they feel their actions are sacred and authorized by God. This is what has happened in Indonesia, and we should not confuse it with fundamentalism.

Understanding liberalism, on the other hand, is less complicated. Montgomery Watt, for one, clearly defines liberal Muslims:

> ... Muslims who appreciated much of the Western outlook and felt that the implicit criticisms of Islam were partly justified, but who at the same time thought of themselves as Muslims and wanted to live their lives as Muslims.[11]

It is true that these liberals have much greater access to Western academic trends and are much more easily accepted in Western academic circles. However, the movement led by "liberals" can only be appreciated by urban elites since their semantic complexity prevents the non-intellectual masses from understanding them. The absence of leadership, according to Watt, would hinder liberal movements in Islam.[12] An Indonesian researcher also points out that the naming of liberal movements – for example, Liberal Islam – is provocative, since it suggests there is a non-liberal Islam.[13] We can also assume that the cause of the rift between fundamentalists and liberals may be psychological.

With regard to its direction, liberalism, like fundamentalism, has both ideological and social qualities. However, liberals also openly admit the necessity of considering social conditions or

---

[11] Watt, *Islamic Fundamentalism and Modernity*, New York, 1988, p. 62.

[12] *Ibid.*, p. 69

[13] K. Zada, "Diversifikasi Islam, 'Why Not'?" *Media Indonesia* (23 August, 2002).

reality in the secular world when determining the course taken by religion. The liberal movement in Indonesia, then, is not only a religious movement but also a social movement that is influenced and encouraged by the condition of society. In short, even though both fundamentalism and liberalism have social and ideological aspects, the former places greater emphasis on religious ideology while the latter includes more societal concerns in its movement.

To understand religious phenomena, it is vital to understand what constitutes religion. Durkheim claims that "beliefs" and "rites" are the two important elements for understanding religion.[14] The former can be related to theology while the latter can be any action or occurrence that goes by the name of religion. Although Durkheim may have meant that rites are only limited to religious rituals conducted in religious buildings, it is the view of this author that rites should be understood more broadly: rites are all phenomena that have a religious aspect. We see two distinctive qualities in RELIGION, which we can call *religion* (which relates to the identity of the people) and *religiosity* (which is related to sociality).

RELIGION comprises two essential elements, that is, Holy Scriptures and appellation. *Religion* mainly deals with principles and dogmas, and religiosity is more broadly connected with occurrences in society, so that one might say that any action carried out with a religious sentiment is the outcome of religiosity. *Religion* is a solid set of ideas and ethics that hardly change, while religiosity flexibly exerts religious emotionalism, which could bring both positivity and negativity towards social realities. A civil war between religions exposes the negative side of religiosity. The volatility of religiosity is affected by social conditions. In other words, it is inappropriate to judge a certain religion by looking only at the negative side of religiosity, as is the case in the Western media's treatment of Islam.

---

[14] E. Durkheim, *The Elementary Forms of the Religious Life* (trans. K.E. Fields), New York,1995, p. 34.

Regarding Islam, Mahmood Mamdani astutely differentiates between political Islam and Islamic fundamentalism.[15] We can understand that fundamentalism as a religious phenomenon is connected with belief or *religion*, while political Islam falls into the category of rites or religiosity. Despite Mamdani's claim that political Islam has little to do with terrorism,[16] terrorist acts can be still the manifestation of religiosity as it pertains to religious emotionalism.

Subjectivity in Understanding Religion

A question arises here in relation to the stability of *religion*. If *religion*, upon which fundamentalism is based, is unchangeable, how can fundamentalism be influenced by social conditions? It is important to note that *religion* exists objectively, but *religion* also can be interpreted by humans subjectively. Since humans are always exposed to and reacting against societal change, fundamentalists vary in terms of their behaviour, but not in their beliefs, which means that what fundamentalists 'hold' can change quickly from *religion* to religiosity. In a way, this is natural and imperative since Islam encourages "the totality of life" that requires involvement in politics.[17]

As society has been industrialized, according to Beckford, it becomes less traditional and more welcoming of individual freedom of choice in religion.[18] As he explains:

> The scope of individual choice also extends to the ways in which individuals choose to express their religious beliefs and to use their religion. 'Individualization' is therefore presented as the key process in religious change.[19]

Although this type of individualization of religion tends to happen to the followers of new religious movements, it also holds true of

---

15 Mamdani, *Good Muslim, Bad Muslim*, New York, 2005, p. 37.

16 *Ibid.*, p. 59.

17 J.L. Esposito, *Islam*, New York, 2002, p.151.

18 J. Beckford, op. cit., p. 209.

19 *Ibid.*, p. 210.

organized world religions, including Islam, of which followers enjoy autonomy in the formation of religious convictions. However, while liberals seem tend more strongly towards individualization of religion, fundamentalists remain attached to values which they believe to be traditional and authentic. Yet the question is: what is truly "traditional" and authentic" in Islam? This sort of individualization relates to "emotional and subjective styles of religiosity,"[20] and is prone to provoking conflict when disagreement occurs between followers of the same religion.

Peter Berger and Thomas Luckmann also emphasize subjectivity in understanding social reality. Comprehending the world, they argue, requires a dialectical process which consists of three steps, namely, externalization, objectivation, and internalization.[21] Externalization takes place when humans "do" something in society. Symbols, as the result of externalization, form the basis of the common understanding of social reality that is objectivation. Finally, humans participate in the process of societal development. The focal point of their argument is that although something exists objectively, it still can be the result of subjective actions such as "interpreting" or "looking." When Muslims build a mosque or read *al-Quran* (externalization), their actions have outcomes, i.e., objects, which "objectively" exist as a religious building or the understanding of the creed of Islam. Muslims engage in their lives as followers of Islam after the goal and truth of Islam have already been revealed. Yet, their understanding of the Islamic teachings and opinions about the design of the Mosque are subjective. Berger and Luckmann explain the inevitability of subjectivity in social reality as follows:

> A society in which discrepant worlds are generally available on a market basis entails specific constellations of subjective reality and identity. There will be an increasingly general consciousness of the relativity of all worlds, including one's

---

[20] *Ibid.*

[21] Berger and Luckmann, *The Social Construction of Reality*, London, 1996, p. 149.

own, which is now subjectively apprehended as 'a world', rather than 'the world'.[22]

There are several factors that encourage an individual and subjective apprehension of religion in an industrialized modern society. Advanced technology is one of the reasons why liberals emphasize the need for peace among religions. Liberals are aware that a single atomic bomb could lead to the destruction of the whole world in which the followers of all religions reside. Therefore, they insist that *jihad* means a struggle of Muslim individuals to become a better Muslim, not physical combat.

Westernization is another momentum to bring about "subjective" religious actions; the value of Western culture is to express "one's opinion" (or individual views) rather straightforwardly. The views of individual city-dwellers are valued more highly in Western society than those of people living in rural communities. Since Muslims in Indonesia are also exposed to the Western culture, it is understandable that there should emerge Muslims who do not hesitate to put a revolutionary interpretation upon Islam. As regards Westernization, the psychological element in the development of fundamentalism should not be overlooked. Because Western civilization is often equated to Christian civilization, fundamentalists undoubtedly feel a strong rivalry with, if not an inferiority complex towards Christianity. This strengthens the religious conviction of fundamentalists, who emphasize the "truth" of Holy Scripture. However, in the eyes of other, liberal, Muslims, fundamentalists are merely presenting their own interpretation.

Materialism, which has accompanied Westernization in Asia, is also an important factor in determining the attitude of people. Kenneth Clark believes that civilization today is epitomized by the appreciation of materialism. According to him, human beings are worshippers in a "religion of gain."[23] He explains the situation of the world after the industrial revolution thus:

---

[22] *Ibid.*, p. 192.
[23] Clark, *Civilization*, Harmondsworth, 1987, p. 230.

> Poverty, hunger, plagues, disease: they were the background of
> history right up to the end of the nineteenth century, and most
> people regarded them as inevitable – like weather.[24]

Although the world has changed, however, the consistently
inhumane realities has never disappeared; we still can see hideous
conditions today, especially in the so-called developing countries,
and including Indonesia.

It is hard to draw a clear line between *religion* and "religiosity"
as they are the both sides of the same coin. However, it is evident
that each religious phenomenon is affected by social conditions.
The orientations of both fundamentalist and liberal Muslims are
subject to social reality. Therefore, the social conditions within
which Islam exists should be carefully observed in order properly
to understand the nature of Islamic movements.

Socio-Political Realities in Indonesia and the Responses from Muslims

The contemporary world is more socially and politically interactive
than ever. Complex international politics affect domestic policies,
and advanced communication systems enable people's
spontaneous access to information about events taking place
anywhere in the world. Ever since the end of Cold War, the United
States (US) government has been in conflict with a number of
Muslim groups, and the attack of 11 September, 2001 showed the
depth of some Muslims' antagonism towards US policies. While
not supporting this extreme terrorist act, there is no question but
that Muslims around the world are generally discontented with
US government approaches to the problems in Palestine,
Afghanistan, and Iraq, and readily point out the hypocrisy of the
US claims to high moral ground. Declassified documents show
that the administration of Ronald Reagan tacitly approved the use
of chemical and biological weapons by the Iraqi government in
order to support Sadddam Hussein in his war with Iran.[25]

---

[24] *Ibid.*, pp. 227-228.

[25] See M. Dobbs, "Not so long Ago, Washington made Iraq a valued
ally," *International Herald Tribune* (31 December 2003).

However, the U.S. attacks on Baghdad in 2002 in order "to stop the use of chemical and biological weapons" aroused the indignation of Muslim communities around the world. Antagonistic and hypocritical US policies towards Islam are one of the key factors behind the fundamentalist view that Muslims should physically defend *umat* Islam when and because Muslims are being attacked.

Abu Bakar Ba'asyir explains that the concept of *jihad*, for instance, is an act of self-defence which results from physical confrontation or a state of war. Thus, Muslims only respond with force when they are physically threatened or attacked by enemies. The idea that "the use of weapons is permissible only in self-defence" is increasingly stated and maintained by fundamentalists these days. The fundamentalist concept of *jihad* gains strength from the situation in Iraq or Afghanistan. However, there is a possibility that Muslim militants who used to be merely fundamentalists are exploiting the situation to justify anonymous acts of terror against anyone. This is the line that separates militants and fundamentalists. Although Abu Bakar Ba'asyir, alleged to have been one of the leaders of *Jamah Isamiyah*, criticizes US policies, he still maintains the idea that, so long as Muslims are not physically threatened, debate should be the tool with which Muslims fight the enemy.[26]

Besides international politics, the domestic situation in Indonesia also affects Muslims' attitude. Their dire economic situation, above all the problem of poverty, offends the pride of many Muslims, and fundamentalists present Islamism as the solution to these problems. The desperate condition today, which was created by the blind glorification of materialism suggested by Clark, can be regarded as the time of darkness or *Jahiliyah* which dominated before Islam was revealed in the Arabian Peninsula during the seventh century. Fundamentalism can therefore be understood as a new 'revivalist' social movement to eradicate neo-*Jahiliyah* in the modern period.

---

[26] Interview with the author in Jakarta (21 January, 2007).

Thus, it is natural for fundamentalists to insist upon the restoration of the Caliphate and the replacement of the current national political system by one of better governance akin to the way Prophet Mohammad and other leaders ruled the Islamic community in the early period of Islam. The masses who advocate conservatism are likely to side with fundamentalists since they are profoundly affected by the dire economic situation. However, it is important to note that these religious conservatives, despite sharing the fundamentalists' view of the incompetence of the government, are not always identical with fundamentalists in that their primary concern is improving the economy, whether or not the Caliphate is restored. Once their worldly problems are solved, their eagerness to support fundamentalism may dwindle.

Social decadence is another problem in Indonesia. Crime and illegal drugs are ubiquitous in Indonesian society, and morality in general seems to be decline, which has contributed to widespread corruption. Fundamentalists find the solution for these social predicaments in the implementation of *syariat* Islam (or Sharia Law). While Islamic ideology teaches Muslims to embrace *syariat* Islam, the social reality of Indonesia further encourages a certain group of Muslims to adopt a legal system based on *syariat* Islam. In other words, the fundamentalists' conviction that *syariat* Islam is the best system has been reaffirmed by the troubled social reality in Indonesia. One fundamentalist group, FPI (Front Pembela Islam or Islam Defenders' Front), is so disturbed by the decadence of Indonesian society that it makes physical interventions to stop "immoral" activities – destroying cafés that serve alcohol during the fasting month of *Ramadan*, for instance, or launching a suit against the publisher of Indonesia's version of *Playboy* magazine.

Moral decay and economic problems in Indonesia are also a concern for liberal Muslims, but their interest lies in realizing a more egalitarian society. Although the majority of Indonesians are Muslim, Indonesian society is highly diversified in the area of religion. Many still remember the horrific Jakarta massacre of ethnic Chinese Indonesians, who are non-Muslim, during the rioting which took place when Suharto was forced to step down in May 1998. Although it has been argued that the riots were provoked and even planned by elements within the Suharto administration, it cannot be denied that some Muslims took part in the killings and attacked non-Muslims in the name of Islam. Note that this is the manifestation of the negative side of religiosity. Islam as a religion never endorses the killing of innocent non-Muslims, but the perpetrators of these crimes used the name of Islam to justify their deeds. Some Muslims in Indonesia, whom we call liberals, realizing the vulnerability of minority groups, have emphasized the importance of reconciliation and cooperation between Islam and other religions.

The establishment of the International Conference of Religion and Peace by liberal Muslim groups in 2000 is a clear response to the social reality that minority groups are exposed to discrimination and insecurity.[27] Here, we see a clear contrast between fundamentalists and liberals in that the former always prioritize the welfare and security of *umat* Islam, while the latter tend to treat all religious communities equally, placing greater emphasis on nationalism than Islamism. Thus it happens that when respective groups exercise their human reasoning or *ijtihad* for the interpretation of Holy Scriptures of Islam, their *ijtihad* will necessarily clash with each other. The cause of such clashes of *ijtihad*, as has been seen, can be found in social conditions as well as international politics. One might say that a complex societal reality contributes to the strengthing of Muslim religious convictions, which results in the clash of *ijtihad* in *umat* Islam in Indonesia.

Historical Construction and Islam

It is now clear that the social condition and the absence of absolute religious authority have brought about different attitudes and opinions among Muslims in Indonesia, which I am here calling the "clash of *ijtihad*." In this light, it is essential to analyse the

---

[27] See, e.g., Kato, "Interfaith Activities in Indonesia," in Z.L. Machackova (ed), *Social Aspect of Religiosity*, Bratislava, 2003.

archives of the historical reality that have affected the current situation in Indonesian society, since events and interactions among the population in the historical past have created the current social condition. Now the world's largest Muslim nation, Indonesia was dominated by Hindu-Buddhist civilizations prior to the arrival of Islam in the archipelago. C. Geertz explains the characteristics of Indonesian Islam thus:

> ... Indonesian Islam, cut off from its centres of orthodoxy at Mecca and Cairo, vegetated, another meandering tropical growth on an already overcrowded religious landscape. Buddhist mystic practices got Arabic names, Hindu Rajas suffered a change of title to become Moslem Sultans, and the common people called some of their wood spirits jinns; but little else changed.[28]

It is true that Islam in Indonesia has been influenced by pre-Islamic civilizations, and its distinguishable feature has been tolerance towards other religions, including animism. The establishment of the modern Muslim organization *Muahammadiya* in 1912, for example, was a reaction against a strongly rooted Indonesian version of Islam. *Adat* or traditional custom has been cherished by Indonesian Muslims throughout history. A prominent Muslim scholar in Indonesia, Dewi Fortuna Anwar, gives an excellent account of this orientation of Islam, replying as follows when asked by Vidiadhar Naipaul about her view of *adat* :

> When it comes to relations between men and God one should adhere to the pure form of Islam, not the syncretic form. We cannot be a good Muslim and adherer to polytheistic or animistic beliefs and practices. But when it comes to ordering the relations between man and his neighbours – how we live in society – each grouping has different need and customs.[29]

The liberal Muslims who came to prominence in the post-Suharto era can be seen as a legacy of the history of religion in Indonesia in which Muslims have traditionally been open-minded towards other faiths. A Javanese Christian poet suggests the complexity

---

[28] C. Geertz, op.cit., p.125.
[29] Naipaul, *Beyond Belief*, New York, 1998, p. 59.

and syncretic feature of religious scene in Indonesia in the following way:

> Six or seven feet below us here are many Hindu temples or Buddha temples or Hindu-Buddha temples, buried by eruption of Merapi a thousand years ago and also two thousand and fifty years ago. ... This creates work for people who want to study about Java culture and religion, because behind these phenomena we can catch the spirit of Javanese people today.[30]

The winner of the Nobel Prize for literature, Naipaul offers an interesting observation about the authenticity of religion, one which liberal Muslims in contemporary Indonesia would readily endorse:

> Religious or cultural purity is a fundamentalist fantasy. Perhaps only shut-away tribal communities can have strong and simple ideas of who they are. ... Converted peoples have to strip themselves of their past; of converted peoples nothing is required but the purest faith (if such a thing can be arrived at), Islam, submission. It is the most uncompromising kind of imperialism.[31]

In a way, the activities of liberal Muslims are tantamount to resistance against "uncompromising kind of imperialism." They are keen to facilitate religious dialogue between Islam and other religions, and they have formed an amicable relationship with non-Muslims. Consequently, they are destined to clash with those demand "religious purity," that is to say, fundamentalists.

In addition to the influence of pre-Islamic civilizations in Indonesia, one also needs to take into account the political history of modern Indonesia when examining the emergence of fundamentalist and hardliner Muslims. The 32-year regime of Suharto was by no means 'Islam friendly': all socio-political organizations, including religious ones, were forced to embrace the state ideology of *Pancacila*, which did not explicitly endorse

---

[30] *Ibid.*, p. 85.
[31] *Ibid.* pp. 59, 64.

the almighty Allah of Islam.[32] The Suharto era witnessed physical clashes between the New Order government and Muslims. One of the most conspicuous challenges made by Muslims to the government was the Tanjung Priok incident in 1984, which resulted in dozens of deaths and the arrest of prominent Muslims leaders.[33] As can easily be imagined, "Islamic indignation" towards a secularly-oriented authoritarian regime was growing, and Muslims enduring physical, psychological and ideological oppression had to wait until the fall of Suharto before they could voice their religious aspirations aloud and in the open. Evidently, both the religious and political history of Indonesia, and both ancient and modern, has contributed to the creation of two distinctive groupings, fundamentalism and liberalism, in *umat* Indonesia.

A Summary of the Contents of this Collection

The main purpose of this book is to present different interpretations of attitudes towards Islamic teachings among Muslims. The authors of the fifteen articles to follow show their *ijtihad* clearly and give us an opportunity to understand the diversity within *umat*. The editor of this book uses the terms "fundamentalist" and "liberal" as outlined above to place the positions of the contributors. However, some "fundamentalists" insist that fundamentalists as such have never existed, only good Muslims. The articles have been arranged in a particular order that is intended to reflect their respective religious perspectives. This has never really been done before. Although there is one related book

---

[32] The *Pancacila* consists of five principles: *Ketuhanan yang Maha Esa* (Belief in the one and only God); *Kemanusiaan yang adlil dan beradab* (Just and civilized humanity); *Persatuan Indonesia* (The unity of Indonesia), *Kerakyatan yang dipimpin oleh kebijaksanaan dalam permusyawaratan/perwakilan* (Democracy led by the wisdom of deliberations among representatives); and *Keadilan sosial* (Social justice of the Indonesian people).

[33] R. Cribb and C. Brown, *Modern Indonesia A History since 1945*, New York, 1995, pp. 142-143. See A.M. Fatwa, *Saya Menghayati dan Mengamalkan Pancasila Justru saya Seorang Muslim*, Jakarta, 1995 for the details of Tanjung Priok incident.

available, it concentrates on theological discussions of Islamic teachings,[34] while in the unique collection that follows the contributors focus much more on the socio-political aspects of Islam in Indonesia.

In Chapter One, Luthfi Assyaukanie, a leading figure of the Islamic liberal movement, clarifies the process of the development of secularism in Indonesia. He also argues that the secularization of a Muslim society such as Indonesia is essential in order to create a democratic state. Moreover, he emphasizes that secularism is not in conflict with Islam. Muslim reformists, who can also be called liberal Muslims, he notes, should strive to "liberate the religion" from conservative clerics. We can see his *ijtihad* clearly, which contrasts with those of other "fundamentalists." In Chapter Two, Lily Munir, a leading female activist in Islamic education, discusses the importance of paying attention to the historical role and treatment of women in Islam. She believes that the apparent discrimination against women in (Quranic) Islam derives from the historical situation in Arabia before the revelation. In her opinion, Muslims should therefore progressively alter their attitudes towards women. In Chapter Three, the late Abdurrahman Wahid, a prominent Muslim scholar and politician (indeed former President), also insists on the importance of the specific location of a religion. Both Munir and Wahid take the view that religions develop progressively over time. What is particularly interesting in Wahid's article is that he shows no antagonism towards fundamentalists and notes that he merely disagrees with some acts of so-called fundamentalists, whose religious convictions are not in question. We see here that Wahid clearly understands the difference between political Islam and fundamentalism. In Chapter Four, Zakiyuddin Baidhawy, a young Muslim intellectual who

---

[34] Abdullah Saeed (ed.), *Approaches to the Qur'an in Contemporary Indonesia*, Oxford, 2005. A reference book comprising some relevant articles by Souutheast Asian (including Indonesian) Muslims is also available: G. Fealy (ed.), *Voices of Islam in Southeast Asia: A Contemporary Sourcebook*, Singapore, 2006.

leads the liberal wing of a modernist organization Muhammadiyah, argues that the concept of *jihad* in Islamic history has been interpreted very diversely, while admitting that *jihad* has in the past taken the form of war. Since the future of humanity depends on how Muslims interpret and exercise *jihad*, he proposes the notion of a Muslim striving for peace, a *mujahid* of peace, who renounces violence in order patiently to endeavour to find solutions for conflicts with other religions. Musdah Mulia presents a theological argument for why Muslim women and men should be treated equally in Chapter Five. She focuses on the problems in current legal provisions, specifically, the Complication of Islamic Law (known as KHI) in Indonesia. She argues that KHI runs contrary to the undeniable fact that Islam affirms the equal status of men and women. In a clear example of the exercise of *ijtihad*, Mulia elaborates upon the origins of her interpretations of *al-Quran* (the Holy Book) and the *Hadith*s (traditions of the Prophet), and how she understands these texts. The suggestions made by Mulia about reforming KHI on the issue of marriage would appear to be not only a statement about marriage but, as an especially vivid manifestation of her *ijtihad*, a profound message to her fellow Muslims as to the future course of Islam. In Chapter Six, Soffa Ihsan presents a controversial view on homosexuals in Islam. He elucidates that Muslims have been no strangers to homosexual activities throughout history. He stresses the humanistic values in Islam and believes that Muslim homosexuals also should be blessed as other Muslims.

In Chapter Seven, the "fundamentalist" champion Abu Bakar Ba'asyir shows a steadfast commitment to the interpretation of Islamic teaching, refusing to deviate from what has been set forth in both *al-Quran* and the *Hadith*s. He rebuts progressive interpretation and arguments based on history, in which he differs radically from the attitudes and the ideas of liberals. However, it should be remarked that Ba'asyir renounces the use of violence as a means of attacking enemies. Rather, he insists that Muslims should limit their use of violence to self-defence and emphasizes the importance of discussion for solving conflicts and forgiving enemies. As discussed earlier, Abu Bakar Ba'asyir, if what he states in the paper is all true, should be seen as a strict fundamentalist, not a terrorist. In Chapter Eight, Ismail Yusanto, one of the leaders of Hizbut Tahrir Indonesia, examines discussions of the relevance of the Caliphate in the contemporary world. His main argument is that the restoration of Caliph and the implementation of *syariat* Islam are the solution for all socio-political problems in the world today. Significantly, he astutely explains the difference between a theocracy and a caliphate; for him the Caliph is a mere representative of the masses and can be replaced according to the will of the people. Liberals, however, would oppose this representative of the people as likely to create a dictatorial system that would stand in the way of recurrent replacement of the Caliph.

In Chapter Nine, Eka Jaya, a young activist from FPI, who attacked a café in Jakarta and was arrested, offers a rare account of activities which are often regarded as destructive. Interestingly, he makes much of his ethnic background as Betawi in relation to his activities. He explains that, as a Muslim and a Betawi, he is obliged to work hard to create a better society, and that his activities should be seen as a part of this process. Needless to say, the implementation of *syariat* Islam is an important item on Jaya's agenda, but he nevertheless tends to concentrate on activities intended to eradicate social evils. The views of Qothrun Nadaa, a female activist from Hizbut Tahrir, which are presented in Chapter Ten, differ from those of both Munir and Mulia. Nadaa insists that the social roles of men and women be inherently different, although both men and women should be treated equally as human beings. Her argument is based on the view that, because the two sexes have different biological attributes, it is, therefore, natural that both men and women be given different tasks in society. Like other "fundamentalists," Nadaa prioritizes the collective welfare of *umat* and believes that men and women alike should live within that paradigm. In Chapter Eleven, Cecep Firdaus, one of the leading figures in Tablig Jammat in Indonesia, discusses the role played by Islam in the pursuit of happiness. It should be noted that Tablig Jammat advocates a non-political stance for social activities. The absolute acceptance of *qadar* or divine will is a noticeable characteristic of this Islamic group, who believe that whatever a political leader does is the will of Allah. They think that inflation, for example, is the will of Allah, and that there will be a change for the better if Allah so desires. Firdaus firmly believes that absolute submission to Allah brings happiness, and that political action, such as encouraging the government to implement *syariat* Islam, is unnecessary.

In Chapter Twelve, Bismar Siregar, a former supreme court judge, gives a passionate account of the importance and the essence of *Pancasila*. A legal expert, he argues that the "values" inherent in *Pancacila* can form the core of a social morality is desperately needed in order to bring about legal justice in the country. At the same time, he enumerates the reasons why he believes that *Pancacila* is the most appropriate state philosophy for maintaining the coherence and the unity of the Republic of Indonesia. The last three articles were contributed by individuals who are deeply involved in politics in Indonesia. In Chapter Thirteen, we find Zulkieflimansyah and Yon Machmudi of the Justice and Prosperous Party (PKS) encourageing all Muslims to participate actively in a nation-building process. The establishment of PKS, according to them, was an important step for that process. It is true that, at the time of PKS's founding, the party was seen as aligned with those who were, politically and religiously, more conservative and rigid. However, the article shows clearly how PKS has shifted its position away from a religious orientation while still emphasizing the role of Islam in politics. It may be that this exemplifies the existence of religiosity in RELIGION by which socio-political circumstances influence the course taken by followers of a religion. In Chapter Fourteen, Andi Muawiyah Ramly, one of the executives of the National Awakening Party (PKB), clearly rejects the employment of any physical feature of *jihad*. He also believes that the role played by traditionalists in *umat* Indonesia represented by Nahdlatul Ulama is vital for the adaptation of Islam to socio-political realities today. In Chapter Fifteen, Andi M. Fatwa, former Vice-Speaker of the parliament and a former political prisoner, proposes a middle-way for enforcing *syariat* Islam. In his view, formal implementation of *syariat* Islam, which would also mean making Islam a state ideology, is irrelevant in a country such as Indonesia that supports cultural diversity. Therefore, Muslims in Indonesia should seek to exert Islamic influence upon existing state laws. Having been arrested and jailed for his involvement in the Tanjung Priok incident, Fatwa is understandably unhappy about seeing physical clashes between the state and Muslim groups or between Muslim groups and non-Muslim groups in Indonesia.

Conclusion

Like Indonesian society itself, the Islamic community in Indonesia is heterogenous, with different interpretations and attitudes towards its chosen religion. However, as we have observed, RELIGION itself has two distinctive features; *religion* and religiosity. The former is rather definite insofar as it deals with the ritualistic concerns of individuals, while the latter is more reactive towards social situations. Islamic movements in the contemporary Indonesia are the eloquence of religiosity; social change, international and national politics, and history etc., in fact, exert influence on the orientation of RELIGION.

However, it should be also remembered that *religion,* of which nature is objective, can be exercised subjectively and interpreted by its followers. Both fundamentalist and liberal Muslims are by no means independent of societal and historical change. One might say that RELIGION (consisting of both *religion* and religiosity) *qua* social entity can never escape social realities. RELIGION is thus a versatile organism that varies with the social reality, bringing either a positive or a negative presence to the world in which all of us live.

Further to the discussion above, several points warrant underscoring. First, it is quite inappropriate to brand a particular RELIGION on the basis of a single aspect of religiosity. This is a trap into which Western media and Westerners in general have tended to fall. Second, it is absolutely vital to examine the socio-cultural condition of society, or more precisely the construction of society, in order to be able to understand religious phenomena. In other words, social construction and history are determining factors on the course taken by a religion. Third, the future of any religion, including that of Islam, of course, lies in how the followers of that religion respond to "social demand" and to what extent they recognize the existence of religiosity. Lastly, it would appear that there are two dominant social discourses that influence the direction taken by both fundamentalist and liberal Muslims: the trajectory of civilization in the secular world, which suboradinates itself to materialism; and Western notions of superiority, which have often been embraced by many in the West.

As we have seen, the triumph of materialism can create social divisions, resulting in the rise of oppressed groups that are inclined to take drastic, even physical, religious measures against affluent ruling groups. Without justifying their brutal and unlawful acts, we might say that oppressed groups are victims of the "religion of gain." We know that modern civilization has brought convenience and efficiency to our lives. However, the irony is that it has created a situation in which people are victimized solely because of the pursuit of faster, better, and more efficient results.[35]

Less appreciation to Islamic civilization would also create social disarray; should that happen, the indignation and the rivalry of Muslims towards non-Muslims would be greater. In this context it is worth considering the statement made by Ferdinand Braudel:

> ... Islam has to modernize and adopt in large measure the technology of the West, on which the world now so much depends. The future hangs on the acceptance or rejection of this world civilization. ... Islam has often been denied the flexibility needed for so drastic a change. So much so, that numerous observers claim that, owing to its 'impermeable,' 'intransigent' heart, spirit and civilization, Islam will find all its efforts to modernize effectively blocked.[36]

---

[35] Kato, "Confrontation between Global and Local Civilizations," *Comparative Civilizations Review* 63, 2010.

[36] Braudel, *A History of Civilizations*, New York, 1993, p. 99.

As they face various problems, including that of the environment, both Muslims and non-Muslims urgently need to rethink the meaning of "modernization", a concept that is so often conflated with materialism. Braudel may be right in his assessment about the necessity of Islam to modernize if he means by modernization the creating of a more civilized society. However, as we have seen, if we continue to accept "modernization" and "materialism" blindly, the negative aspects of religiosity will only continue to proliferate.

References

An-Naim, Abdullahi Ahmed, "Islamic Fundamentalism and social change: Neither the 'End of History' nor a 'Clash of Civilizations'," in Harr, G.T and Busuttil J. J. (eds.), *The Freedom to Do God's Will*, London: Routledge, 2003, pp. 25-48.

Beckford, James, *Social Theory and Religion*, Cambridge: Cambridge University Press, 2003.

Berger, Peter and Luckmann, Thomas, *The Social Construction of Reality*, London: Penguin Books, 1996.

Braudel, Ferdinand, *A History of Civilizations*, New York: Penguin Books, 1993.

Choudhary L.K., "Challenges of Islamic Fundamentalism: Problems and Possibility," *India Quarterly* 57, 3 (July-Sept. 2001): 1-22.

Clark, Kenneth, *Civilization*, Harmondsworth: Penguin Books, 1987.

Cribb, Robert and Brown, Colin, *Modern Indonesia: A History since 1945*, New York: Longman, 1995.

Dobbs, Michael, "Not so Long ago, Washington made Iraq a valued ally", *International Herald Tribute* (1 January, 2003).

Durkheim, Émile, *The Elementary Forms of Religious Life* (trans. K.E. Fields), New York: Free Press, 1995.

Esposito, John L., *Islam*, New York: Oxford University Press, 2002.

Fatwa, Andi M., *Saya Menghayati dan Mengamalkan Pancasila Justru saya Seorang Muslim*, Jakarta: Pt Bina Ilmu, 1995.

Fealy, Greg (ed.), *Voices of Islam in Southeast Asia: A Contemporary Sourcebook*, Singapore: Institute of Southeast Asian Studies, 2006.

Geertz, Clifford, *The Religion of Java*, Chicago: University of Chicago Press, 1976.

Gellner, Ernest, *Nationalism*, London: Phoenix, 1997.

Haar Gerrie ter and Busuttil, James J. (eds.), *The Freedom to Do God's Will*, London: Routledge, 2003.

Kato, Hisanori, *Agama dan Peradaban*, Jakarta: Dian Rakyat, 2002.

———————, "Interfaith activities in Indonesia." In Zastvila Lucia (ed.) *Social Aspects of Religiosity*, Bratislava, 2003, pp. 187-195.

———————, "Confronting between Global and Local Civilizations," *Comparative Civilizations Review* 63 (2010), pp. 37-59.

Machackova, Z.L., (ed), Social *Aspect of Religiosity*, Bratislava: Institute of State-Church Relations, 2003.

Mamdani, Mahmood, *Good Muslim, Bad Muslim: America, the Cold War, and the Roots of Terror*, New York: Tree Leaves Press, 2005.

Naipaul, V.S., *Beyond Belief*, New York: Vintage International, 1999.

Robinson, Richard and Goodman D.S.G. (eds.), *The New Rich in Asia*, London: Routledge, 1996.

———————, "The Middle Class and the Bourgeoisie in Indonesia." In R. Robinson and D.S.G Goodman (eds.), *The New Rich in Asia*, London: Routledge, 1996, pp. 79-104.

Saeed, Abdullah (ed.), *Approaches to the Qur'an in Contemporary Indonesia*, Oxford: Oxford University Press, 2005.

Watt, Montgomery, *Islamic Fundamentalism and Modernity*, New York: Routledge, 1988.

Zada Khamami, "Diversifikasi Islam, 'Why Not'?" *Media Indonesia* (23 August, 2002).

1

Debates on Islam and Secularism in Indonesia

— Luthfi Assyaukanie

Introduction

On 28 July 2005, the Indonesian Council of Ulama (MUI, Majelis Ulama Indonesia) issued a *fatwa* on the illegitimacy (*haram*) of secularism, liberalism, and pluralism. This *fatwa* was among the eleven decreed by MUI and was the longest list of decrees the council had ever made. MUI has routinely released *fatwas* on various issues. Usually, a *fatwa* deals with concrete issues such as food, drink, and bank interest, or human actions such as eating and drinking. It is unusual that a *fatwa* deals with an abstract idea or concept. Therefore, the current *fatwa* on secularism, liberalism, and pluralism is considered by many as exceptional.

The *fatwa* is obviously an emotional reaction of MUI toward the growing number of liberal Islamic movements in the country. Since 1998, more and more Muslims from the younger generation declare themselves liberal. They have formed organizations, held discussions and published articles in the mass media. The central theme that they have promoted has been the idea of progress, freedom, and human liberty. They call for the need for rethinking

Islam and the necessity to be more open and honest about modernity. Most of these liberals are young Muslims of *santri* background. As explained by Geertz, the term *santri* refers to a group of Muslims who are committed to their faith. In the Indonesian socio-political context, *santri* Muslims are often contrasted with *abangan* Muslims. The latter are generally defined as nominal Muslims who are not so much concerned with their religion.[1]

The *fatwa* on secularism, liberalism, and pluralism was issued against this background. Young liberal Muslims have been tirelessly promoting the idea of secularism, liberalism, and pluralism. By decreeing such a *fatwa*, MUI obviously wanted to kill hundreds of flies with one blow. Unfortunately, the flies are too many and too strong to be crushed with one blow. Despite this *fatwa*, liberal Islamic movements remain strong. In fact, they reacted against the *fatwa* in a manner that was probably never imagined by the MUI itself.

The *fatwa* clearly reflects the tension between Islam and secularism and, in fact, between Islam and modern issues in general. In this respect, the *fatwa* is not new. Modern issues have been discussed by Muslims for the last 50 years or even a century as they encountered the modern world. MUI's reaction against secularism is part of the major debate between Islam and modernity that has prevailed in the region since the early twentieth century.

In the mid 1920s, a group of Muslim scholars in Yogyakarta, Bandung, and Jakarta issued a sort of *fatwa* that nationalism is forbidden (*haram*) in Islam. Led by such prominent Muslim figures as Agus Salim, Ahmad Hassan, and Mohammad Natsir, they condemned the nationalist leaders (later dubbed "secular nationalists") for having adopted and promoted nationalism (*kebangsaan*) as the basis of the Indonesian independence struggle. They argued that nationalism is an alien concept that could harm Islamic beliefs. Agus Salim specifically pointed out that the idea

---

[1] C. Geertz, *The Religion of Java*, Chicago, 1976 edn., pp. 125-130.

of nationalism could water down Muslim *tauhid* (divine unity).[2] Meanwhile, Hassan and Natsir associated *kebangsaan* with *'asabiyyah*, a concept of tribal partisanship known before Islam came into existence. By doing so, they wanted to say that nationalism is a concept of *jahiliyyah,* that is, a period in pre-Islamic Arabia regarded as full of disorder. Hassan expressed his view that to "set up a *kebangsaan* organization, to invite and persuade people to join *kebangsaan*, to assist a *kebangsaan* party, is forbidden in Islam."[3]

At the time, the nationalist bloc was led and represented by Soekarno and other nationalist figures considered to be *abangan* Muslims. By associating them with *abangan*, the argument was quite clear that they supported "un-Islamic" ideas (such as nationalism and later also secularism), because they were not concerned with Islam. However, as I will elaborate later, this association is not entirely acceptable, as there is a growing number of Muslims of recent generations from *santri* background who genuinely support nationalism, secularism, and other modern ideas.

The MUI's fatwa on secularism has thus to be seen in the context of this long-standing debate concerning Islam and modernity.

Secularism Denied

Secularism is of course an ambiguous concept. This is fairly understandable since the term even in its original context is vague. In the Western intellectual tradition, secularism has been discussed in various disciplines in such a way that each discipline has a particular definition that is different from the others. In philosophy, for instance, secularism is closely associated with an ideology that denies the existence of religious and mythical authorities. In sociology, it generally means a process by which the religious

---

[2] D. Noer, *The Modernist Muslim Movement in Indonesia, 1900-1942*, Singapore and New York, 1973, p. 254.

[3] *Ibid.*, p. 259.

authorities are declining. In political science, it broadly means a separation of religion and the state.[4] In the Islamic intellectual tradition, secularism, like many other modern terms such as nationalism, democracy, and pluralism, is a new concept. Muslims have different views on how to translate it exactly. In the Arab world, secularism is generally called *'ilmaniyyah* (that derives from *'ilm*) and *'almaniyyah* (deriving from *'alam*). However, several authorities use the word *"la diniyyah"* (literally: non-religious) and *dahriyyah* (deriving from *dahr*; literally: time). In Turkish, it is called *laiklik,* taken from Greek *"laos,"* the same root from which the French word *laicité* originates.[5] As in the Western world, the term secularism is used with different connotations. According to Elmissiri, an Egyptian writer who listed the usage of the word in modern Arabic sources, secularism has at least eighteen different definitions.[6]

---

[4] The word "secularism" was used for the first time in the mid-nineteenth century, when George Jacob Holyoake (1817-1906) introduced it as a political concept rather than a philosophical one. What Holyoake meant by secularism was simply a political ideology that demands a full separation of religion and politics. However, his radical followers such as Charles Bradlaugh (1833-1891), Annie Besant (1847-1933), and Edward Aveling (1849-1898) used the term in such a way that it came close to the idea of the rejection of God (atheism). For a further elaboration on the history of secularism see W.W. Wagar (ed.), *The Secular Mind: Transformations of Faith in Modern Europe: Essays presented to Franklin L. Baumer*, New York, 1982; J.M. Bonham. *Secularism; Its Progress and Its Morals.* New York and London, 1894; Talal Asad, *Formations of the Secular: Christianity, Islam, Modernity, Cultural Memory in the Present*, Stanford, Ca.: 2003.

[5] Aziz Azmeh, *Al-Almaniyah min manzur mukhtalaf*, Beirut, 1992 edn., p. 18; See also S. Morrison, 'Almaniya, Laiklik and Democracy in Egypt and Turkey' (Paper prepared for the American Political Science Association Annual Meeting, San Francisco, California, 29 August-September 2, 2001).

[6] Azzam Tamimi, "The origins of Arab Secularism." In Tamimi and J.L. Esposito (eds.) *Islam and Secularism in the Middle East*, New York, 2000, p. 17.

In Indonesia, the common term used has been *sekularisme*, a direct translation of the English word. However, some Muslim intellectuals also use its Arabic equivalents. Mohammad Natsir, an eminent Muslim leader who discussed this issue, surprisingly used the word *la diniyyah*, an Arabic translation of the term. The way Natsir selected this word illustrates his attitude towards the concept. Indeed, Natsir was one of the staunchest Indonesian Muslim intellectuals who stood out against secularism. He defined secularism as "a way of life which contains belief, aim, and attitude only within the worldly limit," and as an ideology that "does not recognize the afterlife and God."[7] This definition completely covers the Arabic term he used, namely *la diniyyah* (irreligious or anti-religion).

Sekularisme in Indonesia is commonly understood by Muslims as Natsir defines it. By this definition, Pancasila, the philosophical basis of the Indonesian state, is arguably not secular, since it recognizes God and emphasizes the importance of religion. However, for Natsir, Pancasila is a secular platform, since it is not entirely religious. It should be understood here that Natsir's opinion of Pancasila as secular was strongly determined by his own obsession to make Islam the basis of the state (or to support the idea of an Islamic state). He considered that an Islamic basis of the state is superior to Pancasila, since the former comes from God and the latter from humans. In his speech before the Constitutional Assembly on 12 November 1957, Natsir boldly stated:

> In Indonesia, the ideology that drives people has been religion, whose main character I have already explained. Thus, the basis of our nation should be religion, and not an idea that is unlikely to be accepted by all people, namely Pancasila. Pancasila is not considered to be a religion. Although it contains a divine principle (*sila Ketuhanan*), its source is secularism, *la diniyyah*, anti-religion. It does not derive from revelation. It is merely a human creation.[8]

---

[7] M. Natsir, *Islam Sebagai Dasar Negara*, Jakarta, 2000, p. 62.

[8] Idem, *Agama dan Negara dalam Perspektif Islam*, Jakarta, 2001 edn., p. 215.

Natsir's judgment of Pancasila as a secular ideology is crucial to understand Muslims' rejection of Pancasila during the first two years of independence. Although seen from the secular perspective, Pancasila is quite religious (since it puts belief in God as the first principle above any other principles),[9] yet for most *santri* Muslims at the time, it was a secular ideology.

Muslims' rejection of Pancasila as the basis of the state was actually not entirely due to the belief that Pancasila was a secular ideology. What bothered them more was the belief that Pancasila is a rubbery concept in that it can be claimed by many people to justify their political agenda. Natsir repeatedly emphasized this point. For the nationalists, it could be employed to support their secular programmes which might contradict Islamic values. While for the Communists, it could be utilized to fulfil their atheistic agenda which could certainly be against Islamic teaching. Muslims' opposition to Pancasila was mainly driven by these factors. In their view, the secular nationalists (PNI, Indonesian Nationalist Party) and the communists (PKI, Indonesian Communist Party) had used Pancasila to marginalize Islam.

With such a conspiratorial view, it was difficult for the older *santri* generation to see secularism positively, as it was, in their view, the crux of Pancasila ideology. It is important to note that what they meant by "secularism" here was no longer "anti-religion" (*la dini*), but more specifically "anti-Islam" (*la islami*). The reason is quite clear. This generation of *santri* from the very beginning did not want to share an independent Indonesia with their non-Muslim counterparts. They rejected Pancasila not because it was entirely secular or entirely anti-religion, but because it gave equal status to other religions and beliefs with no pre-eminence for Islam. They firmly believed that Islam should be given superiority.

---

[9] Pancasila has five principles: (i) Belief in One God; (ii) A Just and Civilized Humanity; (iii) The Unity of Indonesia; (iv) The Principle of Peoplehood Which is Guarded by the Spirit of Wisdom in Representation; (v) Social Justice.

It was a common view among *santri* Muslims that Islam (and thus Muslims) should be given a higher position to other religions and beliefs. This partly originated from the classical Islamic teaching that says "Islam is the highest religion and none should surpass it" (*al-Islam ya'lu wa la yu'la 'alayh*). Classical Islamic doctrine also considers non-Muslims to be second-class citizens. The concept of *dhimmi,* which is commonly known in Islamic jurisprudential tradition, is an Islamic term for the status of the non-Muslims who live in an Islamic state.[10]

The older generation of *santri* Muslims was strongly influenced by such a doctrine when they discussed such ideas as democracy and secularism. For them, secularism was an alien concept that harms Islam. Of course, what they meant by "Islam" is the particular kind of Islamic ideology that they constructed.

Secularism Justified

Among the older generation of *santri* Muslims, secularism was certainly the most despised political concept apart from communism. Some of them in fact mentioned it in the same breath as communism. The way Natsir used the unusual Arabic phrase *"la diniyyah"* for secularism indicates that he did not see much difference between the two ideas: both are against religion. There was no attempt on the part of *santri* Muslims to reconsider secularism before the early 1970s. Secularism remained a detested concept until Nurcholish Madjid came to the fore and wrote his

---

[10] *Dhimmi* means "under protection," to differentiate it from *harbi,* which means "under attack." The *dhimmi* are protected by the Muslim ruler, but in turn, they have to pay a special tax (*jizyah*), which is much more than Muslims (the first citizens) who have to pay alms (*zakah*). Although some of the older generation of *santri* Muslims tried to reinterpret such a doctrine, the classical Islamic framework was still strongly manifest in their thinking. Abidin Ahmad, Zainal, one of the prolific Muslim authors of the older *santri* generation, for instance, borrowed the classical Islamic doctrine to argue that non-Muslims are not allowed to become the head of state (see Abidin Ahmad, Zainal, *Membentuk Negara Islam,* Jakarta, 1956, p. 64).

controversial article in January 1970. In point of fact, Madjid's article was not only about secularism, but also about many notions that were previously taboo for the older generation of *santri* Muslims.

Madjid did not use any Arabic terms for the word secularism. He just simply used *"sekularisme"* and *"sekularisasi"* for both secularism and secularization respectively. It is important to note here that Madjid drew a clear distinction between the two terms. He defined secularism as "a new closed world view which functions very much like a new religion," and defined secularization as "every form of liberating developments."[11] By distinguishing these two terms, Madjid wanted to make it clear that while secularism could harm Muslim's belief, secularization does not. Muslims can go along with the secularization process without embarking upon secularism. In Madjid's understanding, while secularization deals with the process of liberation of the human mind from any ideological constraints, secularism is a sort of built-in ideology that must be avoided.

Madjid's conception of secularization must first of all be understood sociologically. He held the view that Indonesian Muslims have distorted the understanding of the hierarchy of values. They no longer understand what becomes the transcendental and the temporal values and they are too confused to figure out what is Islam and what is tradition and what is essentially metaphysical (*ukhrawi*) and what is a mere worldly matter (*dunyawi*). As a result, Madjid went on, they equate Islam with tradition; and for them, to defend Islam is equivalent to defending tradition. This confusion, Madjid argued, leads Muslims to an inability to respond to the development of contemporary thought.[12] The role of secularization is thus "to make what is worldly and to release it from the Muslim conception that it is *ukhrawi*."[13]

---

[11] N. Madjid, *Islam, Kemodernan, dan Keindonesiaan*, Bandung, 1987 edn., p. 207.

[12] *Ibid.*, p. 207.

[13] *Ibid.*

Madjid developed the idea of secularization from the modern sociological discourse about religion. He himself acknowledged that he borrowed the term and its meaning from Talcott Parsons and Robert Bellah, two leading sociologists. In Parsons's view, secularization as a sociological concept indicates the liberation of humans from mythological views of their life. And this does not necessarily mean oblivion for their religious faith.[14] As a matter of fact, the process of liberation is greatly inspired by religious belief. Bellah argues, for instance, that the process of liberation of mythologies (*takhyul*) in Islam is mainly due to the Islamic conception of *tauhid*, that is, a concept that requires Muslims to believe in one God by negating other gods (symbolized in the declaration "there is no god but God"). The myths are part of the "gods" that are to be eliminated.[15] Hence, Madjid boldly argues that "secularization is a consequence of *tauhid*."[16]

From this sociological perspective, Madjid elevates the idea of secularization into the political context. Since politics, in his view, is essentially a temporal matter which is different from religion, it is advisable for Muslims to clarify this very distinction. Secularization in the political context is thus to decide what is essentially religious and what is not. Madjid's agenda of secularization is basically targeted to make Indonesian Muslims aware that Islam in Indonesia has developed and changed in such a way that its development has less to do with Islamic political parties.

Islam has been practised not only by traditional Muslims who are generally found in rural areas, but also by "people in the higher social classes" in the urban centers. Whether or not there was an Islamic party, Islam would still develop and Indonesian Muslims were becoming more Islamic than ever. What Madjid wanted to

---

[14] Parsons, *Theories of Society; Foundations of Modern Sociological Theory*, New York, 1961, quoted in Madjid, op. cit., p. 258.

[15] R.N. Bellah, *Beyond Belief; Essays on Religion in a Post-Traditional World*, New York, 1970 edn., p. 151, quoted in Madjid, op. cit., p. 259.

[16] Madjid, op. cit., p. 259.

say is that Muslims have to acknowledge that the struggle to uphold Islam is not necessarily an exclusive right of Islamic political parties. Even, in many cases, "Islamic political parties have failed to build a positive and sympathetic image; they have an image that is opposite (for instance, the reputation of Muslims in corruption is growing)."[17] Finally, Madjid comes to the conclusion, which later becomes his famous catchphrase, "Islam, Yes. Islamic Party, No."

Madjid's criticism of Islamic parties was the first step to criticism of a more fundamental political idea, namely the Islamic state. During the 1950s, the concept of an Islamic state was identical with Islamic political parties. In fact, it was the ultimate agenda of Islamic parties. Muslim leaders such as Mohammad Natsir and Zainal Abidin Ahmad all supported this idea. Although they disagreed about using the term "Islamic state," the state formally based on Islam was the common agenda of most *santri* Muslims of the time.

Nevertheless, the attack on the idea of an Islamic state was not openly addressed until the early 1980s, when more and more intellectuals of the later generation of *santri* came into existence and played their social role. In 1982, Amien Rais, a *santri* intellectual of Muhammadiyah background, made the stunning declaration that "an Islamic state does not exist." What he meant is that Islam has no concept of an Islamic state. The nation-state, Rais argues, is a modern concept which did not exist in classical Islam. There is no specific doctrine, neither in the *Qur'an* nor in *Hadith*s (the Prophetic sayings), that asks Muslims to found an Islamic state.[18]

Amien Rais is certainly not an intellectual type like Madjid who genuinely believes in the integration of Islam and modernity.

---

[17] *Ibid.*, p. 205.

[18] M. Amien Rais, "Tidak Ada Negara Islam." In Nurcholish Majid and Mohamad Roem (eds.), *Tidak Ada Negara Islam: Surat-Surat Politik Nurcholish Madjid-Mohamad Roem*, Jakarta, 2000 edn., pp. xxii-xxiii.

Rais is well-known as a critic of Madjid's ideas. He openly rejected the idea of secularism and secularization altogether. But what should be noted here, despite his condemnation of both terms, Rais's declaration regarding the concept of Islamic state is exactly what Madjid meant by the positive result of secularization. In other words, although Rais rejects secularization, in Madjid's view, he has undergone a practical secularization.[19]

In spite of Rais's attitude towards secularism and secularization, his sharp criticism of the concept of an Islamic state has undermined the pillars of the ideological building of Islamic polity embraced by the older generation of *santri* Muslims. Rais's rejection of the idea of an Islamic state has paved the way for a more inclusive (if not secular) model of the state. This step was crucial in regard to the Muslims' attitude toward Pancasila, an ideology and the philosophical basis of the Indonesian state which used to be seen as secular and un-Islamic.

In 1984 or two years after the death knell of the idea of an Islamic state was sounded by Rais, Nahdlatul Ulama (NU), the biggest Islamic organization in Indonesia, proclaimed that they readily accepted Pancasila as not only the basis of the state, but also as the basis of their very organization. Although this decision was strongly driven by the government policy that all parties

---

[19] Rais's rejection of secularization is a typical example of the *santri* Muslim from the modernist camp. The term modernist Muslim generally refers to the Muhammadiyah. It could be said that most *santri* intellectuals from Muhammadiyah refused the idea of secularization, although in point of fact, they contribute to the secularization process, particularly in Madjid's terms. I have interviewed Dawam Rahardjo, the most liberal Muslim thinker of Muhammadiyah background. Although Rahardjo is very supportive of modern ideas and is known as the leading Muslim with a modern apporoach, he specifically denounced the idea of secularism and secularization. His argument is simply that Islam does not fit with either of these two terms. The same view was expressed by other Muhammadiyah leaders, Ahmad Syafii Maarif (the chairman of Muhammadiyah 2000-2005) and Din Syamsuddin (the Chairman of the Muhammadiyah in 2005-2015).

embrace the sole basis (*asas tunggal*) policy, NU's decision to acknowledge Pancasila as Islamic is a breakthrough in the discourse of Islam and secularism and generally in the relation of Islam and the state in Indonesia. Because of this acceptance, Pancasila was no longer seen as secular. It was rather considered as in line with Islam.

The man behind the NU's acceptance of Pancasila was undoubtedly the late Abdurrahman Wahid, the chairman of NU who is widely known as a liberal thinker. Wahid plays a significant role in the contemporary Islamic discourse in Indonesia. His religious background and education made him an authoritative intellectual, able to speak about religion and other modern issues. Although he rarely speaks about secularism, Wahid is very supportive of this idea. Like Madjid, Wahid believes that Indonesian Muslims are in extreme need of political secularization, since they are often manipulated by what he calls the religious adventurers who (ab)use religion for their own political interest. Wahid himself considers Indonesia not as a religious state, but as "a mild secular state." What he means by "mild" is that the Indonesian constitution and principles (Pancasila) formally recognize religion, but its laws and political administration mostly remain secular.[20]

Nurcholish Madjid, Amien Rais, and Abdurrahman Wahid are all important Muslim leaders of the newer *santri* generation. They have played a significant role in modernizing the religio-political discourse in Indonesia. During the 1980s, the three leaders very actively promoted liberal ideas in their Islamic communities. They campaigned for what is now widely known as "liberal Islam." After the downfall of Soeharto, the three leaders continued to play a crucial role in the national political landscape. In 1999, Abdurrahman Wahid was elected President of the Republic while Amien Rais was chairman of the People's Consultative Assembly (MPR).

---

[20] Abdurrahman Wahid, "Indonesia's Mild Secularism," *SAIS Review* 21, 2 (Summer-Fall 2001): 25-28.

Secularism Defended

Since the 1990s, more and more *santri* Muslims with liberal views came into prominence, engaging in the current Islamic discourse. Dozens of Islamic organizations were founded, promoting progressive and humanistic views of Islam. In Jakarta, Islamic NGOs like JIL,[21] Rahima, Lakpesdam, Puan Amal Hayati, P3M,[22] and LKAJ[23] have been in the frontline in promoting freedom, human rights and gender issues; while in other cities, NGOs like LKiS (Yogyakarta),[24] LKPMP (Makassar),[25] Syarikat (Yogyakarta), MiSPI (Aceh),[26] LK3 (Banjarmasin),[27] and eLSAD (Surabaya) [28] played the same significant role.

This generation of Muslims is generally more confident and more determined in discussing the modern issues. Not only can they accept such modern concepts as democracy, liberalism, pluralism, and secularism, but they also defend them and justify them with strong Islamic arguments. Greatly influenced by the later generation of *santri* intellectuals (Madjid and Wahid particularly), they consider those concepts as nothing but other expressions of certain Islamic values. Said Aqiel Siradj, one of the leading intellectuals of the younger generation, for instance, argues that Islam and secularism (or secularization) are harmoniously compatible, as he writes in the following statement:

---

[21] Jaringan Islam Liberal (Liberal Islam Network).

[22] Perhimpunan Pengembangan Pesantren dan Masyarakat (Association of Pesantren and Society Development).

[23] Lembaga Kajian Agama dan Jender (Institute of Religion and Gender Studies).

[24] Lembaga Kajian Islam dan Sosial (Institute of Islam and Social Studies).

[25] Lembaga Kajian Pengembangan Masyarakat dan Pesantren (Institute of Society and Pesantren Studies).

[26] Mitra Sejati Perempuan Indonesia (Indonesian Woman Coalition).

[27] Lembaga Kajian Keislaman dan Kemasyarakatan (Institute of Islamic and Social Studies).

[28] Lembaga Studi Agama dan Demokrasi (Institute of Religion and Democracy Studies).

> Unlike the doctrine of the church, since the very beginning Islam has tolerated secularism. In fact, it could be said that secularism is a characteristic of Islam! The character of life in Madinah established by the Prophet Muhammad bears historical witness to this. At that time, Muhammad drew a distinction between his position as a prophet on the one hand and as a head of state on the other. The Madinah Charter that formed the foundation of government at the time never mentioned Islam as a political basis. In fact, in a *hadith*, the Prophet says: *antum a'lamu bi umuri dunyakum* (in the worldly matters, you know better than me).[29]

Siradj is not a secular type of man like Soekarno or Soepomo. In fact he is more *santri* than many other *santri* in the 1950s who used to reject secularism (such as Mohammad Natsir). Siradj is a son of a Muslim *kiai* (Islamic scholar) who ran a big *pesantren* (Islamic boarding school) in West Java. He undertook all his studies in Islamic institutions. He holds his BA, MA, and PhD, from Saudi Arabia in Islamic studies.

The main argument that was used by the earlier generation of *santri* to refute the idea of secularism or secularization was that these ideas are against the basic principles of Islam, that is, Islam does not distinguish worldly matters from unworldly ones. However, for the later generation of *santri*, this basic principle is not all-encompassing, since the words "worldly" and "unworldly" are not self-explanatory. Masdar F Mas'udi, another intellectual of the later *santri* generation, distinguishes three kinds of Islamic doctrines to explicate these two ambiguous words. First, there are the doctrines which are characteristically private such as belief in God (creed), the belief in angels, the hereafter, and destiny. All these beliefs, Mas'udi argues, are private matters. What Muslims believe in terms of God and other metaphysical things cannot be made uniform (*diseragamkan*) by the state. Second, there are the doctrines which are characteristically communal (*keummatan*) concerning such things as rituals (prayer, fasting, and pilgrimage).

---

[29] Siradj, *Islam Kebangsaan: Fiqih Demokratik Kaum Santri*, [Jakarta], 1999, p. 164.

Several family laws (*ahwal al-shakhsiyyah*) are also included in this category. In this matter, Mas'udi argues, the state also has no right to interfere, for instance, in delegating the police to compel a Muslim to perform prayers or to fast. Third, there are the doctrines which are characteristically public such as *mu'amalah* (transaction), *jinayah* (criminal codes), and *siyasah* (politics). In this matter, Mas'udi argues, the state can interfere and in fact it has the right to be a regulator.[30]

Given this explanation, Mas'udi suggests that the separation of religion and state in Islam is possible, particularly in view of the first and the second category of Islamic doctrines. Matters like belief, prayer, fasting, and pilgrimage are not in the state's power to regulate. They must be separated from the state's interference.

Secularism is a crucial concept in the idea of liberal democracy. In fact, it is an indispensable foundation of it. It is simply unimaginable to have liberal democracy without political secularization. The younger generation of *santri* is fully aware of this. They consider secularization of Muslim society to be an essential requirement in embarking upon the establishment of a liberal democratic state. Without this secularization, liberal democratic values would not have a firm ground in society.

The rise of liberal Islamic movements in the last two decades has to be understood from this perspective. Organizations like P3M, Lakpesdam, JIL, and Rahima conscientiously believe in freedom and pluralism, and that these concepts will only work if liberal democracy is wholeheartedly accepted. The problem with the earlier generation of *santri* Muslims with regard to the relationship between Islam and democracy was mainly due to their cautious attitude towards the fundamental ideas of liberal democracy. Their total denial of secularism was a big hindrance to fully embarking upon the building of a liberal democratic sate. The later generation, on the other hand, generally look at the

---

[30] Masdar F. Masudi, "Hubungan Agama dan Negara," *Kompas* (7 August 2002).

modern concepts with constructive attitudes. For them, secularism is not a concept that must be contrasted with Islam. On the contrary, it should be understood within the framework of the changing situation of contemporary Islam.

Conclusion

As we can see from the above explanation, the debate on secularism is not new. It has been going on for the last five decades. One interesting point that should be underlined here is that there has been a dramatic shift in Muslims' understanding of the concept. Among the early generation, most *santri* Muslims entirely rejected the idea. However, at the present time, the concept is not only justified, but also is enthusiastically defended. The role of the later generation of Muslim intellectuals is doubly significant. Not only have they introduced liberal Western ideas to their Islamic community, but also they have justified them with Islamic arguments. Islamic arguments for secularism or for socio-cultural change in general, are crucial. They are as real and important as economic and political factors. The current fatwa of MUI must be regarded from this perspective. It is not a mere reaction against such concepts as secularism, liberalism, and pluralism. But it is against Islamic arguments for those concepts developed by *santri* Muslim intellectuals, whom they have long considered to be heretical. As the custodian of orthodoxy, MUI strikingly demonstrate a cautious attitude against any ideas which they considered heretical. But, for Muslim reformists, "heretical" ideas –if heresy is to mean a campaign against orthodoxy - are the correct way to liberate religion from the shackles of rigidity (*kejumudan*) maintained by its clerics.

References

Ahmad, Zainal Abidin, *Membentuk Negara Islam*, Jakarta: Widjaya, 1956.

Asad, Talal, *Formations of the Secular: Christianity, Islam, Modernity, Cultural Memory in the Present*, Stanford, Ca.: Stanford University Press, 2003.

Azmeh, Aziz. *al-Almaniyah min manzur mukhtalaf*, Beirut: Markaz Dirasat al-Wahdah al-Arabiyah, 1992 edn.

Bellah, Robert Neelly, *Beyond Belief: Essays on Religion in a Post-Traditional World*, New York: Harper & Row, 1970 edn.

Bonham, John M., *Secularism; Its Progress and Its Morals*, New York and London: G. P. Putnam's sons, 1894.

Geertz, Clifford, *The Religion of Java*, Chicago: University of Chicago Press, 1976 edn.

Madjid, Nurcholish, *Islam, Kemodernan, dan Keindonesiaan*, Bandung: Mizan, 1987 edn.

Masdar F. Masudi, "Hubungan Agama dan Negara," *Kompas*, (7 August 2002).

Morrison, Scott, 'Almaniya, Laiklik and Democracy in Egypt and Turkey' (Paper prepared for the American Political Science Association Annual Meeting, San Francisco, California, 29 August-September 2, 2001).

Natsir, Mohammad, *Agama dan Negara dalam Perspektif Islam*, Jakarta: Media Da'wah, 2001 edn.

______________, *Islam Sebagai Dasar Negara*, Jakarta: DDII, 2000.

Noer, Deliar, *The Modernist Muslim Movement in Indonesia, 1900-1942*, Singapore and New York: Oxford University Press, 1973.

Parsons, Talcott, *Theories of Society; Foundations of Modern Sociological Theory*, New York: Free Press of Glencoe, 1961.

Rais, M. Amien, "Tidak Ada Negara Islam." In Nurcholish Majid and Mohamad Roem (eds.), *Tidak Ada Negara Islam: Surat-Surat Politik Nurcholish Madjid-Mohamad Roem*, Jakarta: Djambatan, 2000 edn.

Siradj, Said Aqiel, *Islam Kebangsaan: Fiqih Demokratik Kaum Santri*, [Jakarta]: Pustaka Ciganjur, 1999 edn.

Tamimi, Azzam, "The Origins of Arab Secularism." In Azzam Tamimi and John L. Esposito (eds.), *Islam and Secularism in the Middle East*, New York: New York University Press, 2000, pp. 13-28.

Wagar, W. Warren, *The Secular Mind: Transformations of Faith in Modern Europe: Essays presented to Franklin L. Baumer*, New York: Holmes & Meier, 1982, pp. 13-28.

Wahid, Abdurrahman, "Indonesia's Mild Secularism." *SAIS Review* 21, 2, (Summer-Fall 2001): 25-28.

2

Islam, Humanity and the Equality for Women

– Lily Zakiyah Munir

Islam is a religion of great tradition, yet Islam faces some challenges today. One of these challenges is how Muslims can promote the aspect of humanity in Islam in modern life. Islam, which can be understood through the attitudes and behaviour of its followers, presents various images, reflecting the diverse socio-cultural and political backgrounds of the Middle East, North Africa, South Asia, Southeast Asia, and elsewhere in the world. This paper discusses the less understood and less promoted dimension of humanity within Islam, with a focus on issues related to women.

The basic argument conveyed in this paper is that equality between women and men is sanctioned under Islam, which came into existence fifteen centuries ago. Similarly, the rights of women depicted in the universal women's/human rights perfectly cohere with the spirit of liberation, that Islam can bring to oppressed groups. The compatibility between Islam and the concept of universal human rights can be visible if the fundamental values of Islam regarding women and gender in the *Qur'an* and *Hadiths* are understood correctly, without any gender biases as such that one can find in some cultures.

The mission of Islam, which is to bring blessings to the whole universe, can be achieved only if this religion is understood and implemented in a dynamic and progressive way. Only in this way can Islam adjust itself to a continuously changing world, and hence, its teachings on humanity can be materialized. Islamic teachings can be broadly classified into two levels: the universal one and the particular one. The universal teachings, such as principles of justice, equality, public goodness, freedom, etc. are absolute and unchangeable. But how these principles are to be implemented depends on the socio-cultural, economic and political contexts.

The parameter of justice for women today, including in Indonesia, for example, may be different from the one in the seventh century Arabian Peninsula. Therefore, it is necessary to refresh Muslims' understanding of the teachings in line with the course of change in the society. Problems that humans have to deal with are never static, and Islam should be able to respond to these problems properly. This can be done only if the religion exists empirically in dynamic and metamorphic settings.

This paper discusses three major issues. *First,* humanity in Islam will be carefully looked into. This section attempts to uncover how humanity is taught in Islam, a topic to which most Muslims have paid very little attention. Lack of attention to the humanistic features of Islam has resulted in various social ills and the exclusive attitude of many Muslims. *Second,* Quranic injunctions on women, relating to their rights and equality with men, will be discussed. Some verses in the *Qur'an* could be and have been interpreted with some gender bias, which originates in the patriarchal tendency and egoistic attitude of some male readers. This could happen because Islamic texts, more broadly every religious text, is open to different interpretations, depending on each reader's background. After trying to understand the framework of Islamic teachings on women, this paper will present the debates on two specific issues, that is, polygamy and the wearing of the veil. This paper will end with a brief reflection reiterating the importance of understanding the *Qur'an* and *Hadith*s on women or gender issues properly, without gender biases or male ego. Doing so will also suggest universal norms of Islam on women's liberation more clearly.

Islam: Religion for Humanity

Islam, literally, implies peace, submission, justice, and well-being (*maslahah*). Linguistically speaking, it is metamorphose of root words *salima-yaslamu-salaaman*, which means 'safe' and 'peace' and refers to the verb of which meaning is to save or to bring peace. Islam, then, is a religion that intrinsically brings liberation and salvation to humans through a set of new moral values throughout the process of social transformation. It is very true that Islam is a source of morality because of its metaphysical and humanistic character.

The emergence of Islam as a source of norms and morality can be traced in the socio-historical context of the Arab world of the seventh century. At the time, Arabs lived as nomads in open deserts and were susceptible to inter-tribal conflicts and wars. Islam appealed to these nomads and helped them to build their ethical values and moralities. The *Qur'an*, which is filled with aesthetics and messages on humanity and the oneness of God, highly influenced the lives of nomads. Bedouins across the desert were moved by the words of God and were led to a new life, creating a society where social norms and order existed.

Islam gives guidance and discipline to its followers, and the teachings of Islam cover all aspects of human life. The prayer that Muslims conduct at various occasions is the expression of their wish for eternal goodness in the world. In line with this, the Prophet Muhammad asked Muslims to live their present lives rightly as if they would have to stay in this life forever, and at the same time, as if they had to die the very next day. This symbolizes an important set of ideas about relationships that humans have to bear, that is, the vertical relation *(hablul min Allah)*, which is the relation between humans and God, and horizontal relation *(hablul min al-naas)* or the relation between human beings themselves and between humans and their surroundings. Muslims feel so peaceful after performing rituals, such as prayer or fasting, which are vertically oriented, and render a source of peace and goodness given to others. This balance between personal and social piety is important. Muslims are encouraged normatively to spread *salam* (peace) by saying *assalamu alaikum* which means 'may peace be blessed upon you.' This phrase is not only a greeting but is also a prayer for the safety of others. Similarly, Muslims should be reminded that teachings on justice, equality, mutual love, mutual help, etc. have influence on others.

Islam currently faces serious problems in that there are increasing phenomena of violence, wars, and inter-religious conflicts in which many Muslims are involved. Fundamentalism, characterized by rigid and textual approaches to religiosity and the tendency to return to the past, is also a threat to Islam because it erodes the humanistic face of Islam. Fundamentalism always has been "unfriendly" to women. Fundamentalists seem to be exceedingly enthusiastic for finding a way to control women. According to fundamentalists, women have to be covered or domesticated, or have their public activities restricted. They say that women should properly dress and wear headscarf (*jilbab*) so as not to be seductive. Islam is often hijacked by fundamentalists who discriminate and bring injustice to women. The rights of women, as promised in the *Qur'an* and *Hadiths*, are often disregarded. Therefore, it is necessary for us to promote a new paradigm in Islam in order to bridge a wide gap between its ideal universal values and realities in daily life.

The *Qur'an*, Male Ego, and Discrimination Against Woman
The low status of women and the discrimination against women in many Muslim societies have become a major concern of Muslim intellectuals. Women appear to be powerless before deep-rooted patriarchism, male egoism, and hegemony exercised in the name of Islam. This is not an ungrounded worry. The concept of an ideal *Muslimah* (Muslim women) has engineered the image of the ideal woman, that is, obedient and submissive, faithful, loyal, serving and pleasing her husband. In reality, women are encouraged to stay in *dapur* (kitchen), *sumur* (well/washing area),

and *kasur* (mattress); women are marginalized and only appreciated because of their domestic and sexual roles; women are discouraged to participate in public activities. Countless Islamic books, mostly classical ones, have such contents and are widely circulated and used in *pesantrens* (Islamic boarding schools) and other Islamic educational institutions. Written by highly respected religious scholars, these books are often viewed as 'sacred' and treated as if they were the words of God himself. They are unsurprisingly influential on the process of shaping Islamic dogma and paradigm in relation to the position and the status of women. The most often cited Quranic verse to justify male superiority over women is the following:

> And women shall have rights similar to the rights against them, according to what is equitable; but men have a degree (of advantage) over them. And Allah is Exalted in Power, Wise (Q[ur'an] s[ura] *al-Baqarah*/2:228).

This verse should be analyzed carefully and understood properly. In fact, we can find some verses in the *Qur'an* that affirm equal rights between women and men; but the above-mentioned verse states that men are positioned higher than women. These statements obviously contradict each other. In the case of clear contradiction as we see now, one has to consider the social background of when these revelations were made. The verse apparently reflects the then social realities that are iniquitous to women. It was not an easy task to turn the situation in favour of women. The *Qur'an* did not bring an abrupt change by terminating the longtime practices that are detrimental to women. It might have spoilt the social system which, in turn, would have created new problems. Hence, the verse quoted above should be understood in relation to the universal message of the *Qur'an* and its spirit of liberating the oppressed groups. It should not be understood textually by looking at the statement alone. Needless to say, it is absolutely important to read the verse above without a gender-biased mindset.

We also can find a frequently quoted verse to support male dominance in family leadership regardless of men's competence.

It reads as follows:

> Men have authority over women because God has made the one superior to the other, and because they spend their wealth to maintain them. Men are in charge of/are guardians of/are superior to/have authority over/women (*al-rijalu qawwamuuna 'ala l-nisa'*) because God has endowed one with more/because God has preferred some of them over others (*bi-ma faddala Allahu ba'duhum 'ala ba'din*) and they support them from their means (wa-bi-ma anfaqu min amwalihim). Therefore the righteous women are obedient, guarding in secret that which God has guarded. And for those whom you fear may rebel (*nusyuz*), admonish them and banish them to separate beds, and beat them. Then if they obey you, seek not a way against them. For God is Exalted, Great (Q. s. *al-Nisa'*/4:34).

According to classical exegesis, this verse is the illustration of a sexual hierarchy that treats women as sexual objects that provide service to men.[1] Again, this verse should be understood critically. In an ancient Arabic society, women were not expected or required to earn money for living. Men were solely responsible for it. Because men were obliged to provide any necessary commodities for the family, they were granted a status superior to women. That is the wisdom of *Allah*. Knowing that *Allah* is the Most Just, if the social condition changes, and if women start earning money for living (and mind you, there is no prohibition in the *Qur'an* and *Hadiths* that a woman work to support financially herself or her family), there should be no one who would prevent women from obtaining a similar status to men, or even a higher status on certain issues. The *Qur'an* never denies advocating gender equality doctrine as manifested in many verses in the *Qur'an*.[2]

Equality and Justice for Women

To understand how Islam initially elevated the status of women and, therefore, appreciates women's liberation and empowerment,

---

[1] See B.F. Stowasser, *Women in the Qur'an, Traditions, and Interpretation*, New York, 1994.

[2] See A.A. Engineer, *The Qur'an Women and Modern Society*, New Delhi, 1999.

it is crucial to understand the socio-cultural condition of pre-Islamic Arabia. This period is also known as *jahiliya,* where ignorance, a lack of moral values, licentiousness and corruption were widespread in the society. Women had no rights whatsoever and were treated as if they were mere goods rather than human beings; they were not only enslaved but also were inherited as a possession. Females were often viewed as a burden because they could not join the fighting to defend the tribe during war and were regarded as the source of sin and wickedness. In the eyes of men, women were a constant threat to the family's honour, which led to the practice of female infanticide, a barbaric custom of burying female infants alive in the desert. The killing of an infant girl was carried out in many ways. Some would dig a hole and bury her alive; others would throw her from an elevated place; and others would drown or slaughter her.[3] The *Qur'an* illustrates the gruesome fate awaiting female babies and the profound sadness of their fathers at their birth in the following verses:

> And when the news of (the birth of) a female (child) is brought to any of them, his face becomes dark, and he is filled with inward grief. With shame does he hide himself from his people, because of the bad news he has had. Shall he retain it on (sufferance and) contempt, or bury it in the dust? Ah, what an evil (choice) they decide on (*al-Nahl/16:58-9*).

This practice is strongly condemned in the *Qur'an,*

> When the female (infant) buried alive is questioned; for what sin was she buried? (s. *al-Takwir/81:8-9*).

The Prophet Muhammad showed his compassion for female babies and greatly improved the status of women by saying that the one to whom a daughter is born and who does not bury her alive, does not humiliate her, nor prefers a son to a daughter, will be sent by *Allah* to paradise (see Sunan Abi Dawud, *Kitab al Adab,* Bab *Fadl man 'ala yatama*). The Prophet also said that hellfire was

---

[3] See S. El-Bahnassawi, *Women, between Islam and World Legislations: Comparative Study,* Kuwait, 1985, p. 222.

for the ones who have to go through trials and tribulations due to a daughter and yet do not hate her and behave well to her.

Islam was the religion that made these atrocities to women end and granted them a status of human beings and placed them on an equal footing to men. There are more than 30 verses in the *Qur'an* which support equality between women and men and acknowledge the rights of women in various aspects of life. Among them are ones about the creation of human beings. The *Qur'an* has refuted the idea that women are a secondary creation deriving from the rib of men, which is part of Biblical tradition illustrated in Genesis 2:18-24. Instead, women and men are created equally from a single soul (*nafs)* as follows:

> O mankind, reverence your Guardian Lord who created you from a single nafs ... fear Allah, through Whom you demand your mutual (rights)... (s. *al-Nisa*/4: 1).

Women and men were created to be equal.

> And of everything We have created pairs... (s. *al-Dzariyat*/51:49).

Their relationship based on 'love and mercy' is explained in the following verse:

> And among His signs is this, that he created for you mates from among yourselves, that you may dwell in tranquility with them, and He has put love and mercy between your (hearts)... (s. *al-Rum*/30:21).

Both women and men have equal responsibilities and rewards for adhering to the Five Pillars of Islam:

> The believers, men and women, are protectors one of another; they enjoin what is just, and forbid what is evil; they observe regular prayers, practice regular charity, and obey Allah and His Messenger. On them will Allah pour His mercy... (s. *al-Tawbah*/9:71).

In the *Qur'an*, some specific expressions to emphasize the equality of women and men are used in relation to their respective duties, rights, virtues and merits, such as "believing men and women." Thus for example:

> For Muslim men and women, for believing men and women,
> for devout men and women, for true men and women, for men
> and women who are patient and constant, for men and women
> who humble themselves, for men and women who give in
> charity, for men and women who fast, for men and women who
> guard their chastity, and for men and women who engage much
> in Allah's praise, for them has Allah prepared forgiveness and
> great reward (s. *al-Ahzab*/33:35).

All Quranic verses on the cosmic drama, i.e., the story of Adam
and Eva being expelled from heaven, emphasize, through the use
of a pronoun *huma* indicating two actors, that both of them were
actively involved in committing the sin. Contrary to the Bible, the
Qur'an puts equal blame on both Adam and Eva for their mistake.
Nowhere in the *Qur'an* can we find even the slightest hint that
Eva tempted Adam to eat the forbidden fruit or even that she had
eaten before him. Eva in the *Qur'an* is no temptress, no seducer,
and no deceiver. Living in heaven, both were tempted by Satan;
both ate the forbidden fruit; both repented and were forgiven; and
and both fell from heaven (see s. *al-A'raf* /7:19-23).

In Islam, there is no difference between men and women as
far as their relationship to *Allah* is concerned, as both are promised
the same reward for good conduct and the same punishment for
evil conduct. The *Qur'an* says:

> And for women are rights over men similar to those of men
> over women (s. *al-Baqarah*/2:226).

Islam recognizes a distinction between women and men because
of their biological differences, and this should not be mistaken as
discrimination. In spite of biological differences, women and men
remain equal partners as God's creation.

Debatable Issues

Polygamy

Polygamy was widely practised in pre-Islamic society. There was
no limit on the number of wives a man could take. Early
commentators of the *Qur'an* recorded cases of some Arabs having

up to ten wives. The notion of justice towards these wives did not exist in that society. In the time of *jahiliya*, a husband had the unilateral privilege to determine whom he would love most and to whom he would give with his unlimited favors. The wives had to accept their fate without any access to justice.

Islam denies unfair conditions for women. Along with its basic principle to empower women, Islam seems to be a driving force to bring about social change in Arabian society. However, the complete abolition of polygamy and the granting of equal status of women to men in every respect were not practical propositions in that type of society. Thus, the middle-way solution was applied, in what is termed a "pragmatic-ideological" course. While it hinted at equality directly as well as indirectly, it sought solutions which were more acceptable for a society that was dominated by men.

It is clear, judging from verses in the *Qur'an*, that polygamy was not a perfect solution, and yet it had to be advocated in a very restricted manner. The Quranic verse that refers to polygamy is as follows.

> If you fear that you will not be able to deal justly with orphans, marry of your choice, two or three or four; but if you fear that you will not be able to deal justly with them, then only one (s. *al-Nisa'*/4:3).

Seemingly, this rule on polygamy was introduced conditionally; the verse especially refers to the justice for orphans. The verse was revealed immediately after the Battle of *Uhud* when the Muslim community was left with many orphans and widows and captives of war. Their treatment should have been based on principles of the greatest humanity and equity. As argued by Yusuf Ali, the situation changed, but the principles remain. He reads the verse as a possibility for a man to marry the orphans if he is sure that it is the way to protect their interests and their property, and does not diminish the justice shown to the orphans.[4]

---

[4] Ali, *The Holy Qur'an: Text, Translation and Commentary*, Washington D.C., 1989, p. 184.

The verse is not merely limited to orphans, but has a general application to Islamic marriage laws. Muslim jurists, as pointed out by Abdur Rahman Doi[5] lay down the following conditions for a polygamous man: i) he must have sufficient financial resources to look after the needs of the additional wives; ii) he must give equal justice to all of his wives. The wives should be treated equally by the husband in terms of the receipt of their conjugal and other rights. The condition of being just and fair, however, is hardly obtained. One of the verses in the *Qur'an* explicitly states this reality, which makes even clearer the Islamic stance that does not advocate polygamy.

> You are never able to be fair and just as between women; even if it is your ardent desire; but turn not away (from a woman) altogether, so as to leave her (as it were) hanging (in the air) (*al-Nisa'*/4:129).

This verse in the *Qur'an* affirms the rejection of polygamy in Islam. It is quite categorical that human beings cannot treat several wives with fairness. There is a big gap between desire and its fulfilment. As far as polygamy is concerned, the Quranic verse is very clear that men cannot act towards several wives justly, although their initial intention was good and charitable. This may be because, as the *Qur'an* says:

God has not made for any man two hearts (s. *Al-Ahzab*/33:4).

This implies that a man cannot love two women equally at the same time. These verses, then, suggest that Islam reject generalized polygamy (which Muslims derive from reading half a line of sura *al-Nisa'*/4:1).

It seems that the societal condition in the seventh century in Arabia, which was hideous for women, has not been taken into account in the current debates on polygamy. And only generalized ideas about plural marriages are emphasized. Polygamy, which was common in pre-Islamic society or *jahilia*, apparently had a

---

[5] Doi, *Women in Shari'ah (Islamic Law)* Kuala Lumpur, 1992, p. 51.

new meaning in Islam. Islam intended to eradicate detrimental circumstances of women and children and bring about benefit to the weak. If women agree, polygamy may be the way to protect them and give them stability. It should not be forgotten that women outnumbered men at that time. However, there is no reference to a sexual aspect of polygamy in the *Qur'an*. It only refers to the need of ensuring social justice for orphaned girls, and unprotected women who were vulnerable to all kinds of abuse. Polygamy is not the *Qur'an*'s ideal; otherwise, "its admonition to marry only one, its assertion that men cannot do justice between wives, and its reference to the oneness of the human heart would hold no meaning."[6] For believers, the *Qur'an*'s teachings cannot be meaningless. As Asma Barlas has argued further, it is we who must be willing to reread the verses cumulatively in order not to fall into a generalized mode of polygamy.

Veiling (*hijab, jilbab*)

The veil or headscarf of Muslim women is referred to as either *hijab* or *jilbab*. The term *hijab*, which literally means "curtain," appears seven times in the *Qur'an*, indicating a metaphorical meaning, a concrete object, and an eschatological context. Semantically speaking, the general meaning of *hijab* refers to the concept of 'separation,' which can be concrete, metaphorical, or abstract. *Hijab*, then, means to segregate individuals or groups of individuals from the society in general and also refers to the abstract institution of such segregation. In the mediaeval royal circle, the *hijab* was the curtain behind which the ruler was hidden from the eyes of the courtiers and commoners alike. This tradition in the life of nobility was first documented during the Umayyads and the Abbasids periods, and it became a part of an elaborate system of court ceremonies later.[7]

Now, tradition of *hijab* is mentioned in the *Qur'an* after five years of the *hijra* (627 CE).

---

[6] Barlas, *Believing Women in Islam: Unreading Patriarchal Interpretations of the Qur'an*, Austin, Tx., 2002, p. 192.

[7] Stowasser, op.cit., p. 168.

> Oh ye who believe! Enter not the Prophet's houses, until leave is given you for a meal, not to wait for its preparation; but when you are invited, enter; and when ye have taken your meal, disperse without seeking familiar talk. Such (behavior) annoys the Prophet: he is ashamed to dismiss you, but Allah is not ashamed (to tell you) the truth. And when you ask (his ladies) for anything you want, ask them from before a screen; that makes for greater purity for your hearts and for theirs" (s. *al-Ahzab*/33:53).

The wedding of Zainab bint Jahsy with the Prophet seems to be the time of God's imposition of the *hijab*, according to *Hadith* and *Tafsir*. God shielded the Prophet's women from the eyes of visitors of his house. As pointed out by a number of great Islamic scholars,[8] *hijab* "came down" in a double sense: first, it was, literally, a "curtain" that the Prophet loosened while standing on the threshold to Zainab's chamber in order to bar his servant Anas Ibn Malik from entering. Secondly, *hijab* "came down" by way of God's revelation of the verse, which the Prophet recited to Anas. According to other traditions, *hijab* was decreed after the Prophet saw some men loitering in the vicinity of Zainab's house on the morning after the wedding night. It is also said that Umar ibn al-Khattab urged the Prophet to conceal and segregate his wives because both the righteous and the wicked entered into the Prophet's house.

Muslim scholars stipulate that the Prophet's wives fully participated in the communal affairs of Medina until the revelation of the *hijab* verse mentioned above. Their exclusion from public life was due to several factors, among others to provide domestic comfort and privacy for the female elite of Islam (the Prophet's wives). This notion, in turn, connotes an element of "privilege." Indeed, the mediaeval *hadith* states that the *hijab* was imposed upon the Prophet's wives as a criterion of their elite status. In addition, the *hijab* is also seen as a protective device, especially during the periods of civic tension when the hypocrites were instigating disorder and stirring up inter-communal fears. Because of this

---

[8] See *Ibid.*, p. 90.

social condition, the Prophet felt compelled to heed Umar Ibn Khattab's council and seclude his wives.[9]

Soon after the revelation of the *hijab* verse, self-protection of "the Prophet's wives, his daughters, and the women of the believers" was enjoined in the *Qur'an* (*S. al-Ahzab*/33:59-60) by way of God's command that Muslim women cover themselves in their "mantles" or "cloaks" (*jalabib*, singular: *jilbab)* (when abroad), "so that they be known (as free women, not slaves) and not molested (in the streets) by the hypocrites, and those in whose hearts is a disease ...".[10] This legislation differs from the previous verse in two ways: first, it concerned individual female appearance when outside the house, not confinement of women. Secondly, it applied to all Muslim women, not just the Prophet's wives. Once again, classical exegesis has identified Umar Ibn Khattab as the main spokesman in favour of this clothing law.

Given the multiple meanings of *hijab* and the context of its revelation, it is hard to understand how this phenomenon was made obligatory for Muslim women at large. Stowasser relates it to the period after the expansion of Islam beyond the borders of Arabia, and later in the Islamized societies still ruled by pre-existing (Sassanian and Byzantine) traditions.[11] Rules on women's dress and space were formulated in the mid-eighth century in an absolute and categorical way, reflecting the practices and cultures of that time. Meanwhile, Mernissi points out that *hijab* also means a veil that hides God from men and, thus, takes on an eminently negative significance.[12] She further questions how *hijab*, with such a negative meaning, is claimed in our day as a symbol of Muslim identity for Muslim women. Mernissi concludes that the Prophet,

---

[9] *Ibid.*, p. 91.

[10] *Ibid.*

[11] *Ibid.*, p. 93.

[12] F. Mernissi, *The Veil and the Male Elite: A Feminist Interpretation of Women's Rights in Islam* (trans. M.J. Lakeland), Reading, MA, 1991, p. 97.

during a troubled period at the beginning of Islam, introduced a breach in space separating the public from the private, or indeed the profane from the sacred, but which was to turn into a segregation of the sexes.[13] The veil that descended from Heaven was going to cover up women, separate them from men, from the Prophet, and so from God. Is it really the meaning of the *hijab?*

Final Reflection

The discussions above show that Islam urges its followers to keep the balance between the transcendental and social relations; and between personal and social piety. The feelings of security, peace, and good that result from performing rituals can be a strong foundation to promote humanity and human relations. Islam sanctions equal status to women and men as God's creation. The religion recognizes distinction, not discrimination, between the two genders because of their different biological conditions. Equality among all human beings, both women and men, is a basic principle in Islam and is beautifully illustrated in numerous Quranic verses. We should not read texts on particular issues like polygamy or veiling without paying attention to the social condition of early Islamic or pre-Islamic times. If so, it will be clearly understood that these practices appeared from the idea of discrimination. They should be understood within the socio-cultural context of revelation and should not contradict Islam's universal message of justice and equality.

References

Al-Hibri, Azizah, "A Study of Islamic Herstory: Or, How Did We Ever Get into This Mess?" *Women's Studies International Forum* ([Special Issue on:] *Women and Islam*) 5, 2 (1982): 207-19.

Ali, Yusuf, *The Holy Qur'an: Text, Translation and Commentary,* Washington DC: Amana Corporation, 1989.

---

[13] *Ibid.,* p. 101.

Barlas, Asma, *Believing Women in Islam: Unreading Patriarchal Interpretations of the Qur'an*, Austin, Tx: University of Texas Press, 2002.

Doi, Abdur Rahman, *Women in Shari'ah (Islamic Law)*, Kuala Lumpur, A.S. Noordeen, 1992.

El-Bahnassawi, Salem, *Women, Between Islam and World Legislations: Comparative Study* (trans. A.F. El-Shaer), Kuwait: Dar-ul Qalam, 1985.

Engineer, Ali Asghar, *The Qur'an, Women and Modern Society*, New Delhi, Sterling, 1999.

——————, *The Rights of Women in Islam*, New York: St. Martin's Press, 1992.

Mernissi, Fetima, *The Veil and the Male Elite: A Feminist Interpretation of Women's Rights in Islam*, Massachusetts: Perseus Books, 1991.

——————, *Beyond the Veil: Male-Female Dynamics in a Modern Muslim Society* (trans. M.J. Lakeland), New York: Halstead Press Book, 1986.

Stowasser, Barbara Freyer, *Women in the Qur'an, Traditions, and Interpretation*, New York: Oxford University Press, 1994.

3

The Need for Historical Perspectives in Understanding Islam

— Abdurrahman Wahid [†]

There are several important issues that I would like to present in this article. We should remember that history tells us that there have been responses from the Muslim community about the challenges given by others. That historical process should be seen from two different perspectives. First, we see the relationship between Islam and history from a cultural point of view. The establishment of both *Nahdlatul Ulama* (NU) and *Muhammadiyah* in Indonsia is one example of this.[1] It is related to the decision of *ulamas'* or *fiqh* in the fifth century of the Islamic calendar (the twelfth to the thirteenth centuries CE) that prohibits Muslims from visiting tombs, which means that there were some people who disagreed with the *ulama*'s decision.

People who supported the prohibition from visiting tombs founded *Muhammadiyah*. Conversely, people who still think paying

---

[†] Abdurrahman Wahid recently died in Dec. 2009.

[1] [For background discussion, see H. Kato, *Agama dan Peradaban*, Jakarta, 2002. Ed.]

a visit to tombs is permissible gathered under NU. However, many Muslims in Indonesia do not choose the attitude of NU or "its opponents" anymore. Nowadays, some *Muhammadiyah* followers do not mind visiting tombs, and some NU members have not visited tombs at all. In other words, we see the emergence of a third group, which can be coined as *MuhammadihNU*, that is, the hybrid of two groups. Another example is that Dr Ahmad Sugiat has taken the name of *Syadiziliyah* (it is just like an "adopted mother"), which originates in the Sufi tradition.

Another approach for historical understanding lies in institutionalization. People who adopt this approach believe that Islam is in danger and should be given more power, with little hesitation for using violence or any other possible means. They just disregard *fiqh* (Islamic legal obligation) that Muslims are allowed to use physical means only when they are forced to be taken away from their homes (*idza ukhriju jmin diyaribim*). Therefore, it is totally against Islamic law to use physical force or violence. "Institutionalists" do not remember this and do not practise it in their daily lives.

A few years ago, the author was invited to attend the seminar organized by *Yomiuri Shimbun*, one of the largest newspaper companies in the world, to discuss with Prof. Samuel Huntington in Tokyo about his book entitled *The Clash of Civilizations*. The book indeed brought about controversy as he attempts to show the construction of human history until today. According to Prof. Huntington, civilizations in developed countries such as North America and Europe are very different from the civilizations of so-called developing countries. I said to Prof. Huntington that he might be the expert of the "tree" of Islam, the "tree" of Christianity, and other trees, but what is needed is to watch the "tree" of human history from a distance, which is to say that we need to see the "wood[s]" in a comprehensive manner. It is important to see the whole wood (or forest) rather than seeing just one tree. Several hundred thousand young Muslims are and will be studying in industrialized countries. Although they are not Westerners, just like the author, there will be less distinction between them and Westerners.

Prof. Huntington agreed with what I said to him at the time. However, after he came back to Harvard University in the States, he published another book referring to the clash of civilizations. It is evident that truth is hardly found even though prominent universities, academic institutions, and powerful countries exist in this world.

Knowing this, the author often remembers what Mao Zedong once said: "Study Islam objectively. We need to study it fairly and critically." Yet, it is not an easy task to follow what Mao said because we need to have a strong professional attitude for greater understanding of Islam. What is simply needed is an objective study of Islam through a study of the historical development of Islam. And this is surely more beneficial than merely learning literature.

We can also see the empirical data from exisitng areas of the Muslim community, or *umat*, in the world today. There should be new areas of Islamic study regarding Muslim communities. The historical development of Islam differs around the world, and it is necessary for us to learn about how Islam has developed not only in Saudi Arabia but also in other parts of the world. Therefore, the author divides *umat* into six different areas (according to their own historical development): Islam in sub-Sahara Africa; Islam in North Africa and Arabia; Islam in Turkey, Persia, and Afghanistan; Islam in Bangladesh, Nepal, Pakistan, India, and Sri Lanka; Islam in Southeast Asia; Islam in industrialized countries. (Islam in each area has witnessed specific historical development.)

When we aim to study the differences among Islam in the above-mentioned areas, the room for subjective attitudes is very slim. Objectivity in learning brings about a consistent attitude of people who are involved in research. If we lack objectivity in learning or research, it means that we are not mature yet. We constantly need to strive for knowing ourselves.

It is a very distinguished feature of Islam that both spiritual and secular approaches are appreciated. Spiritual matters come first. As the discussion progresses, a secular approach can be adopted. Issues such as *akhirat* can also be discussed from a secular point of view. We need to take argumentation called *Nagli* (scripture) for the matter of spirituality and take *Aqli* (rationality) for the matter of secularity. This dual approach has been adopted by Islam since its beginning. It is very proper for us to appreciate this, right?

An Interview

Would you explain more about the six areas of umat Islam?

I did not mean that there are six different Islams in the world but that there are Islamic study areas where Islam developed. Even in one division, there are "many Islams." We have to differentiate between the basic Islamic teachings, that is, the belief in Allah and prophethood of Muhammad or the classical form of Islam and different presentations of Islam.

What is your view on syariat Islam?

Syaria means the way we live. *Syaria Islamia* means how we live as good Muslims. Legal obligation is not necessary. It is a matter of individuals.

How do you explain the relationship between nationalism and Islam?

Islam needs a place to exist. Since we are obliged to separate Islam from the state, then there is no choice. In fact, NU (in 1935) officially stated that there was no need to establish an Islamic state. I do not intend to create an Islamic state in Indonesia but do appreciate Islam as a religion.

How do you see fundamentalism in Islam?

I do not see any difference between fundamentalists and me myself. I cannot say that fundamentalists are not Muslims or they are out of Islam. Why? According the Prophet, as long as people believe in the God of Almighty Allah and his messenger Muhammad, they are Muslims. I am against some *actions* of fundamentalists, not against themselves as Muslims. I know there are differences in the interpretation of the teachings between fundamentalists and me. For example, speaking of *jihad*, we do not use violence in *jihad*. *Jihad* is the war against ignorance. That is *jihad*. Except for the time when we need to defend ourselves from intruders. In our history, October 1945, NU people in Surabaya formed a sort of logistic group to defend the Republic of Indonesia, it is one of the *jihad*.

What do you think about the Japanese pacifist Constitution, optimized by Article 9?

I think Article 9 of the Japanese Constitution, is one of the reactions of the Japanese to the mistake of the past. And it is good. I support Article 9 of the Japanese Constitution.

Do you think that Islam is behind compared to the non-Muslim world?

It is true that we Muslims are behind in many fields compared to so-called industrial countries. It happens because we care too much about the institutionalization of Islam, which means that we do not see Islam from a cultural point of view. Look at Indonesia, the Department of Religion, MUI, NU, etc. Muslims tend to understand Islam through institutions. Therefore, education is very important. We need to teach the importance of appreciation of non-Muslims. We have to remember that what is emphasized in Islam is justice and prosperity. It is Muslims' duty to make every effort to bring about justice and prosperity. That is what we should do for Islam and for the Republic of Indonesia.

4

The Concept of *Jihad* and *Mujahid* of Peace

– Zakiyuddin Baidhawy

Recent debates on the role of religion in violent conflicts have revealed two different opinions on religion. Some emphasize the negative side of religion. They think that religions can oppose progress, as religion in the Middle East has shown, and that the terrorism and conflicts seen nowadays are evidence of this. For them, religion can be a destructive power. It should be remembered that people who take a cynical attitude towards religion fail to respect the humane nature of religion and its moral rules stressing tolerance.

On the other hand, secularists, who take a more positive stance towards religions, view it as a humane creed and a force of civilization. Enlightened religious followers, according to secularist groups, are well aware of the fact that terrorism, murder, and destruction violate the teachings of all religions. Secularists know that such violent acts can only tarnish the name of religion, whatever that religion might be. Yet, it also should be remembered that so-called liberals fail to understand that religions always require humans to obey the law of God, something one might call an absolute submission to the God.

We can thus find two features of religion in relation to violence, that is to say, the acceptance of violence and the denial of violence. Religion might justify the "utilization" of violence as a means of self-defense and the expansion of religion and might allow the destructive behaviour of followers. In many religions, we find some resonance between the act of violence and the appreciation of the "holy martyr" who sacrifices him- or herself for the sake of religion. This concept leads us to the debate on *jihad* in Islam. It is hard to find a simple explanation for this delicate religious question since the concept of *jihad* is itself ambiguous. However, it is vital to search for the genuine meaning of *jihad*, because terrorism and violence in the name of Islam occur so frequently these days.

Discussions of *jihad* have been very frequent since the spontaneous terrorist attacks on 11 September 2001 in New York, which destroyed the World Trade Center in Manhattan and caused the war in Afghanistan. The current tense situation in Palestine also makes discussion of *jihad* popular among Muslims and non-Muslims alike. Some Westerners connect *jihad* with the uncivilized crusaders who existed hundreds years ago in the time of the rivalry between Christianity and Islam. This view endorses the idea that violence is inherent in the concept of *jihad*. Others consider *jihad* a spiritual struggle rather than a physical martyrdom. One of the reasons why the concept of *jihad* is so varied lies in the history and the process of its theological legitimation, which happened fourteen centuries ago in an area extending from Spain to the Middle East.

It is true that a sensitive relation between Muslims and non-Muslims was caused by various historical affairs. In other words, historical events have exerted a major influence on the lives of Muslims. We know one extreme Islamic group that regards *jihad* as physical war (or "holy war", as it is sometimes translated into English): the *Khawarij* sect. Like *Khawarji*, many theologians and orthodox jurists think that *jihad* is a religious obligation of that kind. However, the understanding of *jihad* varies substantially. It is this author's intention to examine the real meaning of *jihad* and to suggest a future course of Islam in this paper.

Jihad as War (the Meaning of *jihad*)

The word *jihad* comes from an Arabic word *j-h-d*, of which literal meaning is a serious effort or hard-working. "*Mujahid*", the subject form (*ism fa'il*) of *jihad*, means someone who participates in *jihad* enthusiastically. In many contexts, *jihad* is used to mean warfare, even though there are other Arabic words that more obviously mean war, such as *qital* and *harb*. In the *Qur'an* and other Islamic texts, *jihad* is often followed by the word of *sabi lillah*, which means the path of Allah. It can be assumed that *jihad fi-sabi lilla* (war waged by Muslims against their enemies) denoted the physical clashes between tribes during the Pre-Islamic period in Arabia.

Besides the *Qur'an*, *jihad* is often explained as an act of war in *Hadiths*. For example, there are 199 references about *jihad* in *Hadith Sahih al-Bukhari*, which all regard *jihad* as an act of war.[1] Broadly, Bernard Lewis explains that most *mutakallimun* (theologians), jurists and classic *muhaddithun* (traditionalists)[2] regard *jihad* as a military obligation.[3]

Classical jurists[4] explain that *jihad* should be applied to both the land of Muslims (*dar al-lslam*) and the land of non-Muslims (*dar al-harb*). This suggests that that there were frequent conflicts between Muslims and non-Muslims in the early days of Islam.

---

[1] See M. Bukhari, *Sahih Bukhari*, Medina, 1981 edn., vol. 4, pp. 34-204.

[2] *Mutakallimun* means Muslim scholars who deal with theological issues referring to *Qur'an*, *Hadith*, and human reasoning and is usually translated into English as 'theologian.' *Muhaddithun* means Muslim scholars who "study" hadith and convey the content of hadith to his fellow Muslims and they are usually translated into English as 'traditionalists.'

[3] B. Lewis, *The Political Language of Islam*, Chicago, 1988, p. 72.

[4] There are three divisions in Islamic history: the classical period from 750 to 1250; the mediaeval period from 1251 to 1800; and the modern period from 1801 to present time.

This is one of the reasons why *jihad* is understood as war. However, it is important to remember that *dar al-Islam* never means destroying non-Islamic areas or killing non-Muslims. Moreover, *jihad* never brings about forcible conversion. The *Qur'an* (*al-Baqarah* 2:256) states: "There is no compulsion in religion." We should also not overlook the political feature of *jihad* in that it encourages Muslims to establish their own political entity, which would bring two positive results: Islam recognizing the existence of other religions, and giving Muslims the chance to establish social order and political justice.

Jihad is not Compulsory Conversion

Classical Islamic law divides the citizens of *dar al-harb* into two groups: *ahl al-kitab* (People of the Book); and *Mushrikun* (Polytheist). *Ahl al-kitab* consists of Jewi, Christians, and Sabi'in (those who do not worship idols), and these people have the same status as Muslims because they follow the true revelations conveyed by genuine prophets. They live comfortably under Islamic rule as long as they fulfil their duties (*ahl al-dhimmi*) that they pay the *jizyah* (special tax) and do not disturb the lives of Muslims. Meanwhile, according to Islamic law, Muslims should offer two choices to *Mushrikun*: converting to Islam or death. Yet, this action was rarely taken after the Muslim conquest of Arabia. Muslims usually treated all non-Muslims s (*ahl al-harb*) in the same manner as the people of sacred book (*ahl al-kitab*). The classical jurists regarded even Zoroastrians, for example as *ahl al-kitab*. After the Muslim conquest of India, the concept of *ahl al-kitab* even extended to Hindus as well. These historical facts eventually suggest that "conversion or death" approach in propagation was not adopted by Muslims, and terminology such as *mushrikun* (Polytheist) became obsolete among Muslims.

Although it is understood that *jihad* should be continuously carried out until *dar al-Islam* is completely realized in this world, this does not mean that jurists expect Muslims to engage in endless war. The Prophet Muhammad signed a peace contract with the Meccans, the Hudaibiyah Agreement of 630, and some early *khalifah* (caliphs) also signed a peace treaty with the kingdom of Byzantium. Even if there is no mechanism in Islamic law that recognizes non-Muslim governments, Muslim jurists have encouraged Muslims to negotiate with non-Muslims to cease hostilities and sign peace accords. We also know that many jurists have supported the policy that no single party should possess excessive military power. Some other jurists have set up new categories, such as *dar al-'ahd* (territory where a "social contract" binds together different groups) and *dar al-sulh* (territory where peace exists among different groups).

In addition, jurists have seen *jihad* not only as an individual obligation of Muslims (*fard al-'ayn*) but also as a communal obligation of Muslims (*fard al-kifayah*). However, it is expected that all Muslims will participate in *jihad* when *dar al-Islam* is being attacked. And, if the community as a whole fails to fulfil religious obligations, including *jihad*, its members are regarded as sinners. However, when some Muslims in the community exercise *jihad* on behalf of other Muslims, the rest of community members do not need to participate in *jihad*. Some Shia writers explain that offensive *jihad* is allowed only if *Imam al-Muntazar* (the awaited Imam) appears in this world. Thus, offensive *jihad* is not allowed at the present time (since *Imam al-Muntazar* has not yet appeared).

Despite the historical facts, already mentioned, relating to the peaceful side of *jihad*, a prominent philosopher Ibn Taymiyah (1268-1328) took a more aggressive position. He declared that any ruler who fails to implement *shariah* (Islamic Law) thoroughly, including *jihad*, will lose his right to govern the nation. He encouraged all Muslims to take part in the *jihad* struggle by fighting Christian crusaders and Mongols. He clearly followed the *Khawarij* tradition which was popular in the seventh century and which emphasized the physical side of *jihad* against non-Muslims. Another radical group called the *Assassin* emerged in the eleventh century.[5] This

---

[5] T. Sonn, "Irregular Warfare and *Jihad*: Asking the Right Question." In J. Kelsay (eds.), *Cross, Crescent and Sword: The Justification and*

group evidently gave an impetus to radical Muslims to physically resist non-Muslims. Ibn Taymiyah also made it very clear that nominal confession of the faith cannot be recognized as a true confession or *shahada*. Interesting, however, Ibn Taymiyah supported jurists who accepted rulers who did not implement *shariah* in their government. It is better, according to Ibn Taimiyah, to have a government, whatever it might be, than to have no government.

Islamic Expansion and *Jihad*

Islamic law forbids any war that is not recognized as *jihad*, especially war between Muslims. Muslims are allowed to attack their fellow Muslims only when "Muslims" rebels (*bughat*) against the legal authority and are no longer regarded as Muslims.[6] We can see some examples of this in history. When *khalifah* al-Ma'mun and his relative al-Amin argued over the caliphate between 809 and 813, al-Ma'mun regarded al-Amin as a rebel. The internal rift in the Islamic community became apparent a mere hundred years after the revelation. The term *fitnah* (slander) has been used to describe the disintegration of Muslim community. It is true that the state of *fitnah* has been a standard condition of Islamic world since the early period of Islamic history.

One of the earliest Muslim writers, Muhammad ibn al-Hasan Shaybani (the founder of *Hizbut Tahrir*), codified the laws relating to war and peace after Islamic communities became divisive. Nonetheless, these laws seem to have worked rather ineffectively. Other jurists have tried to find solutions to the disintegration of Islamic world and clashes between Muslims and non-Muslims. However, they have failed to present an effective means to stop it. They also failed to establish a legitimate authority, that is, the *khalifah* (Caliph).

Limitation of War in Western and Islamic Tradition, Wesport, Conn., 1990, pp. 132-8.

[6] F.M. Donner, "The Sources of Islamic Conception of War." In *Ibid.,* pp.51-52.

Yet, the disintegration of Islamic world did not prevent the expansion of Islam. *Jihad*, in the sense of physical conflict, continued, and the non-physical feature of *jihad* had very little influence on Islamic government policies. The word *ghazi*, which means raid, is generally considered as synonymous with *jihad*. The Ottoman kingdom was once called the Kingdom of *ghazi* because of its frequent recourse to *jihad*. However, carrying out *jihad* was not the primary purpose of Ottoman expansion. There were other purposes, such as population control, competition with other Muslim countries, and pacification by conquering opposing countries. Besides, the *jihad* doctrine, Ottoman political ideology was mixed with elements of Turkish, Mongol, Persian, and Byzantine traditions and cultures. With this multi-cultural orientation, Islam even reached as far as India. It should be remembered that the rulers of Ottoman Empire, such as Uzun Hasan Aqquyunlu, who reigned from 1453 to 1478, and Safawi Shah Tahmasp, who ruled from 1524 to 1576, conducted *jihad* to expand their territory and to acquire sovereignty over more tax-paying citizens. This provides evidence that the justification for carrying out "physical *jihad*" can be political as well as religious.

Jihad as Spiritual Struggle

"War" is just one of the many interpretations of *jihad*. Discussion of the meaning of *jihad* seems never-ending. *Jihad* can mean either an internal struggle aiming to bring about personal growth or an external struggle with the goal of achieving justice. We can find a passage in *Hadiths* that indicates the substantive meaning of *jihad*. Muhammad said when he came back from the Badar war: "We have just come back from small (*jihad al-asghar*) and will come across to great *jihad* (*jihad al-akbar*)." Then, one of his friends asked: "What is great jihad?" He replied "It is *jihad* towards ourselves (*jihad al-nafs*)." Although this *hadith* is not included in the authoritative canon of *Hadiths*, it has had great impact on Islamic mysticism and Sufism.

Sufis regard *jihad* as a spiritual struggle or *jihad al-naf*, especially in the face of physical desire and polytheism. True understanding of great *jihad* is necessary when looking at one's inner self. Thus, great *jihad* is the most important part of achieving spiritual enlightenment.[7] Sufism exerted a great influence on Muslim spirituality up until the eleventh century. It is true that many Muslims regarded *jihad* as a personal struggle rather than a politically-motivated physical struggle. However, Sufism was challenged by Ibn Taymiyah, who criticized mystics for breaching *shariyah*. His disciple Ibn al-Qayyim al-Jawziyah (1292-1350) condemned the doctrine of *jihad al-akbar* more explicitly, casting doubt on the authenticity of that *hadith*.[8]

In short, we find three contrasting views on *jihad* in the pre-modern period: (1) *jihad* as an obligation and a communal effort to create and maintain *dar al-Islam* (originating in classical *Fiqh*); (2) *jihad* as a physical struggle and governmental duty (originating in the ideas of Ibn Taymiyah); (3) *jihad* as *jihad al-akbar* or a personal struggle (originating in the ideas of Sufism). Since classical jurists failed to present an accord on the concept of *jihad*, it is easy to understand why there have been debates about the true meaning of *jihad*. Let us see in the remainder of this paper how the debate over *jihad* has developed in the modern period.

Various interpretations of *Jihad* in the Modern Period

The first systematic explanation of *jihad* in modern history came after the Indian uprising against British rule in 1857. Sayyid Ahmad Khan and other Muslim scholars expressed their view that *jihad* meant defensive war and did not justify offensive actions against the British government so long as the latter did not contravene Islamic practices. Sayyid Ahmad Khan conceived of Islam as a private concern rather than a public or political matter.[9] Although

---

[7] See J. Renard, "Al-Jihad al-akbar," *Muslim World* 78 (1988): pp. 225-42, and V.J. Hoffman, *Sufism, Mystics and Saints in Modern Egypt* (Studies in Comparative Religion), Columbia, 1995, pp. 196-200.

[8] J.J.G. Jansen, *The Neglected Duty: The Creed of Sadat's Assassins and Islamic Resurgence in the Middle East*, New York, 1986, p.102.

[9] M. V. Ali, *A Critical Exposition of the Popular Jihad*, Delhi, 1984, p. 21.

his view was formed in response to the specific situation of British colonization, his ideas had an impact on the attitude of Muslims in India in general.

Some modern Muslim writers encourage their fellow Muslims to look to the *Qur'an* for guidance in reconciling Islam and the West. They believe that *jihad* is defensive in nature. To prove it, they explain that any war initiated by the Prophet Muhammad and the four rightly guided caliphs (*khalifah*) were defensive. They also say that the *Qur'an* tells Muslims to seek reconciliation when their enemy asks for *dar al-sulh* (the territory where peace prevails among different groups). Such reconciliation deal can last eternally, and Muslims need to take a neutral position when international conflicts arise.[10] Some Muslim scholars in the modern period have also attempted to accommodate *shariah* and secular law. Muhammad Shaltut, former rector of al-Azhar University in Cairo, Egypt, was of the opinion that *shariah* encourages reconciliation between Muslims and non-Muslims, and that the legal right for self-defence advocated in *shariah* is in accordance with the principles of the Charter of the United Nations.[11]

Abul A'la al-Mawdudi (1903-1979), a scholar from India/ Pakistan, also presented a systematic explanation of *jihad*. For him, *jihad* is not only a war to expand an Islamic political domain but also a process for establishing a legal government and ensuring religious freedom. Al-Mawdudi's political life began when he participated in the caliphate movement in India after the First World War. The movement demanded India's independence from Great Britain. He said that *jihad* was a concrete strategy for liberating the people of India, Muslim and non-Muslim alike.[12]

Mawdudi's views significantly changed the concept of *jihad*; he connected a religious concept *jihad* with the secular concepts

---

[10] M.Mir, "Jihad in Islam." In Hadia Shakeel and Ronald A. Messier (eds.), *The Jihad and Its Enemies*, Michigan, 1991, pp.119-22.

[11] R. Peters, *Jihad in Mediaeval and Modern Islam*, Leiden, 1977, p. 66.

[12] A. Mawdudi, *Al-Jihad fi Sabil Allah*, Gujranwala, [n.d.], p. 10.

of the anti-colonialism movement, which meant that *jihad* became a way not only to expand Islamic political influence but also to develop an Islamic polity in an independent nation. Moreover, *jihad*, for him, is the way to ensure the special status of non-Muslims (*ahl al-dhimmi*) by offering them political autonomy. Muslims in Arabia oppose Zionism and Israel because they regard the creation of Israel as an act of colonization. In this regard, the rector of al-Azhar University stated in 1973 that all Egyptians, including Christians, should participate in *jihad* to oppose Israel, and Arafat also should execute *jihad* to liberate Jerusalem.[13]

Other Islamic scholars, such as Hasan al-Banna (1906-1949) and Sayyid Qutb (1906-1956), endorsed the ideas of al-Mawdudi and praised him for having played a significant role in establishing Islamic government. For them, as Ibn Taymiyah notes, *jihad* is an effort to eliminate any government that fails to implement *shariah*. This sort of *jihad* matches the course of revolution which the *Quran* instructs Muslims to bring about. On this view, Muslims may have to enter into conflict with their own government before dealing with external enemies. In the eyes of these Muslim scholars, political leaders such as Gamal Abdel Nasser and Anwar Sadat were not true Muslims; they failed to exercise *jihad* properly (despite stating their opposition to Israel). The aforementioned Muslim scholars insist that *jihad* is a religious obligation for all Muslims and their community as a whole.[14]

One of the assassins of Anwar Sadat, Muhammad Abd al-Salam Faraj, presented his understanding of *jihad* in the booklet titled "The Neglected Duty", which he distributed after killing the President. His view can be seen as giving pure expression to hardliner Muslims' understanding of *jihad*. He said that *jihad* was like a firearm and that it belonged to the core teachings of Islam. He also stated that Islam would be in a disadvantageous situation

---

[13] Peters, *Jihad and Colonialism: the Doctrine of Jihad in the Modern History*, The Hague, 1979, p. 134.

[14] E. Sivan, *Radical Islam: Medieval Theology and Modern Politics*, New Haven, 1990, pp. 16-21, 114-16.

if *jihad* was not properly practiced, and that physical force should be used to destroy paganism. An example of this, according to Faraj, was when Ibrahim and Muhammad destroyed the idols in *Kaba* in the early days of Islam. Farj criticized Muslim political leaders as apostates and insisted that all Muslims should make every effort to realize a true and legitimated Islamic government, to revive the caliphate, and to expand *dar al-islam* (Islamic territory).[15]

Shiite revolutionaries shared the views of Faraj. The Ayatollah Khomeini (1903-1989) said that jurists should struggle to create goodness, eradicate evil, eliminate a tyrannical government so that Muslims could establish their own government. According to Khomeini, true *jihad* and true Islamic teaching encourage all Muslims to be *mujahid* (someone who struggles).[16] Ayatollah Muhammad Mutahhari, a well-known scholar during the Iranian Revolution, regarded *jihad* as a political obligation, too. A.M Mutahhari thought that the "power of gun" was sacred in Islam, and various *fatwas* (Islamic ruling pronounced by religious scholars or authorized religious bodies) supported his view. Mutahhari did not deny the validity of the defensive orientation of *jihad*, but he promoted the offensive side of *jihad* more actively. He insisted that it was legitimate and permissible to attack countries that tolerate polytheism. He also believed that Islam was superior to Christianity because Islam teaches *jihad*, which encourages Muslims to act politically, whereas Christianity has no concept similar to *jihad*.

Jihad as Non-Military Actions in the Modern Period

In the modern period, liberals and Sufi Muslims have clearly expressed their views on *jihad*, advocating its peaceful nature. They believe that *jihad* is a process of socio-political struggle for Muslims. And *jihad* is an important doctrine for the realization of justice in society. Fazlur Rahman, a Pakistani scholar and a

---

[15] J. J. G.Jansen, op. cit., p. 162.

[16] R. Khomeini, *Islamic Government*, Berkeley, 1981, pp. 108, 132.

professor at the University of Chicago, argues that Muslims can never bypass *jihad* when dealing with socio-political matters. According to Rahman, there can be no doubt that the *Quran* teaches Muslims to create a political entity that ensures justice and equality. *Jihad* is one means for achieving this goal.[17] For instance, former Tunisian President Habib Borguiba, exercised *jihad* to bring about economic growth in Tunisia, and his struggle was known as "the War against Poverty." In this case, *jihad* does not imply violence at all. Indeed, it contrasts sharply with the general understanding of *jihad* envisaged by non-Muslims.[18]

The concept of greater *jihad* upheld by Sufis is also important in terms of the development of Islamic philosophy. Although Sufis have little influence on the majority of Muslims compared to voluble Islamists in the political sphere, they have a great impact on Muslims' spiritual life. Egypt is an important place for this peaceful idea of *jihad*, since there are more Sufis than radical Islamists in the country.[19] President Sadat was a pioneering writer on Sufism and was successful in spreading the ideas of Sufism.[20] Some anthropological research conducted in Egypt, Sudan, and Tunisia suggests that *jihad* is deeply connected with Ramahdan fasting.[21] Because Sufi concept of *jihad*, which emphasizes the spiritual side of human struggle, drew a great deal of attention, some Muslim hardliners, such as Hasan al-Banna, became reluctant to criticize Sufis.[22] Sufis now use the term *mujahadah* (greater *jihad*) more than ever as they need to oppose aggressive *jihadist*.

The Impact of *Jihad*

As has been seen, the concept of greater *jihad*, which emphasizes the moral struggle of Muslims, has appealed to the hearts of many

---

[17]See F. Rahman, *The Major Themes of the Qur'an*, Minneapolis, 1980, pp. 3-64.

[18] Peters, *Jihad in Mediaeval*, op. cit., pp. 116-117.

[19] Hoffman, op. cit., pp. 357-358.

[20] Jansen, op. cit., pp. 65-66, 74, 78.

[21] Sonn, loc. cit., pp. 132-138.

[22] *Ibid.*

Muslims, particularly Sufis. On the contrary, the concept of lesser *jihad*, which advocates physical action, has had little impact on the lives of Muslims. Although it is also true that physical *jihad* has caused serious problems in the world today, such *jihad* has never spread to mobilize the masses worldwide. In this regard, physical or little *jihad* has found very little support in Muslim communities in the world. Historically speaking, the Pan-Islamism movement, whose main goal has been defending *dar al-Islam* and promoting the concept of little *jihad*, has only seemed to find success as anti-colonialism movements.

Although there have been many Islamic movements to stop European expansion in Islamic soil, *jihad* has never served as a factor to materialize geographical as well as political unity of Islamic world. The most systematic attempt to mobilize Muslims in opposing the West was made by the Ottoman regime in 1914, but it failed completely. When it declared war on Austria, the Ottoman Empire simultaneously issued *fatwa* on *jihad* that every Muslim, including Muslims in Russia, France, and Britain, should participate in the struggle to improve the lot of Muslims. The *fatwa* was published in Arabic, Urdu, Persian, and Turkish languages, but was not heeded by Muslim communities, with the result that they failed to unify the Islamic world in *jihad*.[23]

Calls for *jihad* have often had very little resonance from Muslim communities. Saddam Hussein's call for *jihad* against Israel while President of Iraq, for example, failed to mobilize Muslims to annihilate Israel. He also called for *jihad* to oppose the U.S. and manoeuvred to lend an Islamic tinge to his secular government. There were some Islamists who responded positively, but S. Hussein gained little support from the masses and never succeeded in resolving his conflict with the USA Ayatollah Ali Khomeini did the same thing when he encouraged his community to go to war against the USA, something he called *jihad*. In the case of Afghanistan, the call for physical resistance or *jihad* against Russia

---

[23] Peters, *Jihad and Colonialism*, op. cit., pp. 90-94.

never gained mass support although many *"mujahidin"*[24] were engaged in fighting. Even though Afghanistan received a great deal of sympathy from Islamic countries, only three states, Saudi Arabia, Iran, and Pakistan, actually sent significant numbers of *mujahidin.* "Lesser *jihad*" has failed to unite an Afghanistan that is divided politically, ethnically, socially, and ideologically. In fact, the recent war involving Afghanistan and the U.S.A. has revealed tensions between the current Afghan government and the Northern Alliance which supported the Taliban government.

It seems to be true that physical *jihad* or little jihad does not function efficiently as a part of Muslim struggle. Most Muslims do not regard war as an obligation for individuals or the community as a whole. Reinhold Loeffler, who worked in a small village in South Iran, found strong evidence that physical *jihad* was not overwhelmingly embraced by the people of Iran at the time of the Islamic Revolution. An informant told Loeffler that "a young man who is not a soldier will be killed in vain. I do not believe that they will be martyrs in the heaven."[25] Another informant, who was aware that Khomeini wrongly modelled himself as Imam Husain, said that "before his last battle, Imam Husain set his followers free from the obligation of *jihad* and many lives were saved.[26] Meanwhile, Khomeini could not be regarded as a saint as he let his followers come to death."[27] Such anecdotal evidence suggests that the call for *jihad* by the Islamic Republic of Iran failed to receive enthusiastic support from the Muslim community.

---

[24] *Mujahidin,* which is a plural form of *mujahid,* is generally known as Muslim fighters who are engaged in physical fighting. However, the author believes that *mujahidin* also means Muslims who struggle for spiritual achievement and peace.

[25] R. Loeffler, *Islam in Practice: Religious Beliefs in a Persian Village,* Albany, 1988, p. 229.

[26] *Ibid.,* p. 235.

[27] *Ibid.,* p. 237.

Mujahid of Terror versus *Mujahid* of Peace

To the aforegoing discussions and analysis, we can add two distinct orientations or types of *mujahid*, namely the "*mujahid* of terror" and the "*mujahid* of peace." The *mujahid* of terror uses violent means to purify his or her religious community and confront other religious communities, believing that the use of violence is a part of his holy obligation. On the other hand, the *mujahid* of peace (peace-maker, peace-builder, peace-keeper) refuses to legitimize the use of violence in the name of religion, athough he will still take to arms when necessary. Both believe in the righteousness of their religious tradition. However, they show a clear contrast in their exercise of *jihad*. It is important to note that the *mujahid* of peace seeks to keep his use of violence to a minimum, resorting to arms only when he faces a tyrant or injustice which cannot be stopped without physical conflict, actions which, for *mujahid* of peace, are self-defence. The *mujahid* of terror regards violence as his religious right and even believes physical fighting is imperative to realize justice.

It is important to recognize that the *mujahid* of terror does not hesitate to employ physical force, including waging war, in order to achieve his religious as well as political goals, while the *mujahid* of peace refuses to glorify the stories of war, concentrating, rather, on the spiritualization of Islamic life. An exemplary *mujahid* of peace in the history of Islam is Khan Abdul Ghaffar Khan, who led the non-violence movement in the Pathan community (Afghanistan) against the British army. In Buddhist and Hindu traditions, "spiritual war" is extremely important, with believers practising severe religious disciplines such as fasting, celibate, prayer and meditation in order to detach themselves from worldly desires. They are permitted to use physical force in self-defence only. This attitude corresponds to the orientation of the *mujahid* of peace. For the *mujahid* of peace, being true to one's principles is extremely important, and he will refuse to use violence as an instrument to express his disappointment, resentment, or frustration. All Muslims should remember that it is not merely evil but shows disrespect to Allah to treat other humans viciously and barbarically.

The special feature of the *mujahid* of peace is that he appreciates humanity and seeks to establish a legal basis for creating a society that is egalitarian, irrespective of religious faith. It is not difficult to imagine that *mujahid* of peace would also face injustice and oppression in their lives. However, they stand resolute in the sight of Allah and choose to coexist with their enemies. Anyone who breaks the law of Allah will be punished, and anyone who fulfils the holy duties of a Muslim will be rewarded. Thus, it is right to understand that the way of *mujahid* of peace is very much in accordance with the teaching of Islam, which also respects human rights. *Muhahid* of peace will be the true creature of Allah, whose good deeds match Allah's will.

A clear contrast can be seen in how the *mujahid* of terror and that of the "*mujahid* of peace" approach the process of conflict resolution. *Mujahidin* of peace always try to find a solution for conflicts by refraining from violence. Reconciliation and peaceful coexistence with the enemy are the primary goal of the *mujahid* of peace. By contrast, *mujahidin* of terror prioritize victory over their enemies and do not scruple to use violence even when it offers little chance of finding a solution.

By now it should be obvious that the source of bloodshed is not religion itself but rather such religious extremism as found with the "*mujahid* of terror." Therefore, the position of the *mujahid* of peace, will be important for the creation of peace and reconciliation between religions.

Conclusion

As we have seen, Muslims have interpreted *jihad* in various ways throughout the history of Islam: classical jurists understood *jihad* as war, bound by certain conditions; Ibn Taymiyah regarded *jihad* as a rebellion against tyranny; Sufis considered *jihad* to be a moral struggle; modernists interpreted *jihad* as a means to bring about social and political reform. Disagreement among Muslims on the interpretation of *jihad* is real, and the ideas of pluralistic Muslims are giving fuel to the discussion. The fact that jurists a thousand years ago offered a number of interpretations of *jihad* does not mean that all Muslims unanimously agreed with them. It is therefore wrong for non-Muslims to believe that *jihad* only means war in Islam, and that Muslims are willing to use violence. The term *jihad* can be confusing because various interpretations of *jihad* have existed in the circle of intellectuals in the Islamic history. The ambivalence of *jihad*, however, would be cleared up only when Muslims with the attitude of *mujahid* of peace show that Islam appreciates peace and the co-existence of different religions in this world.

References

Ali, Maulavi Vheragh, *A Critical Exposition of the Popular Jihad*, Delhi: Idareh-i Adabiyyat-i Delhi, 1984.

Bukhari, Muhammad bin Ismail. *Sahih Bukhari*, Medina: Dar al-Fikr, 1981.

Donner, Fred M., "The Sources of Islamic Conception of War." In John Kelsay and James Turner Johnson (eds.). *Just War and Jihad: Historical and Theoretical Perspectiveson War and Peace in Western and Islamic Tradition*, New York: Greenwood Press, 1991, pp. 31-69.

Hoffman, Valerie, J. *Sufism, Mystics and Saints in Modern Egypt*, Columbia: University of South Carolina Press, 1995.

Hujwiri, 'Ali ibn 'Uthman, *The Kahsf al-Mahjub* (transl. R.A. Nicholson), London: Luzac, 1911.

Jansen, Johannes J.G., *The Neglected Duty: The Creed of Sadat's Assassins and Islamic Resurgence in the Middle East*, New York: Macmillan, 1986.

Kelsay, John and Johson, James Turner (eds.), *Cross, Crescent and Sword: The Justification and Limitation of War in Western and Islamic Tradition*, Wesport, Cn., 1990.

Kelsay, John and Johnson, James Turner (eds.), *Just War and Jihad: Historical and Theoretical Perspective War and Peace in Western Tradition*, New York, Wesport, Cn., 1991.

Khomeini, Ruhullah, *Islamic Government*, Berkeley: Mizan Press, 1981.

Lewis, Bernard, *The Political Language of Islam*, Chicago: University of Chicago Press, 1988.

Loeffler, Reinhold, *Islam in Practice: Religious Beliefs in a Persian Village*, Albany: State University of New York Press, 1988.

Mawdudi, Abul A'la, *Al-Jihad fi-Sabil Allah,* Gujranwala: Dar al-'Arubat li Da'wah al-Islamiyyah, [n.d.].

Mir, Mustansir, "Jihad in Islam." In Hadia Dajami Shakeel and Ronald A. Messier (eds.). *The Jihad and Its Enemies*, Michigan: University of Michigan Center for Near Eastern and North African Studies, 1991, pp. 113-26.

Peters, Rudolph, *Jihad in Mediaeval and Modern Islam*, Leiden: E.J. Brill, 1977.

______________, *Jihad and Colonialism: the Doctrine of Jihad in the Modern History*, The Hague: Mouton, 1979.

Rahman, Fazlur, *The Major Themes of the Qur'an*, Minneapolis: Bibliotheca Islamica, 1980.

Renard, John, "Al-Jihad al-akbar," *Muslim World* 78 (1988): 225-242.

Shakeel, Hadia Dajami and Messier, Ronald A. (eds.), *The Jihad and Its Enemies*, Michigan, University of Michigan Centre For Near Eastern and North African Studies, 1991.

Sivan, Emmanuel, *Radical Islam: Medieval Theology and Modern Politics*, New Haven: Yale University Press, 1990.

Sonn, Tamara, "Irregular Warfare and Jihad: Asking the Right Question." In John Kelsay and James Turner Johnson (eds.). *Cross, Crescent and Sword: The Justification and Limitation of War in Western and Islamic Tradition*. Wesport Cn.: Greenwood Press, 1990, pp. 129-147.

5

The Position of Women in Islam: Criticizing the Compilation of Islam Law in Indonesia

— Siti Musdah Mulia

Islam is believed by its followers to be *rahmatan lil 'alamin* (a religion which brings blessings to the entire universe). One form of such blessings is Islam's acknowledgment of equality in humanity between women and men. A measure of one's honor before Allah is one's achievement and quality of faith, regardless of gender (Q[uran] s[ura] *al-Hujurat*/49:13). Women and men have equal potential to become the most devout. The *Qur'an* does not extend superiority to a certain gender. All of mankind, regardless of gender, has the same potential to become *'abid* and *khalifah* (vicegerent) (ss. *al-Nisa*/4:124 and *al-Nahl*/16:97).

Women at the time of the *Rasulullah* (Messenger) are depicted as active, polite, and moral. *Al-Qur'an* even symbolized the ideal *muslimah* figure as one who is independent in various aspects of life, including independence in politics, *al-Istiqlal al-siyasah* (s. *al-Mumtahanah*/60:12), as portrayed by the figure of Queen Bulqis who led a superpower kingdom (*'arsyun 'azhim*) (s. *al-Naml*/27:23). *Al-Qur'an* allows women to hold "oppositional" movements on various immoralities and to convey the truth (s. *al-Taubah*/9:71). Secondly, women's independence in economics is allowed, *al-istiqlal al-iqtishadi* (s. *al-Nahl*/16:97), as portrayed by the figure of the woman managing the farm in the story of the Noble Prophet Moses in Madyan (s. *al-Qashash*/28:23). Thirdly, women's independence in making a personal choice is allowed, *al-istiqlal al-syakhshi*, the truthfulness of which is believed, even when faced against husbands in the context of married women (s. *al-Tahrim*/66:11) or in opposing public opinion (s. *al-Tahrim*/66:12). It is, therefore, not a surprise that at the time of the Noble Prophet (peace be upon him, "saw"), a number of women were known to have capabilities and achievements no less brilliant than those achieved by men. The *Qur'an* guarantees that women can freely enter into all sectors of life in society, including in politics, economics and other various public sectors.

The above description greatly differs, however, from the realities of today's world. In various Islamic societies, not many women are allowed to play an active role in public sectors, especially in the field of politics. This means that a huge gap on the position of women currently exists, namely between that as set out normatively as against historico-empirical Islamic teachings. Although, normatively speaking, Islam greatly honours and respects women, in the empirical context the position of women is greatly marginalized and subordinated as can be seen from various formulations of Islamic law, particularly those relating to marriage as contained in the Compilations of Islamic Law (*Kompilasi Hukum Islam*, or KHI) of Indonesia.

This piece of writing will particularly focus on KHI with an emphasis on marriage law that has explicitly placed women as sexual objects and clearly confirmed their subordinated position. The writing will commence with a brief explanation of KHI, to be continued with its methodological problem. The writing will then proceed with a critical analysis of the position of women in KHI by laying out a number of crucial issues that have resulted in females becoming subordinated and marginalized. By way of conclusion, a new concept on KHI reform will be offered, which concept shall be based on the essential and universal values of Islam such as fairness, justice, equality and mutual benefit.

Brief Overview on the Compilation of Islamic Law (KHI)

The Compilation of Islamic Law (hereafter KHI) is a compilation produced by the Indonesian government during the New Order, the contents of which were derived from a number of _fiqh_ bibles mostly written during the mid-century. KHI has been compiled based on the joint resolution between the Chairman of the Supreme Court and the Minister of Religious Affairs on March 21, 1985, which eventually led to the Islamic Law Development Project through Jurisprudence (Compilation of Islamic Law Project). Furthermore, after the project was worked on for six years (1985-91), a formulation of Islamic law emerged that consisted of marriage law, inheritance law, and the law on religious foundations (_hukum perwakafan_), which was later called the Compilation of Islamic Law (KHI). Based on Presidential Instruction No.1 of 1991, KHI has been affirmed to be the official guide in the field of material law for judges handling religious affairs under the auspices of the Religious Courts[1] in all of Indonesia. The legal basis for this is art[icle] 4 para[graph] (1) of the 1945 Constitution, namely the power of the President over the State Government. It is interesting to note that the stipulation of KHI did not go through the parliamentary (People's Representative Council) approval process as is the case with statutes, but rather by way of a presidential decree. Although KHI is not legislated as law, its position in reality is strong since it serves as a guideline for all

---

[1] Indonesia has three types of courts, namely District Courts, which handle general cases for all Indonesian citizens irrespective of religion; Religious Courts, which specifically handle cases involving marriage, divorce, reconciliation, _wakaf_ (religious foundations) and other issues of the Indonesian Islamic community; and the Military Courts, which specifically handle military-related cases. Since the legal reform of 1999, these three types of court have all been united under the auspices of the Supreme Court.

judges and leaders of religious affairs, particularly those serving under the auspices of the Department of Religious Affairs.

The main objectives of KHI are threefold, namely to formulate Islamic law in a systematic and concrete fashion; to build a foundation of national scale for the application of Islamic law under the auspices of the Religious Courts; and, most importantly, to assert in uniform legal materials which shall serve as a reference for judges of the Religious Courts. In other words, KHI shall function as both a guideline for all judges within the auspices of the Religious Courts and a guide on Islamic law for all members of society. KHI also consists of three books, namely Book I on Marriage; Book II on Inheritance; and Book III on Religious Foundations (*Perwakafan*). Overall, KHI consists of 229 articles, the largest portion of which concerns marriage law.

KHI has been prepared in several stages. The first stage is by way of review of a number of fiqh bibles. At least thirteen *fiqh* bibles have been used as references, most of which were the classical *fiqh* bibles of the Syafi'i school of thought, such as *Kitab Al-Bajuri, Fathul Mu'in, Fathul Wahab, Tuhfah,* and *Qalyubi* or *Mahalli*, which, previously by the Department of Religious Affairs, have been used as a guideline for all Judges of Religious Affairs. The second stage is by way of interviewing 166 Islamic scholars in Indonesia's ten largest cities, none of whom, unfortunately, were women. The third stage is by way of comparative studies with Islamic countries: Morocco, Turkey and Egypt, so as to ascertain directly how Islamic law has been applied in such countries. The fourth stage is by way of seminars on legal materials held particularly for the Religious Courts. The facts at hand indicated that the preparation and formulation of KHI neglected the aspirations of women, which, among other matters, could be plainly considering the number of women involved in the project, which was highly insignificant given their involvement merely as note keepers. Ideally, the preparation of KHI should involve all women organizations and non-governmental organizations or include interviews with Islamic scholars who are women, particularly those having sound religious viewpoints and gender sensitivity.

KHI constitutes the government's response to some "unrest" in society arising from variations in the decisions of the Religious Courts in similar cases. These varied decisions were a logical consequence to the variations in legal finding sources taking the form of *fiqh* bibles used by judges of religious affairs in trying cases. Speaking of *fiqh* bibles meant speaking of variations in the opinions of religious scholars, whereby, interestingly, none of these scholars claimed that their opinions were the most correct and that those of others were not. This shows that freedom of opinion is greatly appreciated in Islam. Strangely, however, such 'freedom of opinion principle' as guaranteed by Islam was not applied by the government at that time. On the basis of social "unrest," the government produced positive law which was to serve as a uniform legal reference to all judges of religious affairs. Its objective was clearly to prevent the issuance of different decisions in similar cases, as was previous practised.

The government policy of formulating KHI contains two weaknesses: first, that although on the one hand it does facilitate the work of judges of religious affairs and other parties seeking instant legal reference, it has cut down on *ijtihad* creativity and efforts in the field of law. Due to the availability of instant legal materials, the judges generally no longer carry out a review of the *fiqh* bibles. This, in turn, led to stagnancy in the *ijtihad* process whereby the Islamic community has been repressed in legal obstinacy. Secondly, the limited legal materials of the KHI formulation have posed difficulties to judges of religious affairs, since, in reality, a number of new issues have arisen in line with the dynamics of society, such as violence in the home (*kejahatan dalam rumah tangga*, KDRT), the trafficking of women, contractual marriages, private marriages (*kawin sirri*) and inter-religion marriages with no change in legal references. These issues have posed difficulties to the judges of religious affairs in formulating decisions in the religious courts.

In our opinion, KHI, which has existed for the past 14 years, greatly needs to be evaluated in such a way that its effectiveness as a legal source, how society responds towards it, and whether KHI is still relevant for use in today's society can all be ascertained. At the same time, searches in the form of theses, dissertations and others have concluded that reviews and revisions to KHI need to be made, as parts of its contents are no longer relevant to contemporary social realities currently faced by society, that it no longer accommodated the interests of developing an egalitarian and democratic society, and that it is even considered a hindrance in efforts to form a civil society in this nation.

Another reason why KHI should be revised is the presence of a number of new laws and regulations in Indonesia, such as the second amendment to the 1945 Constitution, Law No. 7 on the Ratification of CEDAW, which confirmed the abolishment of all forms of discrimination towards women; Law No. 22 of 1999 on Regional Government, which quite strictly emphasized democratic principles characterized by the participation of all of society, without differentiating between men and women; Law No. 39 of 1999 on Human Rights; Law No. 23 of 2003 on the Protection of Children; Law No. 23 of 2004 on the Abolishment of Violence toward Women in their Homes (KDRT). The last two statutes greatly emphasized the protection of women's and children's rights from various forms of discrimination, exploitation and violence from any party and for whatever reason. In essence, such statutes greatly stressed efforts to protect and strengthen the rights of women with the aim of realizing conditions of gender equality and justice in all aspects of life in society, which shall include: social, economic and political spheres as well as in the family, society, nation and state.

KHI and its Methodological Problems (*Ushul Fiqh*)

KHI is deemed to be insufficiently representative of the needs and interests of the Islamic community in Indonesia, as it has not been thoroughly dug out from the wisdoms of Indonesian society but is rather derived from the classical *fiqh* bibles, which were Arabic in nature. The irrelevance of such classical *fiqh* is attributable to, among other factors, that they have been prepared in an altogether different era, culture and social imagination. There is even an indication that such classical fiqh are not only irrelevant from their material viewpoint, but are also problematic in their methodology. By way of definition, for example, *fiqh* has often been understood as "the mastery of *syara'* laws which are practical in nature and have been derived from *tafshili* argumentations, namely the *Qur'an* and the Sunnah (*al 'ilmu bi al-ahkam al-syar'iyyah al-'amaliyyah al-muktasab min adillatiha al-tafshiliyyah*). Speaking of such *ta'rif*, the truth of the *fiqh* becomes quite normative, as such truth is not only based on the role of the same for humanity but also on the extent of correctness in its reference to the literal meanings of *al-Qur'an* and *al-Sunnah*.

The law is a set of normative rules that regulate the patterns of human behaviour. The law does not grow in a vacuum but rather grows from social consciousness that acknowledges the need for joint rules. Therefore, the law should be able to adopt values which have grown and developed in society, including cultural, traditional and religious values. This is what is referred to as the *al-adat muhkamat* in the theory of Islamic law. This also means that the traditions or customs of society could turn into law.[2] As a consequence, each legal product must be perceived as a product of its time which could not be separated from various influences which surrounded its birth, both socio-cultural and socio-political influences alike. As both a social and cultural product, and even a political product of ideological nature, the law has always been contextual in nature.

Therefore, an alternative methodological structure (*ushul fiqh*) needs to be formulated by bearing in mind the following principles: *First*, that the reactualization of Islamic law is highly likely due to the dynamics and developments of time which give birth to various forms of social change. *Secondly*, that the reactualization of Islamic

---

[2] Jalaludin Al-Suyuthi, *Al-Asybah wa Al-Nazhair*, [n.pl., n.d.], p. 63.

law only relates to issues of *furu'* which are partial and substantial in nature (results of thoughts or interpretations of Islamic scholars on Islamic *syari'ah*, which, of course, are still *insaniyyah* and temporal in nature) and not on issues which involve *ushul al-kulliyat* (basic universal principles). *Thirdly*, that the reactualization of Islamic law is based on the principle of "preserving the old which is still relevant and formulating and offering a better new." *Fourthly*, that the reactualization of Islamic law must be followed with a criticial viewpoint on the world of classical scholars without the loss of due respect towards them. *Fifthly*, that the rationalization and reactualization of Islamic law means an understanding and a re-review of all Islamic traditions, including interpretations of *Al-Qur'an* and the *Hadiths* (*ahadith*, traditions), by understanding the same morally, intellectually and contextually without being tied to their legal-formal forms which tend to be partial and local in nature. *Sixthly*, the reactualization of Islamic law should adhere to the *maqashid al-ahkam al-syar'iyyah* (the essential purpose of Islam) and the well-being of its believers.

In addition, changes in time and place also hold an important position in the process of determining law (*taghayyurul ahkam bi taghayyur al-azminah wa al-amkinah*). Changes in law which are caused by changes in time and place consist of three possibilities, namely: (1) changes to the law itself, (2) changes to *muta'allaq al-hukm* (the object[s] of law), and (3) changes to *mawdu'al-hukm* (the subject[s] of law). Besides observing the above principles and efforts of systemization, another issue which must be considered in the process of inferring law (*istinbath al-ahkam*) is the use of ratio. Ratio holds an important position in Islamic law since it holds the highest place in the hierarchy of the knowledge system. Such importance of ratio has also been supported by the *ushul fiqh* norm which states, "*Kullu ma hakama al-'aqlu bi husnihi aw qubhihi, hakama al-syar'u bi wujubihi aw hurmatihi*" (Truthfully speaking, what is good or bad according to the law is even set out by *syari'at* law [the law of the path to be followed] as expressly enjoined or *haram* [expressly prohibited]). By using such an approach, the methodological structure of *ushul fiqh* will be dynamic, applicable and able to respond to every contemporary issue which may arise at any time. This is what makes Islamic teachings functional at any time and place (*shalihun li kulli zamanin wa makanin*).

Crucial Issues in KHI

As previously discussed, KHI consists of three sections of law, namely that of marriage, inheritance and religious foundations. In this writing, however, a critical analysis will be made only on marriage law, since this section highly deals with the issue of the role of women, particularly in husband-wife relations within households. The position of Muslim women in Indonesia is greatly influenced by the terms of marriage law contained in such KHI. This can be clearly seen from the number of issues discussed in KHI, such as the definition of marriage and provisions on the registration of marriage; the minimum ages to marry; the guardian of the bride in marriage; witnesses to the marriage and the role of husbands-wives; the rights and obligations of husbands-wives; the issue of poligamy; the issue of divorce; the issue of *nusyuz* (disobedience) and the issue of the status of out of wedlock children. These crucial issues will be discussed below.

Definition of Marriage

It is not difficult to explain how the position of women is marginalized under KHI. This can be seen, for example, in its definition of marriage, as set out in chapter II article 2: "Marriage according to Islamic law is (true) marriage, namely a marriage ceremony which is highly strong or *miitsaaqan ghaliidhan* to obey Allah's orders whereby to adhere to the same forms as *ibadah* (worship)." The sentence "to obey Allah's orders whereby to adhere to *same forms as* worship" contains a connotation that marriage is considered a worship or obligation that must be adhered to by all Muslims. This definition has led to the understanding that each Muslim must marry, and that not marrying is deemed to be not abiding by religious orders.

The basic law of marriage in Islam is *mubah* (simply permitted through silence). In other words, it may or may not be carried out. Marriage is a choice, not an obligation. Therefore, as marriage forms part of a person's human rights, he may proceed with the same in accordance with the prevailing rules or not engage in the same should he consider that such would be best. Certain conditions may change such basic law (*mubah*) into *sunah* (recommended but not enjoined), *wajib* (expressly enjoined), *makruh* (disliked but not prohibited), even *haram* (expressly prohibited). For example, if a person is able to marry and can no longer contain his sexual desires, then under such conditions he is obliged to marry. If, however, a person is not yet able to marry due to his not yet having a stable job or still being unable to provide, then marriage will only disadvantage him and his partner or, in the event he cannot function sexually, it would be best for him to avoid marriage altogether.

The meaning of worship in society is often confusing and interpreted narrowly. Truthfully speaking, worship covers all activities of man in his life that are intended to bestow upon him the blessings of Allah. If marriage is intended as a means to gain Allah's blessings, then it shall be deemed to form part of worship. Let alone marriage, even the daily consumption of food and water can fall into the category of worship if it is intended to gain the blessings of Allah. So the meaning of worship can be quite broad as it covers all of man's activities. What differentiates between activities of worship and activities of non-worship is the intention or commitment of the person in carrying out such activities. Accordingly, numerous verses and *hadits* of the Noble Prophet could be found which suggest that man affirms his intention solely to gain Allah's blessings, with no exceptions being made for marriage.

Why then must the definition of marriage be amended? Because defining marriage as part of worship and Allah's orders has, empirically and realistically speaking, brought about unfavourable consequences to women, including their inability to avoid marriage should parents and relatives require them to do so. Refusing to marry is considered a disobedience to religious norms which shall result in women being isolated from both their families and society. It is therefore not a surprise that in society, many cases of women being forced to marry under such theological argument could be found. In such cases, is marriage under Islamic syariat considered to be part of worship? Scholars are of different opinions, as a minority considers it to be worship, such as that of the Zahiri school of thought (the school of thought which strongly upholds the contextual meaning of Islamic teachings). Their understanding is based on a verse in Q[ur'an] s[ura] *an-Nisa'*/4:3 which contains the instruction to marry (*fankihu*) and that marriage is thus expressly enjoined. The majority of the scholars, such as Imam Syafi'i, however, affirmed that marriage forms part of *muamalah*, not worship. Syafi'i has based his arguments on s. *al-Nisa*/4:25, concluding froim his analysis of this verse that marriage is also not worship but rather *mandub* (recommended but not enjoined). He even added that it is highly recommended to avoid marriage for those who are unable to refrain themselves from acts of adultery.[3] Factually speaking, all *fiqh* bibles, both classical and contemporary alike, place marriage in their chapters on *muamalah* (issues of interpersonal relationships), and not in those of worship. The concept of Islam on marriage differs from that of Catholicism, which perceives the same as a form of sacrament. Marriage in Islam is more of a social contract. This contractual nature can be seen in the elements of *ijab* (offer) and *qabul* (acceptance).

For revisions to *the* KHI, we hereby offer the following: first, to affirm the understanding that marriage is not an obligation but rather a right. Men are entitled to freely choose to marry or not to marry. The right to marry, build families and build generations are human rights which are non-derogatory. Secondly, to affirm the meaning of marriage as a social transaction or *akad* which shall involve two equal parties: a man and a woman. The parties entering into the *akad* (transaction) in marriage should be the man (groom-to-be) and woman (bride-to-be), not the man (groom-to-be) and man (father in-law to be or guardian of the bride-to-be) as is the current practice in Islamic societies.

---

[3] Abu Hasan al-Mawardi, *Laws of Governance, al-Ahkam al-Sultaniyyah*, London, 1996.

We also suggest that the (new) definition of marriage at least contain the following two principles. First, the principle of *mitsaqan ghalidzan* as referred to in the Quranic ss. *a-Ahzab 7; an-Nisa 21 and 154* which all contain the understanding that marriage is a sacred agreement between two parties. Accordingly, marriage is a sacred agreement between a man and a woman that is entered into under full consciousness and willingness without any coercions on the basis of love and care (*mawaddah wa rahmah*). Both parties are obliged to maintain the sacredness and longevity of such agreement. Secondly, the principle of equality between husband and wife is referred in the following verses: *al-Zariyat 49; Fatir 11; an-Naba' 78; an-Nisa' 20; Yasin 36; as-Syura 11; az-Zukhruf 12; al-Baqarah 187;* and *an-Najm 53;* and a number of the Noble Prophet's *Hadiths* or traditions.

Registration of Marriage

The registration of marriage is regulated in articles 5, 6 and 7 of KHI. The provisions contained in such articles explain the importance of registration of marriage. However, society in general is of the understanding that a marriage is deemed valid if carried out in accordance with Islamic law, although it has not been registered. A majority of the Islamic community adopts the Syafi'i school of thought, which is of the belief that a marriage is deemed valid if the following five elements are available: the groom, the bride, *ijab qabul* (matrimonial vows), witnesses and guardian. Registration is not required for a marriage to be deemed valid. Is it therefore not a surprise that there are many cases of unregistered marriages, commonly known as *kawin sirri* or *kawin di bawah tangan* (privately held marriages). In such cases, the victims are most often women and children as, in the event of divorces, they generally can not demand their civil rights, such as monthly support, inheritance and *harta gono-gini* (joint property gained during marriage) due to the non-existence of legal documentation in the form of a *Akta Nikah* (Marriage Deed). The revision offered herein is to make registration one of the requirements for a marriage to be valid. The theological basis for such is the use of *qiyas* or analogy of the *Qur'an's al-Baqarah*/2:282 which ordered the registration of debts.[4] In essence, marriage is a highly important transaction, much more important than any other transaction in a man's life. If a debt transaction must be registered, shouldn't it be more crucial for a marriage transaction to be registered as well? Another basis is the *hadith* of the Noble Prophet which said: …do not subject yourself to prostitution and enter into a *pernikahan sirri* (*sirri* marriage)" (see the *an-Nikah* and *Sunan at-Tirmizi* bibles, *hadith* no. 1008; *an-Nikah Sunan an-Nasai* bible nos. 3316-3317; *an-Nikah Sunan Ibn Majah* no. 1886). In addition, there are also a number of *hadiths* which encourage the publication of marriage (See as-Sarakhsi, *al-Mabsut*, V:31; Sunan at-Tirmidzi no. 1009; Sunan Ibn Majah no. 1885; and Musnad Ahmad no. 15545), and other *hadiths* again which require the fulfilment of the (above) four elements in *akad nikah* for a marriage to be considered valid. There is also a saying of Umar ibn Khattab which does not acknowledge the validity of a marriage which is attended by only one witness.

Unregistered marriages are truly disadvantageous to wives and children alike. Legally speaking, the wives are not considered to be lawfully wed as they do not own the *Akta Nikah* as an authentic legal document. As a result, such wives are not entitled to *harta gono-gini* in the event of divorces as, legally speaking, such marriages are deemed to have never existed. In addition, they are also not entitled to monthly support and inheritance in the event of divorces or the deaths of their husbands. Besides the above legal effects, privately-held marriages also bring about social effects to the women, who will have a difficult time socializing in society as they are deemed to be mistresses or engaging in *kumpul kebo* (living together without being married). As for children born under these kinds of marriages, they will bear the status of an *anak tidak sah* (children born out of wedlock), a status that will also be written on their birth certificates. Such children will also only have civil ties with their mothers and their mothers' families, with no legal ties whatsoever with their fathers (articles 42 and 43 of the Marriage Law: *Undang-undang Perkawinan*, UUP). The statement "child born

---

[4] Al-Baqarah, 2:282.

out of wedlock" on birth certificates will surely bring adverse social and psychological effects to these children and their mothers. The unclear legal statuses of these children will also result in their not being entitled to receive monthly allowances, inheritances as well as costs of living and education, from their fathers.

According to Abu Hasan al-Mawardi,[5] governments under Islamic law are obliged to protect their citizens from all forms of exploitation and unfair treatment by formulating rules which shall create harmony and peace. As *uli al-amr*, governments have two main functions, namely that of *fi harasah al-din* (protector of religion) and *fi siyasah al-dunya* (regulator of wordly affairs). In implementing these two functions, citizens must abide with their governments, so long as they do not endorse acts which deny (Allah) or are not beneficial (to society). It is in the context of implementing these functions that governments are allowed to formulate laws and regulations in the field of *siyasah al-syar'iyah*. *Siyasah al-syar'iyah* is a set of rules which has been prepared by governments in order to support the application of teachings of *Al-Qur'an* and the *Hadiths* of the *Rasul*, even if such a set has not yet been formulated by previous scholars.

Age to Enter into Marriage

The minimum age to enter into marriage under KHI is nineteen for men and sixteen for women (art. 7 para. 1). The fact that the age limit is lower for women substantially confirms the subordinated position of women (wives) versus men (husbands). Why must there be differing minimum ages? This truly also goes against the contents of Indonesia's Law No. 4 of 1979 on the Welfare of Children. art. 1 para. 2 of such Law sets out that: "A child is one who is not yet 21 years of age and has never been married." It is also contrary to the contents of the International Convention of the Children's Rights as ratified by Indonesia in 1990. The Convention confirms that eighteen is the age limit of a child, as is the case with the Law on the Protection of Children of 2003. In other words, the government's act of legalizing marriages of

---

[5] See Abu Hasan, op. cit.

women aged sixteen means that it has legitimized child marriages, a form of child abuse.

Research results at the Center for Women Studies at the Universitas Islam Negeri Syarif Hidayatullah Jakarta (2000) have indicated that the average ideal age for women to marry ranges from 19,9 years whereas for men, 23.4 years. It is important to note that such maturity in age ideally results from an accumulation of physical, economic, social, mental and psychological, religious and cultural readiness. Marriages require maturity which should not only be biological but psychological and social as well. The minimum age to marry for men and women alike should be at least 21, approximately after they graduate from high school. Marriages at a young age for women may subject them to various risks, both biological, such as damage to their reproductive organs, or pregnancies at a young age, and psychological, such as the inability to carry out their reproductive functions. Family life requires that significant roles be played and significant responsibilities be borne by men and women alike.

By way of comparison, in Syria, not only is the minimum age to marry regulated but also the age difference between the man and woman to be married is regulated. If the age gap between the two is too wide, the court may prohibit such a marriage from taking place. The same also applies in Jordan, whereby a marriage is prohibited if the age difference between both parties exceeds more than twenty years, unless the court decides otherwise by way of a special permit. The objective of the governments of these two countries in regulating the age gap between the two parties is solely to protect their citizens from acts of extortion and exploitation, as large age gaps may give one party the potential to take advantage of the other. Scholars must think about increasing the minimum age to marry, as lately there have been many cases of child trafficking hidden under the modus operandi of marriage.

Marriage Guardian (*Wali Nikah*)

Art. 19 of KHI states that a marriage guardian of a woman in marriage is a must, and such guardian must be male and a Muslim.

This requirement clearly exemplies the subordinated position of women within the family, besides also confirming that they are neither free nor independent. This is due to the fact that the father of the bride-to-be shall serve as guardian, failing which a male relative may take his place, even if of a younger age than that of the bride-to-be. A man is more accepted to become a guardian than a mature woman, even the mother of the bride-to-be. It could be clearly seen here that the human rights of women is not appreciated since, even as the biological mother of the bride-to-be, a woman is not allowed to see her daughter be wed due solely to the fact that she is a woman. In addition, the existence of a guardian may give rise to a crisis of existence on the part of the woman: allowing the guardian to see that she be wed indirectly means that she does not have the autonomy and power to act, two of the most basic rights in a man's life. In other words, the requirement of a guardian could be deemed an emasculation of women's rights.

We propose that guardians be required only for women who are still underaged or under 21 years of age. The eradication of the requirement for a woman's guardian in marriage is actually not new, since such has already been practised by Imam Abu Hanafiah, who lived during the ninth century. The requirement of a guardian does not have a basis in either the *Qur'an* or *Sunnah*. Its only basis is in interpretations of the *Hadiths* of the Noble Prophet. In the meantime, a number of verses and *Hadiths* has explicitly affirmed the existence of women as whole beings who are equal to men. There are no essential differences between the two in exercising religious teachings, including those on marriage.

Witnesses to a Marriage

Art. 25 of KHI states that the presence of two witnesses is a must in a marriage ceremony, and that these witnesses must be male, Muslim, and able-bodied (neither deaf nor blind). There clearly is an element of discrimination in this case, not only against women but also against a group of people who are coincidentally physically handicapped (disabled) from a general human rights perspective. Why cannot women, the blind and the deaf be allowed to act as witnesses in marriage? With reference to the *Qur'an*, witnesses are not required in the context of marriage but rather that of divorce. Witnesses are only allowed at the time of divorce (*thalaq*) as explained in s. *al-Thalaq*, 2. The proposed KHI revision in this case is that registration should form one of the requirements for a marriage to be valid. The function of witnesses, which is basically to witness and inform that a marriage has taken place, could be with registration. Cannot the party registering the marriage, either man or woman alike, simultaneously become a witness to such marriage as well? Should the requirement for witnesses still be upheld, then it is proposed that those who could serve as witnesses are men and women as well as the handicapped, including those who are deaf and blind.

Position of Husband-Wife

The position of husband-wife in KHI is stated in art. 79 as follows: (1) A husband shall serve as head of the family whereas the wife, as a homemaker. (2) The rights and position of a wife are equal to those of a husband within both the household and interactions in society. (3) Each party is entitled to carry out a legal act. Plainly viewed, the contents of the three paragraphs of article 79 appear to contradict one another. In para. 2 it is stated that the positions of husband and wife are equal, but how could they be equal when in the preceding paragraph, a husband is set out as head of the family? The use of the word "head" in explaining the position of husband contains a connotation of power and is authoritarian in such a way that the public perceives a husband as identical with authority in social life. The implication of this understanding in society is, among others, that husbands become extremely dominant and hold authoritarian power in households so as to impose upon wives the carrying out of all domestic tasks as well as the serving of all their husbands' physical and mental needs. The practice of domination by husbands is quite contrary to the moral message of the *Qur'an*. Through a number of Quranic verses, Allah the Almighty has reiterated the equal position of husband and wife whereby both should complement one another (*hunna libasun lakum wa antum libasun lahunna* (a wife shall protect her husband and, vice versa, a husband shall protect his wife) (s. *al-Baqarah*/2:187).

The unequal position of husband-wife as referred to in art. 79, para. 1 of KHI has led to women not being able to enjoy equal position and rights as set out in para. 2. Although both are entitled to carry out legal acts (para. 3), in reality the position of women or wives is not always equal from a legal perspective. The position of wives, which is subordinate to that of their husbands, has imposed a structural hindrance on them in being able to carry out legal acts. This is a fact which, besides affirming the marginalized position of women as homemakers, has also standardized their domestic roles. In turn, this domestication has led to "taming", segregation and to efforts at de-politicizing women. This domestication has also led to discrimination against women in the work force. Generally speaking, women workers are paid less than their male counterparts.

Positing the position of husband as head of the family also reflects a denial of the realities currently existing in society, as this article only accomodates one pattern of family, that consisting of a father (husband), mother (wife) and children. The reality of society, on the other hand, shows variations in the form of families and households. Many families consist of only one parent, namely mothers or wives with several children, thus resulting in such mothers playing the role of family heads. There are also families which consist of several children whose parents have left (both father and mother), thus resulting in the eldest daughters playing the role of heads of such families or households. Accordingly, many women have on a *de facto* basis already played the role of family heads, although such is not yet acknowledged on a *de jure* basis. This latest phenomenon clearly shows that there is an increasing role of women acting as family heads, which matter could not be explained by KHI. As a result of wars (such as in Aceh) and the migration of workers abroad, women have indeed been forced to take up the roles of family heads. Statistics in 2003 from the

National Central Statistics Bureau have even stated that one out of every nine heads of families in Indonesia are women.

Islam teaches that, generally speaking, each man is a leader, at a minimum for his own self. All leaders will also be held accountable before Allah for all of their actions. There is a *hadith* which states that: "Each of you is a leader, and each of you will be asked about your leadership; a wife is a leader and will be asked about her leadership; an aide is a leader in maintaining the property of his master; and will be asked about his leadership; and all of you are leaders, and will be asked about your leaderships" (H.R. Bukhari Muslim). This *hadith* shows and gives an opportunity to everyone, men or women alike, to become leaders. The biological label which is attached to gender is not a main requirement for one to become a leader, but rather one's competence for his leadership in being held accountable before Allah.

The Rights and Obligations of Husband-Wife

KHI states that "A husband shall give guidance to his wife and household, although important household decisions shall be made jointly by both husband and wife" (art. 80, para. 1). The imposition of duty on the husband to guide his wife affirms the subordinate role of women. This subordinated position is emphasized in the following statement: "A husband shall protect his wife and provide all household needs in accordance with his capabilities" (para. 2). With such a statement, the figure of the wife is depicted as helpless and always in need of protection, whereas a husband is strong and powerful. The sociological reality shown that wives are not always weak and helpless, and that many are able to bear living costs alone. Cases of work termination have shown that husbands who are terminated at work find it difficult to bear household burdens, which matter has ultimately led to their wives being active despite their being stereotyped as weak.

Another of a husband's obligations under KHI has it that: "A husband must ensure that his wife receives religious education and ample opportunity to gain knowledge which is useful and valuable to her religion, country and nation" (art. 80, para. 3). It appears that the formulators of KHI have already predicted that a husband must have superior knowledge than his wife in various aspects, including in religion, since, if such is not the case, how could the husband carry out the above obligation? A question then arises as to the possibility of a wife coincidentally being an expert in the field of religion. Logically speaking, a man who does not have or lacks knowledge in religion should be prohibited from marrying such a woman due to the concern that he may not be able to fulfil the above obligation after the marriage takes place. Another question also arises as to why the husband-wife relationship is often depicted as a vertical and structural relationship instead of a horizontal relationship with synergy, where both shall help and complement one another? As required under the *Qur'an (ul-Baqarah/2:187)* "...wives shall be like clothing to you, and husbands shall be like clothing to their wives."

Further, the following is the obligation of a wife: "The main obligation of a wife is to physically and mentally serve her husband within boundaries allowed by Islamic law" (art. 83, para. 1). Why are the words physically and mentally only emphasized for wives and not applicable to husbands? Are the obligations of husbands purely limited to matters that are material and physical in nature? Furthermore, it is quite difficult to explain the valid measure of what to serve physically and mentally means. If a wife is unable to carry out her obligation of serving physically and mentally, then she shall be deemed to be *nusyuz*. Worse still, *nusyuz* serves as justification on the part of a husband to to fulfil his obligations. KHI only places *nusyuz* on wives, whereas the *Qur'an (an-Nisa'/4:128)* explicitly mentions the *nusyuz* of husbands. This means that *nusyuz* accusations are not only applicable to women but also men. Unfortunately, the words "within boundaries allowed by Islamic law" as set out in KHI are rarely socialized in society, although such is the substance of Allah's saying in *s. an-Nisa/4:19*: *wa'asyiruuhunna bilmakruf* (do exchange in gentle intercourses with your wife). Another obligation is "A wife shall with best efforts manage and arrange for the daily needs of the household" (art. 83

para. 2). This stipulation justifies the stereotypical perception in society that women are best placed in beds, wells and kitchens. As a result, women working outside their homes are deemed dishonorable due to their having neglected their obligations. This has also brought unfavourable implications to women in the workplace, as wives working for a living outside their homes are only valued as additional workers earning additional incomes. Women workers are often categorized as single workers, although they may, realistically speaking, have husbands and children. In this case, they do not receive support for their husbands and children as is the case with their male counterparts.

Polygamy

KHI, as is the case with the Marriage Law of 1974, adopts that husbands are allowed to engage in polygamy (although the number is limited to four wives). This provision is set out in chapter IX, arts. 55-59, which mentions *inter alia*: The main requirement that a husband may have more than one wife is that he must be able to accord fair treatment to all of his wives and children (art. 55, para. 2). Besides the above, another requirement that must be fulfilled as set out in art. 5 of Law No.1 of 1974 is spousal consent and certainty that the husband is capable of providing the daily needs of his wives and children. Ironically, art. 59 states: "In the event a wife refuses to grant consent and an application for permission to have more than one wife based on one of the reasons referred to in arts. 55, paras. (2) and 57 has been duly filed, the Religious Court may stipulate on the granting of such permission after having examined and heard the relevant wife/wives at a court session of the Religious Court, which stipulation can be appealed or filed for cessation by the wife/wives or husband. This article clearly indicates the weak position of a wife since, in the event she should refuse to grant consent, the Religious Court may simultaneously take over her position as the party granting consent, although the same article provided a clause at the end which allowed her to file for an appeal. In reality, however, wives are generally ashamed and reluctant to appeal court decisions concerning polygamy.

The reasons used by Religious Courts in granting permission to a husband to engage in polygamy are as follows: 1) that the wife is unable to carry out obligations as a wife; 2) the wife becomes physically handicapped or suffers an incurable illness; and 3) the wife could not conceive. These reasons as referred to by Religious Courts have in no way reflected the guidance of Allah under *s. al-Nisa*/4:19, which means: "…and do gently engage in intercourse with your wives. If you are not fond of them, (then be patient) as it could be that Allah has bestowed much good behind things you are not fond of."

In addition, the above reasons for husbands to engage in polygamy are only seen from the perspective of their interests without any consideration whatsoever to the interests of women. It has never been considered, for instance, that husbands may be unable to carry out their obligations, incur handicap or disease, or be unable to conceive. In such cases, can the Religious Court grant permission to wives to re-marry? The provisions of KHI on polygamy, then, clearly show the subordinated position of women.

Does Islam endorse polygamy? Let us take a look at history. When Islam was first introduced in the seventh century, polygamy had already existed as a widely spread practice in various societies, including the Arab *Jahiliyah* society. Islam has brought about radical changes to such a practice as polygamy, which had already become tradition. First, it has limited the number of wives to four, whereas previously no limit was set. Several tribal heads were even known to have hundreds of wives. The next change involves the requirement for fairness, whereby if such is not possible, it would be best to have only one wife. This fairness requirement covers quite a wide aspect, but as *mufassirs* (experts in *Qur'an*) generally reduce this requirement to material fairness, this interpretation is, expectedly, detrimental to women. The changes brought about by Islam should have served as an incentive for Muslims to improve the condition of women by not tolerating polygamy as is the case in Tunisia, a Muslim country. Tunisian marriage law prohibits polygamy, as it is considered to be a crime against humanity and no longer relevant to civilized modern society.

Theologically speaking, the only verse which has often been used as a basis to endorse polygamy is the *sura an-Nisa*/4, vs. 3. If the *asbab nuzul* (reason for revelation) of this verse is researched, however, it could be seen it does not speak in the context of marriage but rather the maintenance of orphans. Islam is a religion which brings with it the mission for freedom. Such freedom is particularly addressed to three groups within society, namely the slaves, orphans and women. Orphans receive attention which is no less important than that accorded to slaves and women, since they often become objects of property confiscation as a result of their not being duly protected by their guardians. At that time, marriages taking place with orphans were often solely intended as a means to control their property. To men who are unable to act fairly to orphans, Allah has suggested that they do not marry orphans and that as an alternative, they are allowed to marry other women whom they are fond of up to two, three or four persons. The latter, too, is only allowed if they are able to act fairly to all wives, failing which one wife shall suffice since it will be closest to the fairness concept. Based on the above, it can be concluded that the principle of marriage in Islam is monogamy, not polygamy.

Another point which should be noted with respect to polygamy is the attitude of the Noble Prophet Muhammad, who has engaged in the same only after reaching the age of 53, after the death of his wife Khadijah and his children had reached adulthood with the exception of Fatimah. If polygamy is endorsed in Islam, then why did the Noble Prophet Muhammad not engage in the same from the beginning of his marriage? It is also interesting to note here that a number of *hadiths* have shown that the Prophet did not allow his daughter to be an object of polygamy. When Ali ibn Abi Thalib, Fatimah's husband, intended to re-marry, the Prophet became furious and said, "Fatimah's pain is also mine, and Fatimah's suffering is mine as well."[6] The above *hadith* of the

---

[6] Siti Musdah Mulia, *Islam Menggugat Poligami* (Islam sues Polygamy), Gramedia, Jakarta, 2004, pp. 82-84.

Prophet has clearly explained his disliking of the concept of polygamy.

Consequences of an Ended Marriage

In KHI chapter XVII regarding Consequences of an Ended Marriage, it is stated among others that: An ex-husband is allowed to reconcilie with his wife during the *iddah* (three menstruating cycles) stage (art. 150). The dominant position of a man in marriage could be clearly seen here, whereby he may at any time reconcile with his wife without having to request her consent. A wife, on the other hand, does not have such a right, but rather only has to wait for her husband's wish to do so. The preceding article further states that: "During the *iddah* period, an ex-wife must maintain herself well, not accept any marriage proposals and not marry another man" (art. 151). The obligation to maintain oneself is always emphasized on the part of a wife, not the husband. A question then arises as to why only wives are obliged to maintain themselves, in this case their reproductive organs. This also reaffirms the existing negative impression on women, namely that they are weak, vulnerable, and easily susceptible to sexual disorders and, that accordingly, they must be confined to their homes. In this regard, KHI clearly shows its support of the stereotypical perspective that is paternally biased, and not the egalitarian perspective of Islam. Islam teaches that all mankind, both men and women alike, must maintain their reproductive organs so as to not fall in acts of sin. In the *Al-Qur'an* there is even a number of verses that explain the same, with indications that the instruction to maintain reproductive organs is more addressed to men rather than women *(ss. al Mukminun/23:5, al-Nur/24:30-31, al-Ahzab/33:35,* and *al-Ma'arij/70:29).*

The negative impression on wives could also be seen in the last chapter, namely chapter XIX on Mourning Period. It is stated there that "A wife whose husband has passed away must go through a mourning period during her *iddah* stage as a token of her grief and to avoid slander." The emphasis that a wife must go through an *iddah* stage is acceptable, since such shall serve as a transitional period for the wife to further consider whether she will or will not re-marry. What is questionable, however, is the reason behind such a period, namely to avoid the occurrence of slander. The mentioning of such reason in this provision only strengthens the stereotype currently existing that women are a source of slander and therefore must be confined to their homes so as not to create chaos in society.

Nusyuz (Disobedience)

Terminologically speaking, *nusyuz* shall mean to rebel or be disobedient to orders. Unfortunately, however, society only perceives *nusyuz* as the rebellion of wives against their husbands and not vice versa. *Nusyuz* has led to the rise of violent acts in households. The concept of *nusyuz* is not attached to husbands, which matter clearly shows the existence of a double standard. As normal human beings, even men have the potential to engage in *nusyuz*, although such has never been attached to them (as husbands). The verse on *nusyuz* (*s. an-Nisa*/4:34) emerged in the context of Arab society at the time that was accustomed to violence against women (as wives). Battery was the form of violence which most often occurred. Therefore, we can see that such a verse has descended in the context of prohibiting battery and not, as often said, to legitimate violence. At the time, Ummu Habibah came to the Noble Prophet to tell of her experiences after being beaten by her husband, after which the Noble Prophet advised that she should *qishash* (hit back). After she had left, however, the above verse descended (*s. an-Nisa'*/4:34), which referred to husbands as *qawamuuna* (protectors) of their wives. In other words, husbands are supposed to protect their wives, not oppress or make them suffer. At the same time, the verse also prohibits wives from hitting back as violence could not be settled with similar violence.

Then how do we give meaning to the verse which is deemed to give legitimacy to violence? If there is concern that a wife has committed *nusyuz*, then the husband shall first give advice, failing which both should sleep distantly in bed. In the event of no change, then the husband may give a lesson to his wife without hurting her physically. The word *dharaba*, which is often defined as "hit," actually has various meanings (*interpretable*), one of which is to "provide instances" which shows that the word does not always refer to physical beatings. Therefore, the word *dharaba* as linked with the concept of *nusyuz* shall mean the exertion of (mental) beatings to the wife by using various analogies. In reality, however, this verse has been used as legitimation of the beating of wives. It is therefore not a surprise that the amount of domestic violence taking place in Islamic societies is extremely high, with no exceptions being made for Indonesia.

Status of Children born out of Wedlock

KHI does not accord adequate treatment to children born out of wedlock. This is evinced by art. 100, which states that children born out of wedlock shall only have family ties with their mothers and their mothers' families and shall not in any way have ties with their fathers. This perception, which is an utter harassment to children born out of wedlock, falls against Islamic teachings which reaffirm that equal treatment be accorded to all men without due regard to their origins. Has not Islam taught that all men are born innocent, sinless and without any hereditary sins whatsoever? Accordingly, for the good of these children as honourable human beings who should not bear the sins of their parents, we suggest that KHI grant a right to these children to trace family ties from their fathers' side. The tracing of one's biological father is no longer such a difficult task, as such could be done through DNA testing. KHI should not close the opportunity for these children to acquire the love and care of both their fathers and their fathers' families. KHI should also give a solution for the fulfilment of children's rights as regarding inheritance from their biological fathers. In order for the welfare of these innocent children to still be maintained, it is suggested that KHI give adequate protection to these children. Such protection could be accorded by stating that the status of children resulting from unwed pregnancies shall not differ from those born in valid marriages. These children born out of wedlock shall also be entitled to child care, education and judicial legality on the status of their family ties.

The Patriarchally Biased Fiqh Perception

At the beginning of this writing, it was mentioned that the sources used in formulating KHI are classical *fiqh* bibles which are biased with patriarchal values so that its contents contain perspectives which discredit women. *Fiqh* bibles, which have been written periodically, generally contain the guidance of a person or several *fiqh* experts. In other words, *fiqh* consists of cultural interpretations of the *syariat* that have been developed by *fiqh* scholars since the second decade of the hijrah period. It is common knowledge that *fiqh* often places women as sexual objects, particularly in husband-wife relations. Discussions on marriage in *fiqh* bibles display a strikingly explicit difference between men and women, in that men are allowed to engage in polygamy, whereas women can only engage in monogamous relationships. Even from the stage of selecting a partner-to-be, women are stated to not have the right to decide but rather their fathers or guardians, of which right is referred to as the *hak ijbar* in *fiqh*. Further, men have the right to "take a peek" at their future wives during marriage proposals, whereas none of this exists for women.

Fiqh bibles are actually bibles which contain cultural interpretations or explanations on verses of the *Qur'an*. In the intellectual history of Islam, *syari'ah* has been differentiated from *fiqh*. The first contains basic teachings, is universal in nature, absolute and permanent, whereas the latter contains non-basic teachings, is local, elastic and relative or not permanent. *Fiqh* bibles are greatly influenced by the environmental situations and conditions of their writers. Writers who lived through situations and conditions of male-dominated societies, such as those of Middle Eastern regions, were prone to writing *fiqh* bibles of a patriarchal nature and vice versa. A *fiqh* bible which is often used as a reference in schools of Quranic studies, particularly those under the auspices of Nahdlatul Ulama, is the *'Uqud al-Lujain fi Bayani Huquq az-Zaujain'* bible. This bible has been written by Imam Nawawi al-Bantani, a great scholar from Banten who married an Arab woman and lived in Mecca. The perceptions contained in this bible were highly gender biased with patriarchal values. The following is a quotation from this bible in that regard: "A wife's obligation to her husband is to obey him and not to be disobedient, not to leave the home without his permission, not to engage in *sunat* fasting without his permission, and not to refuse his request for sexual intercourse even when riding a camel."

The above bible has mentioned more than once that:

> A wife who leaves home without her husband's permission shall be cursed by a number of angels, among them the angel of blessings, the angel guarding the skies and even the angel guarding the earth, up until the time she returns home.

The bible also often mentioned the rage of angels towards wives who are disobedient or not submissive to their husbands. Another perception which could be found in such bible is the following:

> A wife is prohibited from taking her husband's property without his permission since her sins in this case shall be heavier than taking the property of another person. Punishment for stealing the property of a husband shall equal that of 70 thieves, whereas punishment for stealing another person's property shall equal that of one thief.

Logically speaking, if a wife intends to steal, it would be best to steal another person's property rather than that of her husband, since punishment for the former is lighter. The above statement also justifies the stereotypical perception of a wife as an individual who does not have her own property and is therefore always dependent on her husband's property. In conclusion, women are always depicted as inferior in *fiqh* bibles.

Truthfully speaking, the writers of *fiqh* bibles, particularly leaders (*imam*) of the large schools of thought, have never mentioned that their *fiqh* perceptions must be used as a reference or source in formulating law. Almost all of these writers even humbly stated that if the opinions written in the *fiqh* bibles are correct, they came from Allah, whereas if not, it is because they came from the writers themselves as human beings. At the end of each discussion in the *fiqh* bibles, the writers always insert the sentence: *wallahu a'lam* (only Allah is the All Knowing), which meant that if my opinion is correct, do adopt it whereas if not, do not adopt the same. This also meant that the writer as of the *fiqh* bibles themselves still give room for possible corrections and revisions to their perceptions. Why, then, do subsequent generations tend to treat the perceptions set out in the *fiqh* bibles as final and unchangeable? In other words, *fiqh* bibles have been treated as sacred, even more so than the *Qur'an*, which matter is highly un-proportional.

Improvements on the Position of Women through KHI Revisions
To raise the position and status of women in proportion to the teachings of Islam, reform in various fields needs to be made, such as reconstruction on the understanding of Islam, particularly that on the position and status of women; improvements in the quality of women's education; and revision of statutes, particularly those on marriage. This last solution is utterly important, since improvements in the field of law will ultimately influence other fields. For this, we propose a concept for revision by offering a new paradigm on marriage which shall be based on the following four basic principles. First, that marriage is a highly strong contract (*mitsaaqan ghaliidzan*) which has been entered into consciously by a man and a woman in order to form a family whose running shall be based on the willingness and consent of both parties. Secondly, that the principle of marriage is monogamy (*tawahhud al-zawj*) and not polygamy. Thirdly, that marriage is entered into on the basis of willingness (*al-taraadli*), equality (*al-musaawah*), justice (*al'adaalah*), welfare (*al-mashlahat*), pluralism (*al-ta'addudiyah*), and democracy (*al-diimuqrathiyyah*). Fourthly, that the purpose of marriage is to create a happy and prosperous (*sakiinah*) household based on love and care (*mawaddah* and *rahmah*) as well as to fulfil biological needs in a legal, healthy, safe, comfortable and responsible manner. These four paradigms form strong grounds for gender equality foundation in husband-wife relations.

The above four principles have been derived from the main source of Islamic teachings, namely the *Qur'an* and the *Hadith*s of the *Rasul. Al-Qur'an* (*ss. al-Ahzab*/33:7 and *an-Nisa*/4:21 and 154), for example, always depicts marriage as *mitsaaqan ghalidzan*, a sacred agreement between two equal parties which is filled with love and care. Therefore, both parties are obliged to maintain the sacredness and longevity of such agreement. Further, the *Qur'an* also affirms the egalitarian relationship between husband-wife, as could be seen in the following verses: *ss. az*-Zariyat/51:49; Fatir/ 35:11; *an-Naba'*/78; *an-Nisa'*/4:20; *Yasin*/36; *as-Syura*/42:11; *az-Zukhruf*/43:12; *al-Baqarah*/2:187; and *an-Najm*/53. Affirmations on the equal nature of the relations could also be found in a number of the Prophet's *hadiths*. All of the above verses and *hadiths* clearly conclude that a marriage in Islam is more of an agreement or contract.[7] Such contract could be seen from the element of *ijab* (offer) and *qabul* (acceptance). Therefore, a marriage is an agreement or contract which binds two equal parties, namely a man and a woman who have each fulfilled certain requirements based on prevailing laws and on the basis of their mutual willingness and fondness to form a family.

The highest essence of marriage is eloquently described in the *Qur'an*, namely in *s. al-A'raf*/7:18. According to this verse, marriage is a re-uniting of man to his most fundamental form of humanity, namely the *nafsin wahidah* (a united self). Allah the Almighty has used the term *nafsin wahidah* on purpose, since this term is intended to basically depict marriage as a reunification between man and woman at the practical level, after reunification at the basic stage has first taken place, namely sameness in the origins of man from a united self.

In another verse (*al-Rum*/30:21), emphasis is placed on ties between fundamental unity, *min anfusikun*, as a form of unity at the theoretical and idealistic level with practical unity (marriage) that is harmonious and full of care. This harmony and care could never exist in unequal husband-wife relations or in circumstances where a husband or wife is more dominant. Dominance in its truest

---

[7] *An-Nisa'*/4:21 and *Al-Baqarah*/2:231.

form has always led to ignorance of the partner's rights and existence. If the dominance element in *husband*-wife relations are taken out, what takes place in its stead is a just relationship which is full of love and care (*mawaddah wa rahmah*).

It is iteresting to note that the *Qur'an* discusses marriage in detail in numerous verses. In no less than 104 verses, marriage is discussed through use of the term *nikah* (to unite) which is repeated 23 times as well as the term *zauwj* (spouse) which is mentioned 80 times. Understanding the essence of marriage in Islam is a must, unless all verses which discuss marriage are elaborated by simultaneously using a thematic and holistic approach, after which the common thread between such verses shall be sought surely 30?

From all of the verses which discuss marriage, it may be concluded that the following five basic principles should be used as grounds for a marriage in Islam. First, the principle of monogamy.[8] Secondly, the principle of *mawaddah wa rahmah* (love and care);[9] thirdly, the principle of complementing and protecting one another;[10] fourthly, the principle of *mu'asyarah bil ma'ruf* (polite social relations),[11] both in sexual and human relations alike; and fifthly, the principle of freedom in selecting a partner for men and women alike, so long as such freedom does not violate the rules of the syari'ah. The above five and highly ideal principles are apparently not well accommodated in KHI, which matter has naturally led to the position of women being highly marginalized and subordinated. In other words, KHI does not reflect the essential values of Islam which respect and honour women. We hope this writing is beneficial and can be of use. *In uridu illa al-ishlah mastatha'tu. Wa ma tawfiqiy illa billah.*

---

[8] *An-Nisa'/4:3 and 129.*
[9] *Al-Rum/30:21.*
[10] *Al-Baqarah/2:187.*
[11] *An-Nisa'/4:19; at-Taubah/9:24; al-Hajj/22:13.*

References

Abu Hasan al-Mawardi, *Laws of Governance, al-Ahkam al-Sulthaniyyah*, London, Ta-Ha Publishing, 1996.

El Alami, Dawoud and Doreen Hinchcliffe, *Islamic Marriage and Divorce Laws of the Arab World*, Boston: Kluwer Law International, 1996.

Anderson, J.N.D., *Law Reform in the Modern World*, London: Anthone Press, 1967.

Department of Religious Affairs of RI, *Kompilasi Hukum Islam di Indonesia* (Compilation of Islamic Law in Indonesia), Jakarta: Directorate for the Guidance of Religious Courts, 2002.

Khallaf, 'Abd al-Wahhab, *'Ilm Ushul al-Fiqh* [Cairo]: Dar al-Qalam, 1978 (12th edn.).

Madjid, Nurcholish, *Islam Doktrin dan Peradaban: Sebuah Telaah Kritis Tentang Masalah Keislaman, Kemanusiaan dan Kemordenan* (Islam in Doctrine and Civilization: A Critical Analysis on Problems concerning Islam, Humanity and Modernism), Jakarta: Paramadina, 1995 (3rd edn.).

Mahmood, Tahir, *Personal Law in Islamic Countries (History, Text and Comparative Analysis)*, New Delhi: Academy of Law and Religion, 1987.

___________, *Family Law Reform in the Muslim World*, Bombay: N.M. Tripathi Pvt. Ltd., Bombay, 1972.

Mahfud, Sahal, *Nuansa Fiqhi Sosial* (Nuances of Social Fiqh), Yogyakarta: LkiS, 1994.

Mulia, Siti Musdah. *Islam Menggugat Poligamy* (Islam Sues Poligamy), Jakarta: Gramedia, 2004.

___________, *Negara Islam: Pemikiran Politik Haikal* (The Islamic State: Haikal's Political Thoughts), Jakarta: Paramadina, 2002.

___________, *Perempuan dan Politik* (Women and Politics), Jakarta: Gramedia, 2005.

___________, *Muslimah Reformis: Perempuan Pembaru Keagamaan* (Muslimah Reformists: Women Modernizing Religion), Bandung: Mizan, 2005.

Nasution, Khoiruddin, *Status Wanita Di Asia Tenggara: Studi Terhadap Perundang-undangan Perkawinan Muslim Kontemporer di Indonesia dan Malaysia* (Status of Women in Southeast Asia: A Study of Contemporary Islamic Marriage Laws in Indonesia and Malaysia), Leiden and Jakarta: INIS, 2002.

Sjadzali, Munawir, "Makna UU No.7 tahun 1989 dan KHI bagi Pembangunan Hukum di Indonesia" (The Impact of Law No.7 of 1989 and KHI to Legal Development in Indonesia), *Mimbar Hukum* 17 (1994): 8.

__________, "Reaktualisasi Ajaran Islam" ("Reactualization of Islamic Teachings") in Iqbal Abdurrauf Saimima (eds.), *Polemik Reaktualisasi Ajaran Islam* (Polemics in the Reactualization of Islamic Teachings), Jakarta: Pustaka Panjimas, 1988, pp. 1-12.

Al-Suyuthi, Jalal al-Din, 'Abd Rahman bin Abi Bakr, *al-Jami' al-Shagir fo Ahadits al-Basyir wa al-Nazhir* (Juz 1), n.p.: Dar al-Fikr, [n.d.].

__________, *Al-Asybah wa al-Nadzair fi al-Furu'*, Jeddah: Al-Harramain, 1960.

Prodojodikoro, Wirjono. *Hukum Perkawinan di Indonesia* (Marriage Law in Indonesia), Nandung: Vorkink van Hoeve.

UNFPA, PP and BKKBN State Secretariat Office, *Bunga Rampai Bahan Pembelajaran Pelatihan Pengarusutamaan Gender* (Anthology of Course Materials on the Importance of Gender Issues), Jakarta, UNFPA, etc., 2001.

Tim Pengarusutamaan Gender, *Pembaruan Hukum Islam: Counter Legal Draft KHI* (Reformations on Islamic Law: Counterarguments to the KHI Legal Draft), Department of Religious Affairs, Jakarta, 2004 [not yet published].

6

Homosexuality in Islam: Coming Out of the Dark

– Soffa Ihsan

The human body is a gift from God. It is clearly connected with something both holy and profane. Life and spirit exist together in all living human bodies. In general terms, the human body visibly shows two distinguishable characteristics, namely, men and women. The human body, which retains its biological feature and function, creates a certain meaning, depending on the value system, culture, and religion in society.

Obviously, the tendency to categorize the human body is a phenomenon throughout human history. On the one hand, people living in a "secular society" treat the human body as a passive object for pleasure. On the other hand, people living in a "religious society" think that the human body is potentially seductive and ought thus to be strictly controlled. Although these two attitudes towards the human body seem to be quite different, they are, in fact, quite similar in that both groups like to control the human body, believing that it belongs to them.

In general, people usually fall into a dichotomous mode of thinking which leaves no room for relativity as regards black or white, rich or poor, clever or stupid. With regard to gender and sexual orientation, people only accept the paring of man and woman. The paring of the same sex is not accepted by society, and only men with masculinity and women with femininity are respected. Same-sex pairing is regarded as a social and religious deviation. As a result, homosexuals are easily marginalized, both socially and religiously.

This social and religious environment creates the view that homosexuals are "freaks." The perspective which rejects homosexuality stems ultimately from the family. Consequently, society as a whole alienates homosexuals on the grounds that they are "queer." This homophobia is a fundamental feature of our society. Homophobia has been created and maintained by a socially dominant group, namely, heterosexuals. This majority group justifies their orientation on ethical, cultural, and religious grounds. Homophobic attitudes are often caused by narrow-mindedness, originating in religious dogmas that feature a negative view of homosexuals. On the pretext that they are a disgrace to religion, homosexuals are regularly discriminated against, physically abused, and marginalized.

We know that there are various bearings in sexuality. Allah did not intend to create a single-oriented sexuality. What is obvious is that the social norms that exist in our society require us to follow existing models regarding our ideas, behaviour and sexual tendency. Men should be with women, and women should be with men. This is the heterosexual norm. However, we should be aware of the fact that there is also a homosexual norm in our society.

In fact, debates over homosexuality have been taking place for a long time. The question frequently asked is that whether homosexuals are contagious, as if they had a disease and their sexual behaviour were unnatural. Another popular topic is whether homosexual acts are based on inherited nature or are the result of experiences in one's immediate environment. Is homosexuality genetically inherited or acquired? Compared with heterosexuals, homosexuals certainly face an array of problems. Heterosexuals have been accepted by society throughout history.

Homosexuals, on the other hand, have been a minority group throughout the history of human sexuality. The important question now is whether moral and religious prejudices against homosexuals have any basis in scinence. The most rational view is that homosexuality is a natural phenomenon. We should accept the fact that homosexuals were born "that way."

However, debating scientific discovery and religious morality is unlikely to solve the problem of homosexuality. These discussions do not cover all aspects of the problem. Both scientific explanations and religious views on morality are insufficient for finding the answer. What is needed is a clear and sensible view homosexuality is neither an infectious disease nor contradictory to human nature. Seen in this way, we will be able to maintain a more objective and humane perspective towards homosexuals, who are clearly a minority. We could then let anyone who feels that they might have a homosexual orientation explore their own sexuality in order to find their own identity. It is important to affirm our intention to encourage explorations of sexuality without rushing to judgement. The fact is that gays and lesbians unquestionably exist in our society. Who could deny this fact? We will see how Islam views homosexuals in the following parts of the paper.

Homosexuality in Islamic History

Homosexuality is certainly not new. Sexual intercourse between members of the same sex has existed throughout the history of human society. History shows that homosexuality has been a consistent strand in the sexual life of human beings. We can find several stories about homosexuality in the religious books, such as *al-Quran*, the Old Testament and the New Testament. Despite the fact that homosexuality is denounced and prohibited in Islam, it is also true that some Muslims have practised such an act. Needless to say, homosexuals were ubiquitous in all social classes, that is to say, all the way from nobles to commoners.

Homosexual intercourse and fondling young boys or paedophilia while drinking wine were not bizarre or alien practices among some Muslims in Islamic history. The atmosphere in several Islamic Empires, including those of the Umayyads, Abbasids, Fatimids and Ottomans, was sexually quite lax. They enjoyed not only harems and concubinage but also some sexual practices which were seen as deviations from the way of Allah. Homosexual activities have unquestionably played a part in the process of creating a good Islamic society. This historical fact, first pointed out by Khalil Abdul Karim, has since analysed by historians such as Ibnu Jabir, Ibnu Khaldun, Abu Umar al-Kindi, Ibnu Ilyas, and Nashir Khasru.[1]

At the beginning of the tenth century in Spain, there was a Caliph with homosexual tendencies, Abdurrahaman III, during the time of the second Umayyad caliphate. It is said that the caliph was fond of a cleric named Palaguis, who was in prison at the time. The caliph often had sexual intercourse with him. When Egypt was controlled by Mameluke Dynasty in 1249, male prostitution was widespread. Handsome young boys were usually taken from the rural areas. Most of them worked for soldiers in the field. Such sexual acts were so frequent that there was even a division within the military in charge of male prostitution. In Persia, it was a common practice for a desert caravan to take with them a handsome young boy dressed as a woman. These homosexual acts were practised not only by military personnel and the nobility but also by commoners. Male prostitution, in general, was widely practised in Africa and the Middle East, such as Morocco, Libya, and Syria. In Siwah, a city in Libya, gay prostitution was common, and it was even said that the parents sometimes had homosexual intercourse with their young children. In Iraq, it was not uncommon for parents to make their sons work as prostitutes. Male prostitution was also observed in Oman. At the beginning of the eighteenth century in Morocco, the abduction of the young boys for the purposes of trafficking in homosexual adults occurred frequently. For these reasons, it is understandable

---

[1] See Khalil Abdul Karim, *Al-Shahabah Wa Al-Shahabah vol 2*, Cairo, 1997, vol. 2, p. 223.

that Islamic jurisprudence (*fiqh*) should have always discouraged Muslims from permitting handsome young boys to attend the collective prayers in mosques. At the beginning of the nineteenth century in Syria, a group of para-Shia Muslims called the Druzes commonly practised homosexuality. Likewise, sexual intercourse among members of the same sex also frequently took place in the time of the Shah in Iran. Only after the 1979 Iranian Revolution led by Imam Khomaeni were homosexual practices stopped. It is said that thousands of homosexuals were executed around that time.

Homosexuals in predominantly Islamic Saudi Arabia, where Islamic law or *syariat* Islam is currently implemented, cannot avoid being attacked. In Saudi Arabia, homosexual acts are forbidden, and carry the death penalty. Homosexuals in Saudi Arabai are less free than those in the West. They have not been liberated yet. However, times are changing, and new norms slowly starting to emerge. Many shopping malls in Riyadh have become meeting places for homosexuals. Gay couples can now socialize in more public places than previously. Carmen bin Laden, who is a relative of Osama bin Laden, published a book revealing how popular homosexual relationships are among the jet-set class and single aristocratic women in Saudi Arabia.[2] Some affluent Saudi Arabian women like to hire premises such as discotheques for lesbian events. It is said that even some women of noble birth often visit a lesbian club in Riyadh to meet their fellow lesbians. According to Carmen bin Laden, many Saudi Arabian men, especially those who are still young and single, have homosexual partners.[3] In Saudi Arabia, if a man and a woman walk shoulder to shoulder or hand in hand on the street, there is a great deal of commotion, and the police will arrest them. On the contrary, when a man walks with another man holding hands in public, people do not find it at all unusual or sexual. Carmen bin Laden writes that "A man

---

[2] Carmen bin Ladin, *Inside The Kingdom*, New York, 2005.
[3] *Ibid.*, p. 182

dealing with European interior once told me that there could be more gays in Saudi Arabia than in Europe."[4] The homosexual scene in Saudi Arabia, which is regarded as the centre of Islam, has also been disclosed by Abd al-Ula al-Taqawi.[5]

Nor is life in Islamic boarding schools (*pesantren*) in Indonesia free from homosexual practices. Muslim male students in *pesantren* are separated from female students. Under these conditions, they are forced to restrain their sexual desires, and it is unhealthy. Consequently, homosexual acts become a solution for them. In *pesantren, mairil* or *sempetan* is the term that denotes homosexual acts. However, their "homosexual acts" are not tantamount to sodomy *per se*. What is usually practised there is called *mufakhadzah*, namely, that male Muslims students mutually masturbate. Research on the sexual life of Muslims in the past was conducted by BF Musalam.[6]

In the Middle Ages among Arabs, there was already a widespread understanding of homosexuality as a means of avoiding pregnancy. For instance, it is said that when a lesbian was asked by a female prostitute why she chose to be a lesbian, she answered: "It is better to be like this than to be pregnant and a scandal."[7] Some men chose to be homosexual because they like to avoid any burdens in life, including marriage and having offspring.[8]

Jalaluddin al-Suyuthi also explained in his book that homosexuality has existed since the beginning of Islam.[9] One reason why homosexuality was common in the history of Islam is that there were so many wars, which forced men to spend long

---

[4] *Ibid.*

[5] See Abd al-Ula al-Taqawi, *Al-Firqah al-Wahabiah Fi Khidmati Man?* Beirut, n.d.

[6] See B.F. Musallam, *Seks Dan Masyarakat Dalam Islam*, Bandung, 1985.

[7] *Ibid.*, p. 50.

[8] *Ibid.*, p. 131.

[9] Jalaluddin al-Suyuthi, *al-Wasa'il Fi Musamarah al-Awa'il*, Beirut, 1991.

periods far from homes in the battlefield. After a Muslim victory, many non-Muslims became slaves for Muslims, and since Muslim male fighters were far away from their wives they felt lonely. Muslims had many more opportunities to encounter male than female non-Muslim slaves, which encouraged same-sex interactions. It was in this social environment that homosexual relations gradually appeared in the history of Islam.

The Mystery of the story of Lut

The community of Lut is usually referred to as a group of homosexuals.[10] It is usually assumed that Allah was furious about the homosexual orientation of the people led by a prophet Lut. His indignation was shown when the rain of stones fell onto 'the Lut community,' and the earth was turned upside down. As a result, the Lut community was completely destroyed, and the people were terminated, including the wife of Lut. The only survivors were the followers of Lut. These events can be found in *al-Quran ss. al-'Araf/7:80-84, al-Shu'ara/26:160, al-'Ankabut/29:29,* and *al-Qamar/54:38.* Ali al-Shabuni describes the Lut community as the most decadent Islamic society in its history.[11]

Thabathaba'i explains that the people of Lut community were the first group to indulge in homosexual intercourse.[12] One of the *hadiths* also acknowledges that the Lut group engaged in homosexual acts.[13] In *al-Quran*, the people of Lut are usually branded as idolaters, robbers and homosexuals. The community as a whole adopted homosexuality. Lut earnestly preached to those who had a special sexual orientation: preference for men rather than women.

---

[10] The community of Lut is originally narrated in the Genesis 19. Lut is also regarded as one of the prophets in Islam.

[11] Ali al-Shabuni, *Qabas Min Nur al-Quran*, Damascus, 1988, p. 176.

[12] Thabathaba'i, *Tafsir al-Mizan*, Beirut, 1991, vol. 10, pp. 345-346.

[13] *Ibid.*

What led them to homosexual acts? According to some scholars, the Lut community was originally blessed by Allah.[14] The people in Lut community were also highly family-oriented. Men usually went to work all together, and women followed after them. Because of their diligence, they grew in wealth. However, one day they found that their savings had been stolen. From that time on, they were continually robbed of their savings. One day, they managed to capture a robber who was very young and handsome. Immediately, they agreed to punish him by terminating his life. The young and handsome robber was taken to one of the community members' house before the execution. The robber suddenly started to call to the owner of the house for something in the middle of the night. Wondering about what happened, the owner of the house came to him. Then, the robber asked him to sleep together, and in fact, granted the robber a favour. The next day, the owner of the house told the whole community what he experienced with the robber. His fellow community male members were so attracted to his story that they wanted to do the same. As a result, the execution of the young and handsome robber never took place. After this incident, all men in the community started to neglect women in favour of men. The robber was regarded as the incarnation of Satan. The women in the community were also encouraged by this satanic figure to become lesbian.[15]

This story tells us that the homosexual orientation of the members of the Lut community was not inherited but acquired. Environment and personal experience were the main factors behind the Lut community's members becoming homosexual. The temptation of Satan epitomizes the existence of the external factor of creating homosexuality. Because of the story of the Lut community, the belief that homosexuality is malevolent has been deeply rooted in the minds of Muslims. Fakhruddin al-Razi, however, explains that homosexuality is a natural phenomenon,

---

[14] See *Ibid.*, p.344.
[15] *Ibid.*

and that no further explanation is needed.[16] Although al-Razi admits that some pleasure can be found in homosexual activities, he believes that the sexual intercourse between the same sexes should be prevented simply because it does not create any offspring.[17] Allah granted human beings the joy of having children. We are now in a position to appreciate how homophobic views were fostered in Islamic communities. Up until the present day, there is no Islamic document of record which suggests that homosexuality is a genetic phenomenon. The scientific research which proposes a genetic basis for homosexuality has not been generally accepted by Islamic communities.

There is another interpretation of the annihilation of the Luth, which focuses on the fact that the community of Lut had a very serious political conflict with another community. The homosexuals in the community were vanished as a severe punishment for political transgression. This interpretation suggests that the people of Lut were not punished because Allah was furious at them. Rather, they simply lost a political battle. We can also find a third explanation for the disaster visited upon the people of Lut, namely, that the homosexual community was violently attacked by Lut himself, who was angry with them because his daughter had failed to find a man to marry in this community of homosexuals. The extermination of the Lut community could also be attributed to a massive natural disaster, such as an earthquake. Some think that the earthquake that took place in the Lut community was merely a natural phenomenon. Even so, some traditionalists and mystics have preferred to regard the termination of the Lut community as some kind of supernatural occurrence.

Even today, some people like to predict that the same natural disaster will take place in Holland and Belgium, countries which have legalized homosexual marriage. However, the fact is that these two European countries have not experienced any such

---

[16] Fakhruddin al-Razi, *Tafsir Fakhruddin al-Razi*, Beirut, vol. 1, p.151.
[17] *Ibid.*, p. 155.

disaster. It is no surprise that there are various interpretations about the story of the Lut; in itself *al-Quran* does not provide a full explanation of the Lut disaster.

Islamic Jurisprudence (*fiqh*) on Homosexuality

The existence of homosexuality has, in fact, been acknowledged by Islamic jurisprudence or *fiqh*. Apart from denouncing and punishing (*bab al-hadd*) homosexuality, *fiqh* deals with various issues, such as the formulae of prayer, and problems of judicature and political administration. *Fiqh* formulates a practical law as a solution for people in the community. We can find realistic answers about the public issues in *fiqh*. Regarding the issue of homosexuality, *fiqh* only acknowledges two genders, namely, males with a penis (*dzakar*) and females with a vagina (*farji*). In *fiqh*, we often find a term *khuntsa*, which literally means someone effeminate or transvestite in Arabic. *Khuntsa* generally is referred to the males who are physically masculine but have the appearance of a female. According to dictionaries, such as *al-Munjid* (edited by Louis Makluf) and *Lisan al-Arab* (edited by Ibnu al-Mundzir), *khuntsa* means someone who possesses both male and female biological characteristics, that is, a hermaphrodite in medical terminology. The usual understanding is that transsexuals (or/and transvestites), who bear conflicting sexual identities, can also be categorized in this group. *Khuntsa* can be applied to anyone who acts contrary to their biological gender.

Islamic scholars (*ulama*) have presented a *fiqh* which divides *khuntsa* into two groups. The first group is termed as *khuntsa musykil,* (indistinct/disguised homosexual) which refers to people who have both male and female genitals. However, this kind of individual is very rare among homosexuals. The second group, which is coined as *khuntsa ghairu musykil,* (openly homosexual) denotes people who clearly belong to either gender but prefer sexual intercourse with the same sex. These people are called gay. The term gay is usually referred to lthe male homosexuals, and their appearance is still masculine.

We can find several references to homosexuals in the Islamic classical literature. For instance, a book titled *al-Iqna'* by Syarbini Khathib contains a *fiqh* that someone with a *khuntsa ghairu musykil* (openly homosexual) orientation cannot attend prayers led by either man or female.[18] Only when a *khuntsa ghairu musykil* (distinct homosexual) person becomes a woman may "she" be allowed to pray normally. The same principle is applied to the male. There are also practical instructions in *fiqh* when people need to deal with *khuntsa ghairu musykil* (distinct homosexual). What about people who attend prayers led by *khuntsa ghairu musykil* (openly homosexual)? They realized that the prayer leader has a homosesxual orientation only after the prayer session. Would that prayer be valid? According to Zakariya al-Anshari and other scholars, the prayer itself is valid, provided that they do not repeat the same mistake.[19] Imam Nawawi, who was an Indonesian native and lived in Saudi Arabia, discussed the issue of homosexuality in his book, viz *Nihayat al-Zain*. The book gives no definition of *khuntsa*. There are contrasting views as to how the collective prayer should be understood, with some asserting that it be *fardhu kifayah* (not an obligation), with some others believing it is *sunnah mu'akkad* (an obligation).[20] These arrangements apply only to men. Both *khuntsa* and women are exempted from joining the collective prayer. A *khuntsa ghairu musykil* (openly homosexual) should pray at his own place rather than at a mosque. *Khuntsa ghairu musykil* (open homosexuals) are treated in the same way as women in the matter of collective prayers. What is interesting is that *khuntsa ghairu musykil* (openly homosexual) people are treated in the same way as the handsome boys who are discouraged from attending prayer in the mosque. Children are, needless to say, encouraged to visit the Mosque to attend prayers, except when they are young and handsome. This is a precaution for avoiding problems.

---

[18] Syarbini Khathib, *al-Iqna*, Bandung, [n.d. as yet], p. 124.

[19] Ahmad Abid, *Al-I'lam Wa al-Ihtimam Bi Jam'i Fatawa Syaikh al-Islam Zakariya al-Anshori*, Beirut,1984, p. 59.

[20] See Nawawi al-Bantani, *Nihayah al-Zain*, Semarang, [n.d.], p. 112.

It seems that there are various interpretations of *umalas* (*fiqh*) on homosexuality. Sexual orientation, which is determined by biological factors, that is to say, the balance of hormones and chromosomes, is the result of *qadar* (the power of Allah to determine all the matters in the world). In this regard, there is nothing humans can do. Only the discovery of new hormones could alter the sexual orientation of a homosexual.

On the other hand, there are *ulamas* who believe that gayness is the result of experiences since birth. In their opinion, psychological therapy to change one's gay orientation is the only remedy available. In this case, wisdom (human endeavour) can be the means by which to change the sexual orientation, as it is obviously not something that humans are unable to deal with. There is also a view that gayness is an attribute "given" to homosexuals in childhood. Should a gay person wish to have a sex change, he is allowed to do so; this act aims to eradicate the vagueness of his identity and to bring about a more sexually appropriate physical appearance. If homosexuality is the result of socio-cultural environment, the alternation of sexuality is possible because it is not *qadar*.

The question today is whether homosexuals in the time of Prophet Muhammad were punished for their orientation. The answer is negative. Unlike heterosexuals who committed adultery, who were stoned to death, homosexuals received no punishment. It was only in the reign of Caliph Abu Bakar that homosexuals were punished for the first time. One day, Khalid bin Walid, who was one of the generals, found an Arabian community whose members were homosexual. Learning that there was a male-married couple, Khalid bin Walid informed Abu Bakar of this peculiar marriage and asked how he should deal with them. The Caliph, who felt that it was such a delicate case, immediately called for a meeting with other authorities in order to discuss the matter. At the meeting, Ali bin Abi Thalib gave his opinion that these homosexuals should be burned to death. Abu Bakar ordered Khalid to execute them as Ali suggested. It is important to bear in mind that the decision to execute the homosexuals was based solely on Abu Bakar's *ijtihad* (individual interpretation), and is not the final word on punishing homosexuals in Islam. In other words, Abu Bakar's order was not an ideal choice for treating homosexuals.

In Islamic law, which is codified in the books of *fiqh*, we find no special references to punishments against homosexuals and people who engage in unacceptable forms of sexual intercourse. The legal sanctions against homosexual activities, whether rape or voluntary, are usually mentioned in the context of cases involving violations of decency. Although there is a general consensus that homosexual acts are forbidden, the procedure of the sanctions is obviously controversial; there is no consensus on this matter in the authentic sources of Islamic teachings, namely, *al-Quran* and the *Hadiths*. In these two important guides for Muslims, we find no complete or uniform explanation of the sanctions against homosexuals. It is, therefore, necessary for us to situate the treatment of homosexuals in relation to the social context.

The three important schools of thought in Islam, namely, Syafi'i, Maliki, and Hambali, concur that, as with as cases of indecent sexual intercourse, four honest and trustworthy male witnesses are required to prove the offence of a homosexual act, provided that at least one the two men accused of engaging in a homosexual act admits his guilt. However, the school of Hanafi, which is dominant in the Arab world, takes a different view: homosexual acts and *zina* or indecent sexual intercourse should not be treated similarly because the dangers of homosexual activities are smaller than those caused by *zina*. For this reason, the Hanafi School directs that one honest and trustworthy male witness shall suffice in cases of homosexuality. The Hanafi School does not regard homosexual activities as *zina*, and homosexual relationships, for them, are not formal contracts like ordinary marriage. As we can see, the ways in which Islamic law deals with homosexuality are not identical, and, thus, religious obligations, such as pilgrimage and fasting, counducted by homosexual Muslims, are still valid. Abu Daud al-Dzahiri, for one, agrees with the Hanafi School and believes that only sexual intercourse involving women's genitals should be understood as *zina*.[21] What al-Dzahiri means is that harsh punishment against homosexuals is unnecessary; imprisonment or *ta'zir* is enough.

There is also an argument that, since homosexual relations do not create any offspring unlike *zina*, punishment of homosexuals should be lighter than that of those who commit *zina*. We remember a story narrated in one of the *Hadith*s, which reads: "If you encounter someone who engages in homosexual activities, you should kill both of them."[22] However, there are debates over this *hadith*, and Abu Hanifah himself disagreed with this passage.[23] There is no unanimous agreement among the experts of *fiqh* in relation to how homosexuals should be sanctioned. They even debate the total number of witnesses. We can find at least three opinions in the legal documents on the sanction against homosexuals. First, homosexuals should be executed; second, homosexuals should be punished in the same way as those who commit *zina*, that is to say, when the offender is unmarried he/she should be caned, and when the offender is married he/she should be stoned to death; and third, homosexuals should be imprisoned (*ta'zir*) for a certain period of time to be determined by judges.

Generally speaking, sanctions against homosexuals seem to be far more prevalent in the sphere of morality, and less consistent, indicating that punishment of homosexuals is dependent upon the context. This means that the way in which homosexuals should be handled by Islamic law remains a matter of *ijtihad*. It is important to know that when someone insists that homosexuals should be burned or thrown from a mountain top, this is merely a personal interpretation of Islamic law.[24] This sort of radical view cannot be

---

[21] Ibnu Hazm, *al-Muhalla*, Mecca, 2005, vol. 8, p. 219

[22] Hadith from Abu Dawud, Turmudzi dan Ibnu Maja. See *Ibnu Atsir* (juz IV), Beirut, [n.d. a yet], p. 305.

[23] Sirajuddin Abu Hafsh, *al-Ghurrah al-Munifah*, Beirut, vol. 2, 1988, p. 87.

[24] Abu Ja'far Ali al-Thusi, *al-Nihayah*, Beirut, 1980 , vol. 2, p. 704.

the basis for punishing homosexuals in general. In fact, it clearly contradicts the humanistic values and the mercy which the teachings of Islam endorse. Imam Malik, a founder of the school of Maliki, once reminded us not to let the judges alone deal with the issue of homosexuality. He said that: "Any man who accuses someone else of homosexuality should himself be caned."[25]

In any discussion of enforcing Islamic law on homosexuality takes place, it should be pointed out that homosexuality has been already recognised in the field of *fiqh* (Islamic jurisprudence). It is also true that the *fiqh* make numerous references to debates about homosexuality, suggesting that the religion itself recognises the existence of homosexuals. Studies of Islamic jurisprudence (*fiqh*), in fact, show "flexibility" with regard to acknowledging the existence of homosexuals. In addition, the punishment given to homosexuals in the past does not represent the only and final view of homosexuality in Islam. In other words, we should fully exercise our *ijtihad* to determine the position and treatment of homosexuals in accordance with the merciful and humane values of Islam. The impact on society should also be taken into account when determining the punishment for homosexuality. If no one is actually harmed by someone's homosexual activities, why should homosexuals be punished at all?

Do Muslims still refuse to accept the result of the scientific research, the abundant medical evidence and psychiatric findings which show that homosexuality is a genetic phenomenon, not a moral disorder? Has not the extensive research on homosexuality clearly given the last word on the issue of punishing homosexuals? A good analogy is that when a doctor uses medicine for an operation, no *ulamas* would question the validity of the doctor's decision. Is it not true that the doctor's choice to utilize medicine is based on scientific research? If so, should not we respect the results of scientific research and accept homosexuals?

---

[25] See Ibnu Hazm, op. cit., vol. 10, . p. 536.

How about the issue of same-sex marriage? No *fiqh* has ever offered a proper explanation on this matter. Even in the story of Lut, there was no mention whether the same sex marriage really existed as an institution within the community. All we find in the story is the fact that the Lut community was unquestionabley a home of "evil doers." It is worth analysing one of the verses in al-Quran in relation to the pairing of humans.

> By another sign He gave you spouses from among yourselves, that yo might live in peace with them, and planted love and kindness in your hearts.[26]

We should understand the words "among yourselves" in the *Qur'an* rather "broadly" in order to understand those who are attracted to the same sex. They have also been born human and should be blessed. They deserve to receive the love of Allah. There is an interesting explanation in relation to the verse in *al-Qur'an* cited above. According to Raghib al-Asfahani, any human being, whether male or female, in the *Qur'an* is supposed to have a "partner", which is termed as "husband" (*zauji*).[27] The word *zaujatun*, meaning wife, is not used in *al-Qur'an* at all. It is possible to assume that the word *zauji* can be applied, not only to men and women respectively but also to all human kind. In other words, any human experience, regardless of one's gender, should be equally valued.

Conclusion

It is time for Muslims to re-examine the texts of Islam in order to find sound and fair answers to the question of homosexuality. Their decisions should be based on the principle of the equality among humans (*al-musawab bain al-nas*), which is valued in Islam. Isn't it true that Islam as a religion has been embraced by people

---

[26] *Al-Qur'an, s. al-Rum*/30:21. There are various translations available for this verse. The Arabic word here is being translated as "among yourselves." In the Indonesian version, it is being translated as *jenismu sendiri* or your own race/kind/gender.

[27] See Thabathaba'i, op. cit., vol. 4, p. 188.

throughout human history? If we only literally read the texts without any further contemplation we would become "textual cannibals" and "textual idolators" (*taqdis al-nash*). Rather, it is necessary for Muslims to understand the texts and contexts (*muqtadha al-hal, siyaq al-lisan and dhuruf al-ijtima'iyah*) in a comprehensive manner. To borrow Hassan Hanafi's words, the dynamism and history of real life in this world contain values which can be shared by society as a whole.[28] Lastly, it should be remembered that *syariat Islam* or Islamic law has been given to us in order to bring about universal well-being.

References

Abd al-Ula al-Taqawi, *al-Firqah al-Wahabiah Fi Khidmati Man?* Beirut: Al-Irsyad, [n.d.].

Abu Ja'far Ali al-Thusi, *al-Nihayah vol 2*, Beirut: Dar al-Kutub al-Arabi, 1980.

Ali al-Shabuni, *Qabas Min Nur al-Quran*, Damascus: Dar al-Qalam, 1988.

Ahmad Abid, *Al-I'lam Wa al-Ihtimam Bi Jam'i Fatawa Syaikh al-Islam Zakariya al-Anshori*, Beirut: Alim al-Kutub,1984.

Carmen bin Ladin, *Inside The Kingdom*, New York: Warner Book, 2005.

Fakhruddin al-Razi, *Tafsir Fakhruddin al-Razi*, Beirut: Dar al-Fikr, vol. 1.

Ibnu Atsir, Beirut (juz IV) [n.d. as yet.].

Hassan Hanafi, *al-Turats wa al-Tajdid Mauqifuna min al-Turats al-Qadim*, Cairo: Al-Muassasah al-Jami'iyah li al-Dirasah wa al-Nasyr wa al-Tauzi'*, 1992.

Ibnu Hazm, *al-Muhalla*, Mecca: Maktabah Dar al-Turats, 2005, vol. 10.

Jalaluddin al-Suyuthi, *al-Wasa'il Fi Musamarah al-Awa'il*, Beirut: Dar al-Fikr, 1991.

---

[28] Hassan Hanafi, *Al-Turats wa al-Tajdid Mauqifuna min al-Turats al-Qadim*, Cairo, 1992, p. 15.

Khalil Abdul Karim, *Al-Shahabah Wa Al-Shahabah*, Cairo: Sina Li al-Nasyr, 1997, vol. 2.

Musallam, B.F., *Seks Dan Masyarakat Dalam Islam*, Penerbit Pustaka, Bandung, 1985.

Nawawi al-Bantani, *Nihayah al-Zain*, Searang: Thaha Putera, Semarang, [n.d. as yet].

Sirajuddin Abu Hafsh, *al-Ghurrah al-Munifah*, Beirut: Maktabah Imam Abu Hanifah, 1988, vol. 2.

Syarbini Khathib, *al-Iqna*, Bandung, Al-Maarif, [n.d as yet].

Thabathaba'i, *Tafsir al-Mizan*, Beirut: Muassasah al-A'lami, 1991, vols. 4, 10.

7

What is Right in Islam? – Ideas of Abu Bakar Ba'asyir

An Interview with Abu Bakar Ba'asyir

In your opinion, what is right and what is wrong with *umat* Islam in Indonesia today?

In an Islamic community, what is right for Muslims is to obey *syariat* Islam strictly, applying it for themselves, for the society, and for the nation. On the other hand, what is wrong for Muslims is to oppose the implementation of *syariat* Islam as the basic law of the nation.

1. I understand that what is important in Islam is to create an Islamic world (*al-dar Islam*), which is more important than the country. What is your view on this?

Islam divides the human race into two categories, Muslim and non-Muslim (*kafir*). Although all Muslims in the world should be under one leadership, it cannot be realized at once, thus, it has to be materialized step by step. For example, Indonesia can be the very first place (to lead the movement of the creation of the Islamic world), and other countries will follow. If this happens, an ultimate goal of Islam, which is to have one leadership or Caliph, will be achieved.

2.   It seems that many Indonesians appreciate the country (the Republic of Indonesia) more than they do Islam. What do you think about this?

It happens because some Muslims are stupid or they have not understood the truth of Islam yet. Or although they know a decent goal as Muslims, they lack the intention to protect Islam. These people surely practice Islam; however, they take secular issues more seriously and care less about their religion. True Muslims should criticise the government of the Republic of Indonesia because their country is not on the right path in that *syariat* Islam has not been implemented.

3.   Why do you think an Islamic liberal movement emerged in Indonesia?

Liberal groups emerged in Indonesia as a tool of non-believers (*kafir*) who just exploit Muslims. These so-called liberal Muslims, in Prophet Muhamad's words, are attached to this secular world and are afraid of dying. Heathens (*kafir*) created liberal Muslim groups that would harm the Islamic community. Liberal groups, in fact, do not have any influence on religious behaviours of Muslims but only on the financial condition of Muslims.

4.   Should they (liberal Muslims) be punished?

Yes, when *syariat* Islam is implemented, they should be punished because they damage Islam from within.

5.   The social condition of Mecca when Islam was for the first time revealed to the people and the social condition of today are very different. Do you think when the social condition changes, religion also changes?

I do not believe that religion changes. Although there are different civilizations such as Indonesian and Arabic, *syariat* Islam is applicable to any situation. Having said this, civilizations in Indonesia are not always in conflict with *syariat* Islam. If they do not contradict each other, Indonesian locality can be permitted. In other words, the attribute of *syariat* Islam is extraordinary in that it can be featured in any condition regardless of civilizations.

6. Some Muslim scholars think that it is inappropriate and unrealistic to cut off the hand of a thief in this modern world. Do you think that this punishment is still applicable?

Yes, as *syariat* Islam has a superior quality, it is applicable to any country and any time in a human society. Cutting off the hand of a criminal is the most modern way of punishment for it is quick to be done; it is economical to carry out; and it is most effective in preventing crimes. If you say that that punishment is unrealistic, it is just one opinion.

7. What is the difference between the time of Suharto and the time of current President Susilo Bambang Yudhoyono (SBY) in Indonesia?

With regard to their attitudes towards Islam, there is no difference in that they do not support Islam and actually damage Islam. Suharto was more extreme than Susilo Bambang Yudhoyono. SBY is moderate and slow on the matter of Islam. Yet, we should remember that the United States of America is behind him to control him.

8. What policy do you think is wrong in SBY's government?

SBY's attitude towards Islam is the same as that of Suharto. He does not think that *syariat* Islam is the law of the nation so that *syariat* Islam has never been implemented. The failure to enact the anti-pornography law was one of the examples of this. Consequently, SBY's era is tantamount to the violation of God's law. SYB is not the only president who destroys Islam but all presidents in Indonesian history did so. They did not have any intention to make *syariat* Islam as a law of the nation although *syariat* Islam is the core of Islam.

10. How about the position of non-Muslims in the country where *syariat* Islam is adapted as the law of the nation?

Non-Muslims, for example Buddhists, are not forced to embrace the faith of Islam. On the contrary, non-Muslims are assured that they can practice their own faith, provided that they do not disturb the exercise of *syariat* Islam. At the same time, non-Muslims are not disturbed living in an Islamic society. They are free to maintain their faith, and Muslims should not impose Islam on them. Only when non-Muslims wish to convert to Islam, should Muslims give advice and propagate their faith to them. Note that conversion should take place with true realization and understanding of Islam; if non-Muslims do not wish to convert to Islam, there should not be any forcible propagation. *Syariat* Islam regarding religious matters is only applied to the followers of Islam, while *syariat* Islam regarding criminal acts such as theft is applied to both Muslims and non-Muslims without any exception.

11. What criteria should be used for determining who is eligible to exercise *ijtihad*?

Ijtihad is required when there is no clear explanation found in the *al-Quran* and the *Sunnah* (the description of the lifestyle of the Prophet) on specific matters. Speaking of the criteria, the one who exercises *ijtihad* should have a very good command of the Arabic language and should understand the *Hadith*s and the *Quran* very well.

12. Is there anyone who can meet these criteria in Indonesia?

There are some in Indonesia. In fact, we can find those people anywhere, but not many.

13. Do you see anyone who meets the criteria for exercising *ijtihad* in the group of so-called liberal Islam?

Probably, they have an ability to exercise *ijtihad*; however, they are not honest and alter Islamic norms. Any legal decision based on *al-Quran* in Islam can only be invalidated by another recitation which is clearly stipulated in either *al-Quran* or the *Hadith*s. Yet, liberal groups themselves create new norms in Islam, which is to say that they modify the *Quran*, interpreting it according to the situation of society today. For example, although a Muslim woman is not permitted to marry a non-Muslim man in Islamic teaching, liberal groups do not accept this, saying that that tradition is valid only in the past, and it is permissible in the present day. It is misleading and wrong.

14. What do you think of the rightness in the teaching of Islam? For example, the matter of *qadar* (fatalism) has been interpreted in various ways that the group of *Jabriyah* and *Qadariyah* have presented different views on this matter. What is your opinion about this?

Both *Jabriyah* and *Qadariyah* are deviated from the truth of Islam. What is right in Islam is the group of *ahlus sunnah wal jama'ah*, that is, the followers of Prophet Muhammad and his friends (*Sunni* group). Therefore, *Jabriyah* and *Qadariyah* groups are just as wrong as liberal groups today, which are more misleading.

15. What are the parameters to determine the rightness in Islam?

Of course, there is a measurement. What is considered as right in Islam is that Muslims appreciate policies set by prophets and his followers. The one who understands Islam most is Prophet Muhammad, and his friends and pupils are next. As long as your deeds accord with the examples set by Muhammad and his comrades, you are not deviating from the true teaching of Islam. On the contrary, groups such as *Qadariyah*, *Jabriyah*, and *Syiah* do not follow the way of Prophet Muhammad. In fact, they contend with what has been set by predecessors who correctly understood Islam. This deed itself is very wrong and misleading.

16. How about your opinion concerning the deed of the *Taliban* destroying the Buddha statue? Was their action right?

In my opinion, their action to destroy the Buddha statue was right. I say this because the U.S. provided financial support for the Afghan government to restore the Buddha statue, while the people of Afghanistan were suffering from starvation. It was wrong that the U.S. did that on purpose.

17. What is your position about taking physical actions and using weapons?

The utilization of weapons is not excluded from an Islamic doctrine. However, Muslims are only permitted to take weapons when they need to protect themselves from an enemy's attack or warn non-Muslims who disturb Islamic society. Muslims do not take a sword to force non-Muslims to convert to Islam. I think it is logical and believe that there is no ideology that denies the use of weapons.

18. Can the September 11 attack be justified?

That event gave the U.S. justification and a pretext for starting a war against _Taliban_ and _al-Qaida_. Osama bin Laden has been accused as a perpetrator, but they have not found any evidence that Osama bin Laden was involved in that attack. As the U.S. with its economic influence always attempts to destroy Islam anywhere in the world, I believe it was not wrong to defend Islam so that Osama bin Laden can destroy the U.S. economy.

19. How about the executors of bombings in Indonesia?

All Muslims who were involved in bombings in Indonesia are not terrorists. They are "counter-terrorists" or _mujahid_ (defenders of Islam); they protect Islam and Muslims. In fact, the U.S. is the terrorist that constantly terrifies the Islamic community. The purpose of those bombers was to defend Islam from the attack of the U.S. or Australia, and it was right. However, what was wrong and imprudent was that they used bombs in areas where physical conflicts were not taking place. This point gives the U.S. the pretext to accuse them.

20. What is your view on the conspiracy theory? For example, Abdurrahman Wahid (Gus Dur) stated in an Australian TV programme that those bombings were perpetrated by some groups within the government or military.

The Bali bombing resulted in 88 deaths of Australians. It is natural to assume that it was conducted by them (Muslims), but the CIA profited from it.

21. Do you believe in the conspiracy theory, then?

Not conspiracy. They (Muslim bombers) had their own aim to destroy the interests of the U.S., but were not competent enough to make powerful bombs. The U.S. understood this very point and used this opportunity only for realizing their purpose to suppress Indonesia. As I said before, the bombers had a genuine intention that is anti-terror, but they did not examine the situation well enough. I would say that their deeds were not "action" but "reaction" towards the U.S., which attacked and killed the people of Afghanistan. In Islamic teaching, fellow Muslims are obliged to help one another even when they are physically distanced. Having said this, I believe it is better for us, Muslims, to face the U.S. with our propagation activities because the U.S. also "attacks" us through argumentation, which is non-physical. We should take our weapons only when the U.S. starts to bomb us.

22. Japan has a pacifist constitution in that the Article 9 stipulates that Japan has abandoned its right to start war and to use any physical means to solve international conflicts. It is surely different from the teaching of Islam. What do you think about this constitution?

It is not effective from a religious point of view. I do not know how the Japanese people would defend themselves if they are attacked physically. What is logical is that when we are attacked verbally we should fight back in the same manner, but when we are attacked physically we need to use weapons. If Muslims are forbidden to adopt a physical way of fighting, Islam will be surely destroyed. If we follow the Article 9 of the Japanese Constitution, we will not be able to fight in order to help other countries.

23. Do you think Islamic countries and Japan can work together?

Muslims are able to work with not only Japan but also any country, provided that non-Muslims do not trouble Muslims, and both non-Muslims and Muslims are assured to maintain their faiths. Muslims can work together with non-Muslims on the secular issues but not the religious issues, for the *Quran Al-Mumtahanah*/60:8 states: "God does not forbid you to be kind and equitable to those who have neither made war on your religion nor driven you from your home."

24. What is your opinion about Japan?

Japan is surely a country of *kafir* or infidels. However, it is good that Japan has given religious freedom to its citizens to convert to Islam. In addition, Muslims can work together with Japan on secular matters such as technology and the economy. Yet, if Japan troubles Islamic countries, we should cut off diplomatic relations, which is the case where the U.S. has attacked Islamic soils physically.

25. When someone or some countries try to destroy Islam, would Muslims be able to stop it without taking up weapons?

Stopping physical attacks without using weapons sounds very illogical. A country that lacks morality, like the U.S., keeps attacking enemies even though they already know that the opponent no longer possesses weapons. It is simply because they like to dominate them. We defend ourselves with weapons when we are physically attacked. Islam orders Muslims to do the same thing, that Muslims should take up weapons when they need to protect themselves and to warn anyone who potentially troubles Muslims.

26. You state in your book that a woman is not supposed to be president of the country. Yet, we still can find some verses in *al-Quran* that affirm the equality of human beings. What is your view on the position and role of women in society?

According to God's will, men and women have different duties. In fact, some researchers say that the size of the brain also differs between men and women. Surely women are not as strong as men physically, but they have their special abilities, such as giving education to children. Women have certain skills. The medical doctor is one of the suitable professions for women. Women can be the leaders of some specific fields in accordance with their special abilities. All hospitals, for example, can be headed by women. Prophet Muhammad once said that women are not successful for being a leader in Islam because there are certain restrictions applied for women. A woman, for instance, needs to be accompanied by a male relative when she goes out. Knowing this, it is not effective if a woman becomes a leader of the nation.

27. What is your view on polygamy?

Polygamy is permitted in Islam as long as the marriage is based on justice. However, *al-Quran* explains that human beings are not able to divide love equally. When one exercises polygamy, the love of that person cannot be given to all of his wives equally. Thus, justice should be realised in a realistic way. That man should provide the same amount of financial support to his wives.

This interview was conducted in Jakarta Barat on 22 January 2007.

8

Caliphate, *Sharia* and the Future of Umat

– *M. Ismail Yusanto*

ndonesia weeps! A country once prosperous and fertile, the emerald of the equator, is now in dire straits. Economically, Indonesia has again become a poor country whose *per capita* GNP is barely higher than that of another poor country in Africa, Zimbabwe. Its debt is huge. The total amount of debt is Rp 1,400 quintillion, consisting of Rp 742 quintillion in international debts and the rest national.[1]

In fact, everyone knows that Indonesia is a rich and vast country. Indonesia's forests are among the largest in the world, and its land is fertile and beautiful. Indonesia's marine industry also has huge potential. Indonesia's maritime territory can boast fisheries, pearls, oil, and other minerals, amounting to about 6.2 million tons annually. Let us not forget, too, how breathtaking its underwater coral reefs are. The fishing industry alone generates more than eight billion dollars every year. In addition, Indonesia is rich in gold, nickel, tin, copper, and coal. Moreover, there are

---

[1] *Forum* (5 March, 2002).

huge gas and oil deposits, and the eastern province of Papua contains the largest gold mine in the world.

However, everyone also knows that Indonesia has been declining. A prolonged economic crisis has forced ten million people to live below the poverty line, and millions of others lost their jobs. Meanwhile, 4.5 million children have been forced to give up school and millions of others suffer from malnutrition. For many citizens, life has become more and more difficult, even simply earning a bowl of rice. Moreover, prices are kept getting higher and higher. People with weak character or simple opportunists have committed crimes such as robbery, theft, and murder. The decline of morality is evident from the "permissive culture" which encourages pornography. The publication of pornographic material has even been justified as a "necessary" contribution to the economic recovery which deserves to be prioritized. As the crisis continues, crime has increased by 1,000%, divorce by 400%, and admissions to mental hospitals by 300%.

Although the government has changed several times, the political situation has never been stable. In fact, political problems in several provinces seem to be more serious than previously. We need to ask why such things are taking place. What is the origin of these mistakes? Is the system adopted in Indonesia wrong? Or, are the people in charge of politics incompetent and untrustworthy?

The Root of Indonesia's Problems and the Fundamental Solution
There are at least three possible explanations for the crisis in Indonesia.[2] First, an economic perspective: the problem stems from a weak economic foundation, massive foreign debt, a balance of trade deficit, and so on. Its solution is increased export, debt restructuring, and measures to combat the deficit. Second, a political perspective: the crisis occurred because the government

---

[2] See Saidi Zaim, *Soeharto menjaring matahari: talik ulur reformasi ekonomi Orde Baru pasca -1980*, Jakarta, 1998.

in charge was corrupt and undemocratic. Its solution is to facilitate the process of democratization and to change the government, something that has already happened since Suharto gave up power. And a third perspective, known as the radical-philosophical perspective: the crisis which afflicts our country has its roots in none of these problems. Rather, the root of the problem is the system adopted in Indonesia: liberal capitalism, which is inherently weak, defective, and self-destructive.

According to the Islamic point of view, all crises are caused by men's own misdeeds. As *Allah* in *al-Quran* revealed:

> Corruption has become rife on land and sea in consequence of mankind's misdeeds (*s[ura] Ar-Rum/30:41*).

Maksiyat refers to all transgressions of divine law, such as doing something that is forbidden, neglecting Islamic obligations, and creating mischief among people. Every breach from divine law causes sin. Each sin causes destruction (*fasad*).

Meanwhile, it has been shown that deviation from divine law is rife in the daily life of people and the country. Islamic rules have never been applied comprehensively within the confines of the secular system. Islam has been seen as an individual or private matter relating to God, in the same way as other religions are seen in Western societies. Therefore, Islam has been excluded from discussions of social issues. Consequently, unIslamic social order prevails in a society with the rampant of capitalistic economy, opportunistic political behaviour, hedonistic culture, egoistic and individualistic attitudes, and syncretic religiosity along with materialistic education.

Sharia: the Solution

The almighty *Allah* makes it obligatory for every Muslim who believes in *Allah* to follow *syariat* (*Sharia* law) and to see to it that all aspects of individual, societal, and national affairs are in accordance with *syariat*.

> When true believers are called to God and His apostle that he may pass judgment (syariat Islam) upon them, their only reply

is: 'We hear and obey.' Such Men will surely prosper (*s. al-Nuur*/
24:51).

(therefore) give judgement among men according to God's
revelations(*syariat* Islam) and do not yield to their fancies or
swerve from the truth made known to you (*s. al-Maidah*/5:48).

Pronounce judgement among them according to God's
revelations(syariat Islam) and do not be led by their desires.
Take heed lest they turn you away from a part of that which
God has revealed to you (*al-Maidah* 49).

Religious issues regulated by *syariat* Islam, such as prayer, fasting,
charity, pilgrimage, dietary restriction, and clothing are the concern
of dividual Muslims. Likewise, there are matters in which Muslims
are bound to obey *syariat Islam* as members of a community.
However, issues related to political, social, economy, and education
should be managed by the nation. Here, it is critical and obligatory
for the nation to implement and execute *syariat* Islam. Therefore,
both individual and communal entities of a nation are bound to
comply with *syariat* Islam. Without the support of the nation,
individuals and communal entities cannot apply *syariat* Islam,
especially when the nation itself opposes it. Full implementation
of *syariat* Islam can only be realiszd when a nation shares and
believes in Islamic principles of *syariat* and is committed to it.

Anything that is Required in order to Fulfil an Obligation is itself Obligatory

There is no nation without a leader. Therefore, Islam has ruled
that the people must appoint a leader to lead the nation and
implement Islamic *Syariat*, from the time of Prophet Muhammad
to the fall of Caliph Ustmani in 1924. Since then, no Caliph has
lead the Islamic World. Instead, the Islamic community or *umat*
Islam has been divided into over 50 nations headed by leaders
who either do not implement *syariat* Islam at all or implement it
partially. *Al-Quran* states:

Believers obey God and obey the Apostle and those in authority
among you (*s. al-Nisa*/4:59).

Allah enjoins obedience to leaders. The verse cited above makes it clear that the sole duty of the leader is to uphold *syariat* Islam, and obedience to authority also means obedience to *Allah* and His Prophet. Establishing *waliyul amri,* an institution of power that upholds Islamic *Sharia,* is therefore obligatory. By contrast, secular powers that refuse to implement *syariat* Islam, and instead endorse secular laws, are leading the people and the country away from the divine commands of *Allah* and His Prophet. Following *Allah* and His Prophet is obligatory, and straying (*maksiyat*) from the rules of *Allah* is forbidden.

> When my guidance is revealed to you, he that follows it shall neither err nor grieve; but he that rejects My warning shall live in woe and come before Us blind on the Day of Resuurection (*s. Taha*/20:123~124).

> It is better for the people to be given one punishment rather than the punishment to force them being in the rain for forty days (*Hadith* narrated by an-Nasa'I and Ibn Majah).

The mercy of Islam that is given by *Allah* will be truly realized only when *syariat* Islam is implemented completely, consistently, and comprehensively. National leaders who are obedient to *Allah* should lead their country and society with full implementation of *syariat* Islam. They will encourage all Muslims to be pious, to observe dietary restrictions, to cover their bodies in compliance to Islamic standards of modesty, and to uphold morality as prescribed by Islam. Following *syariat,* they will lead their country to a place where morality is upheld, and safety, peace, and prosperity exist. Social welfare, such as education, health and infrastructures for transportation, communication, water and electricity, will be properly provided and overseen by an efficient civil service or bureaucracy. All of these things will be realized by means of good governance and honest government. Moreover, the leader of the country will solve the problems by implementing *syariat.* He can forbid pornography and gambling and punish those who engage in corruption and other criminals. Poverty will be diminished as economy grows, and business activities will grow. He will forbid people to earn money by means of interest rates, and he will encourage the active circulation of money, which stimulates economic growth.

Obviously, the leader of an Islamic system differs from that of a secular democratic system. Although both are chosen by the people, the head of state in a secular democratic system is chosen to protect or assure the sovereignty of the people, which means that the people have the right to make laws. Thus, the head of state will carry out his duty to administer laws made by representatives of the people. This is not compatible with *syariat* Islam. In other words, the head of state in a secular democratic society is obligated to lead the country with secular laws, not with *syariat* Islam.

In Islam, neither people nor the head of the state have the right to make laws, except the almighty *Allah*. The head of state is chosen by the people in order to implement the law of *Allah*, drawing upon *al-Quran* and *al-Sunnah*. The head of state then implements those laws to ensure the welfare of the people.

Therefore, the head of the state in an Islamic political system, though elected by the people, is actually the guardian of the *syariat* sovereignty (not the people). The Islamic community or people need to decide which should be applied, *syariat* Islam or secular law, and whether sovereignty should remain in the hands of the people, as has been the case, or whether sovereignty should be in the hands of *syariat*.

For these reasons, every Muslim should remember the following issues when choosing a head of state:

1. When choosing the head of state, appoint *(surutu al-in'iqadz)* someone who is a Muslim (it is forbidden to appoint a non-Muslim as head of state), who is male (it is forbidden to appoint a woman as head of state), who has reached maturity, who is intelligent, who is just (who consistently performs Islamic duties), who is independent and competent when responding to the mandate of head of state. Other desirable criteria include being born from a *quraish* lineage, expertise in Islamic law, bravery, and political acumen.

2. Choose a head of state who is able to protect the security and independence of the country and who champions the cause of Muslim communities and Muslim nations. Do not choose someone who supports a country that is imperialistic or is under the influence of warring non-Muslim believers. In other words, the head of state should be able to bring about the full independence of Muslims, and not allow his nation to be dominated by foreign powers, socially, politically, economically, legally, or culturally.

> God will not let the unbelievers triumph over the faithful (*s. al-Nisa'*/4:141).

Umat Islam is a united community, and Muslims should have one country, i.e., the Caliphate, and a single head of state, i.e., a Caliph who rules the country based on what *Allah* has revealed. A Muslim cannot live without the presence of the of the caliphate and disobedience to the caliph is not permitted, as the words of the Prophet clearly stated:

> Whoever detaches from the loyalty to Allah, he or she surely will meet Allah on the Day of Judgment without having any proof (of being a good Muslim). Whoever has no oath of allegiance, he or she will die as an unbelieving person (Narrated by Muslim).

> If there are two caliphs who took the oath of allegiance, kill the second one (Narrated by Muslim).

In the Madina Charter that was written and ratified by Prophet Muhammad after the time of Hijra (migration from Mecca to Medina), it is stated that:

> In the name of God the compassionate and merciful, this is a document ratified by Prophet Muhammad. Muslims, both Quraisy and Yatsrib, and whoever follow them are the same. Their status is the same. They fight *jihad* as one unit. They are one Islamic community that faces other communities. ... In fact, Muslims in an Islamic community should protect each other. Then, the safety of Islamic community is one thing: a Muslim is not permitted to be given up to the non-Muslim enemies during the course of battle in the way of God.

Imams from all four schools of thoughts have already explained this issue. *Imamah* (unitary Islamic political leadership) existence is obligatory, and the Islamic community must have an *imam* who promotes Islamic duties and gives justice to the oppressed from tyrannical rulers. At the same time, whether or not the *imams* are in agreement, the Islamic community should not have two *imams* (the law prohibits having two heads of states/Caliphs).

3. Implement *syariat* Islam comprehensively and consistently. The head of the state (caliph) should have authority to make law, in which case there is no excuse for delaying or rejecting the implementation of *syariat* Islam.

   Judgement rests only with God. He has commanded you to worship none but Him (*s. Yusuf/*12:40).

   ...they will not be true believers until they seek your arbitration in their disputes. Then they will not doubt the justice of your verdicts and will submit to you entirely (*s. al- Nisa/*4:65).

Finally, *umat Islam* must choose. Is our country to be ruled by a tyrant under a secular system? Can we accept the fact that *syariat* Islam has not been implemented comprehensively? Or, should we choose a leader who is trustworthy and intends to implement *syariat* Islam for the realization of peace, prosperity, and justice? *Umat Islam* holds the key to choosing the President (of Indonesia), and Muslim people should know it. In fact, we have to yet to find competent people who meet the criteria of caliph in *umat* Islam (in Indonesia). Therefore, *Umat* Islam must continue the struggle, preparing to appoint the head of state (Caliph) in order to implement *syariat* Islam. We have to abandon a secular system and work to realize Islam across the board so that it can unite Islamic countries under the *daulah khilafah Islamiyah* (greater Islamic superstate). It is the time to take the right step. Reject secular leadership!

Understanding the History of the Caliphate

One of the arguments against the caliphate system is historical. The history of the Caliphate is seen as having been full of bloodshed, confusion, and conflict. At least three false claims about the history of caliphate system are always presented: (1) the caliph is authoritarian and dictatorial; (2) mass killings occurred during the times of the rightly guided caliphs; (3) it discriminates against non-Muslims and women. These claims lead people to conclude that the caliphate system is unsuitable because it is dictatorial and lacks a mechanism for preventing degeneration and chaos. In addition, it does not respect non-Muslims and women.

These views are quite false. We can find several fundamental misunderstandings in these arguments. First, there is a mistake in understanding the position or role of Islamic history in the entire debate. The obligation to implement a caliphate system is not merely an historical argument. The caliphate system, in history, should not be discussed in terms of whether it should be accepted or rejected. In Islam, the main credible sources on *syariat*, including the issue of the caliphate system, are *al-Quran*, *al-Sunnah* (the Prophetic tradition), *ijma* (consultation), and *qiyas* (analogy). Therefore, any discussion of the forcible implementation of the caliphate system must refer to these four sources.

However, this does not necessarily mean that history (*târîkh*) has no meaning. We can still learn how *syariat* Islam has been implemented from time to time. We are able to know whether *syariat Islam* has really worked or not, and what the consequences would be without it. Perhaps human beings were the cause of mistakes, not *syariat* Islam itself. As a human being, the Caliph could do wrong and deviate from what *syariat* Islam stipulates, with the exception of prophets and messengers of God, who do not commit sins. As a system practised by human beings, the caliphate system is, in a way, a "humanized political system." Thus, human errors are inevitable. Yet, what is important to remember is that even if the Caliph or the head of state makes a mistake, the caliphate system itself is not necessarily wrong. It is wrong to blame an ideal system by judging at the mistakes of those ones who run it.

There are plenty of examples of this. Some people say that Islam is a bad religion on the basis of the behaviour of followers of Islam. Consider some examples from Indonesia, where the majority of criminals are Muslim; many corrupt people are Muslim; many Muslims do not care about cleanliness and health. Is it right then to conclude that Islam is a bad religion? One must judge Islam according to its sources, not its followers. Islam never teaches bad things to its followers. Islam clearly forbids criminal acts; there are punishments for misdeeds. Islam also teaches the need for "cleanliness." Muslims from time to time behave badly and do wrong because they are not practising Islam; *syariat* Islam has nothing to do with these deeds. Similarly, the examples of negative conduct of Muslims in the past should not be attributed to the system itself. Rather, we need to remember that they occurred because *syariat* Islam was not properly implemented by the Caliph (the head of state) and his subjects. For example, when *Muawiyah* forced the people to pay allegiance to his son, Yazid, this was a clear misapplication of the Islamic *syariat*. The Caliph should be appointed by a majority vote that reflects the will of the people. Lineage or nepotism should not accepted as a way of choosing the caliph. It was *Muawiyah* who was wrong, not the caliphate system itself. Thus, we cannot conclude that caliphate system is authoritarian from a selective survey of history.

Second, generalizing is another trap that leads to false conclusions. One perspective that rejects the caliphate system is based on several historical factors. Examples of the Caliph's leadership do not reflect the goodness of caliphate system. Furthermore, there are some cases in history when the Caliph did not act in accordance with the principle of caliphate system. To cite the mistakes made by Yazid in order to blame the entire *Bani Umayah* government, or to focus on the behaviour of few Caliphs of *Bani Abbasiya* (Abbasid dynasty) as historical facts in order to paint a negative picture of the caliphate as a whole, is uncritical and unfair. This is especially true of those interpretations of historical misapplications of *syariat* that quote books written by historians who have a deep antipathy towards Islam.

Another mistake with regard to the government or caliphate of *Bani Abbas* is that people only read *al-Aghani*, which was written as a tale of singers, drunkards, poets, and novelists. Moreover, people also get their information from books of mysticism which contain incorrect accounts of Islam. What we should remember is that many books describing the government of *Bani Abbas* are unconvincing. The majority of them are critics or mere idolators whose narrations are hardly credible. Reliable historical sources show that every historical event can be clearly explained in a way that allows us to comprehend history properly. Thus, examination of historical accounts should be at least as rigorous as our methods of studying the *Hadith* (or the tradition of the Prophet Mohammad).

Third, it is improper to use democracy as a standard for judging the caliphate system. Those who see it as incompatible with democracy regard the caliphate system as dictatorial, authoritarian, and evil. In fact, democracy itself is weak and imperfect, and it cannot be a standard for judging other systems. For example, according to the principles of democracy, any system that prescribes the separation of political powers into legislative, judicial, and executive powers is good. Therefore, when one man holds all of those three powers (such as European theocracies of the past), he tends to be dictatorial.

The caliphate system stipulates that a Caliph has judicial authority to take people to court when public transgressions take place, and that he has executive power to govern as well. According to "democratic principles," the caliphate system is therefore authoritarian and dictatorial. Moreover, it has been argued that the Caliph has legislative authority, as in a theocracy which treats the laws of the King as the voice of God. The king is never wrong. One might conclude that caliphate system is the same as theocracy, since a ruler uses his power in the name of the God. It is a big mistake to equate the caliphate system with theocracy because what the Caliph says is not the voice of God.

We need to remember that the caliphate system is very different from a theocracy. Sheikh Taqiyyudin an-Nabhani, the founder of Hizbut Tahrir (the movement for a united Islam started in Jerusalem, 1953), presents a clear explanation about the difference between the two in his book *Nidhamul hukmi fi al Islam*. Taqiyyudin differentiates the term 'sovereignty' (al-siyadah) from 'authority' (al-sultan) in the caliphate system. In his view, sovereignty clearly belongs to almighty God, *Allah*, while political authority is still held by the people. This means that no one has the right to claim to be Caliph without having been elected by the people. When someone is chosen as caliph, his duty is to implement God's law (*syariat* Islam). Therefore, policies enacted by a Caliph do not automatically mean the will of God.

Prophet Muhammad once said that, "You need to follow any instructions given by fellow humans when these instructions are not in accordance with God's law." This means that decisions taken by the Caliph are only valid as long as they are derived from divine revelation. Any deviation from revelation must be challenged and criticized. Therefore, it is a duty as noble as *jihad* for Muslims to correct political authority. The Prophet also said, "The best *jihad* is to convey the truth to a tyrannical ruler." Those who are killed for speaking the truth have earned the praise of being the best of martyrs. This duty also implies that the Caliph can make mistakes and that his words are not divine. Thus, the claim that nobody can criticize the Caliph is wrong. There is definitely a clear distinction between a caliphate and theocracy.

The Caliph has to refer to *syariat* Islam when making decision and policies. There is always the possibility that the Caliph himself can be wrong and deviate from Islamic teaching. Moreover, Islam itself requires the *umat* (Islamic community) to correct the ruler if he deviates from *syariat* Islam. Muslims are obliged to correct the Caliph when the Caliph makes mistakes. Muslims are very much aware that even a Caliph can be wrong from time to time. If what a Caliph says can never be questioned, then why there is an obligation for Muslims to do good and to forbid evil, and why are Muslims who die correcting an oppressive ruler seen as carrying out *jihad*?

Fourth, there are those who might conclude that the caliphate system is not stable; there have been conflicts, assassinations, and chaos in the history of caliphate system. However, what we have to question is the root cause of these occurrences, whether it was an inherent weaknesses of the system itself or popular deviation from correct implementation of the system. Conflicts that led to bloodsheds in the past were evidently the result of deviation from the ideal system, that is, *syariat* Islam, and were not the result of the application of *syariat* Islam. Does *syariat* Islam have the means to prevent conflict? The answer is, emphatically, yes.

If chaos and assassination are criteria for judging the system, then democracy may also lack a stable mechanism for historical succession. For instance, assassinations of the head of the state and politicians have also taken place in "democratic societies" such as the United States of America and European countries. The history of so-called democratic countries is not free of the same conflict which took place during the time of Islamic caliphate. The United States of America, a self-proclaimed champion of democracy has itself experienced bloody chapters in its history, which consumed its people and rulers, especially during the great Civil War of the nineteenth century. If the assassination of the Caliph as the head of state is grounds for rejecting the caliphate system, how does one explain the murder of J.F. Kennedy and the attempted assassinations of Ronald Reagan and other US political leaders? Have these historical events in the West been taken as grounds for rejecting democracy? The French Revolution, which is regarded as an important event in the history of democracy, was also full of bloodshed. The fall of Communist countries, which brought about the creation of democratic countries, have also witnessed much bloodshed in the former Soviet Union and Eastern Europe. This issue has been more thoroughly discussed by Jack Snyder in his book titled *From Voting to Violence*, which has been translated into Indonesian as *Dari Pemugutan Suara ke Pertumpahan Darah* (2003).

Islamic Mechanisms Prevent the Caliph from Deviating

In *syariat* Islam, there is a mechanism that prevents conflict. Generally speaking, Islam, for instance, forbids mutual killing and oppression between political authorities and people, and requires the followers of Islam to maintain unity while forcing them to reject rebellion. And Islam offers detailed rules to prevent the Caliph from deviating. They are:

1. Instilling political awareness in the people. Whatever system is in force, application of the system depends entirely on the people. The reason for the decline of Islamic society can be attributed to the poor application of Islam. Shallow understanding of Islam only results in deviation (from *syariat* Islam). Therefore, it is extremely important for Muslims to build up and maintain awareness of Islam in the caliphate system. It is nation's duty to provide citizens with an Islamic education. This responsibility is also shared by the political parties. This is the first step to prevent the Caliph from deviating. As long as this knowledge of political Islam exists, people will consistently maintain the caliphate system and will not allow the caliph to abuse, neglect, or deviate from *syariat* Islam.

2. Voluntarily giving the elected Caliph the oath of allegiance. The people, who are not under pressure, elect the Caliph. People cannot be forced to choose or reject someone. This principle prevents the emergence of a tyrant who is already known to be unsuitable, and he will not be elected.

3. Requiring Muslims to control and to correct the political authorities (see the Quranic *s. Ali-Imran*/3:103). Islam praised a person as martyr when he dies with the intention of correcting political authorities. Political parties and individual Muslims can participate in correcting the rulers. Representatives from the *Umat* Council (Islamic Community Council), that always strives for the aspiration of the people, are also able to carry out this task.

4. Having a Court of *Mazhalim* that can settle disputes or disagreements between the Caliph and the people. This court has authority to dismiss the Caliph for serious violations of the law.

5. Mobilizing against the Caliph if the Court of *Mazhalim* fails to settle the matter by means of a process of correction and control. People have the right to take up arms to oust the Caliph. Fighting is allowed when the caliph has committed clear acts of *kufr* (heresy) and has rejected *syariat* Islam. This is a last resort for stopping the emergence of a tyrannical Caliph.

Those five mechanisms will prevent the rise of tyrannical Caliph if practised properly. The deviation of Caliphs in the past occurred because some or all of these mechanisms were not in place. It is obvious that there is nothing wrong with the caliphate system itself, but the people who dealt with the system were wrong. Even an ideal system will produce chaos if people fail to handle it in a consistent manner.

Success of the Caliphate System

To dismiss historical facts that bear witness to the successful implementation of the caliphate in the past is foolish. It cannot be denied that any objective person can appreciate the positive side of the caliphate system, if it is applied correctly. The caliphate system propagated ideological leadership (*qiyâdah fikriyah*) and brought respect to Arab nations, which had lagged behind. The caliphate system has succeeded in bringing welfare to human beings, Muslim and non-Muslim alike. It also played an important part in uniting the Arabian Peninsula, Persia, Africa, and some parts of Europe by means of religious summons (*dakwah*) and physical force (*jihad*).

The Islamic community, thanks to the caliphate system, became a respected nation in the history of human civilization. The writings of honest and objective historians recall the glory of Islam. Evidence for this is easy to find: scientific discoveries and technological inventions during the caliphate period are still valid;

the books written by *ulama* (Muslim scholars) and Muslim intellectuals are useful; and a considerable number of actual relics that marks Islamic glory can be still seen today.

Major Obstacles

One of the chapters of the Holy *Quran, s. Ali Imran*/3:110, states that Muslim community or *umat* is the best community *(khayru al-ummah)* of all communities in the world. It says, "You are the noblest community ever raised up for mankind." However, it is obvious that *umat Islam* is not the best community at the moment. *Umat* has experienced a drastic decline in the fields of education, culture, economy, politics, science, and technology. What we are witnessing today is just the remnant of a once glorious Islamic civilization.

Before its collapse in 1924, the Ottoman Caliphate controlled vast Islamic territories, reigning over the entire Arabian peninsula, North Africa, some parts of Europe, Central Asia, Eastern Asia, and Southern Asia. Since then, these Islamic regions have been carved up and turned into independent states. Intellectually, Muslims have suffered from *westoxication* and alienation from Islamic teaching, a legacy of western colonial rule. Thus, weakened Muslim minds are unable to withstand the onslaught of erroneous ideas, and fail to achieve balanced intellectual dialogue with the West. Such intellectual impotence must have its roots in the political decline which began with the fall of Caliph Utsmani.

The fall of the last Caliph, who had served as a protector of the Islamic world, has proven disastrous for *umat* welfare. Internationally, we witness the sufferings of our brothers in Palestine. Despite having agreed to a peace deal with the PLO (Palestinian Liberation Organization), the Israeli Zionists have continued to show cruelty towards the people in Palestine. Not just in Palestine but Muslims in other parts of the world, such as Bosnia, Kosovo, Chechnya, Dagestan, Jammu Khasmir, Pattani, Muang Thai, and Moro in the Philippines, have also suffered. Muslims in Afghanistan and Iraq are the latest victims. The United States and its allies have attacked cities in both countries upon the pretext of waging war against terrorism and eradicating weapons of mass destruction. America and its allies have destroyed and occupied cities in both Iraq and Afghanistan. With regard to the situation in Indonesia, *umat* is no better than anywhere else, as has been mentioned earlier. The incompetence of the government makes the life of the people more difficult. Most of those who suffer are part of *umat Islam*. Those grim realities have demonstrated that *umat Islam* has been in serious decline. This situation is similar to what the Prophet Muhammad said 1,400 years ago.

Why is the *Umat* in Retreat?

Why has the *umat*, described by *Allah* as the best community, fallen into so dire a condition? In his book on *Our Decline, its Causes and Remedies* (*Lamadz Ta'akhara al-Muslimun wa Taqaddama Ghyruhum*), Sheikh Emir Syakib Arsalan attributes this to factors, internal as well as external, relating to the body of the *umat*.

First, there have been endless attacks on the *umat* from external enemies. The enemies of Islam, comprised of people who resent the establishing of Islam, instigate disunity among the *umat*, distance the *umat* from the correct Islamic teachings, and promote nationalism to make Muslims more attached to their nation and their ethnic group than to Islam. They achieve these goals by spreading the idea (*fikrah*) of secularism, either subtly or overtly, using their own words or those of key Muslims. Consequently, Muslims have been alienated from their own Islamic heritage. In spite of gaining independence from Western colonial powers, the populations of Muslim countries have not freed their minds from Western ideas.

Colonialism (*isti'mar*) or imperialism is the power to control the politics, economy, military, and culture of its target countries. According to Sheikh Abu Yusuf in *Mafahim Siyasiyah* (Political Concepts), capitalist countries have adopted a specific method (*thariqah*) to spread their ideology of secularism. This method is currently spread all over the world, including Muslim countries. Colonialists use secularism to control a country by encouraging people to subscribe to its ideology. This is the real ideological war or *al-ghazwu al-fikriy* being waged against the Muslim world in order to to spread Western ideas and provoke conflict or *al-ghazwu al-'askary*.

Second, the internal factor, according to Syakib Arsalan, is that members of the *umat* itself have disregarded the teachings of Islam. Muslims' poor understanding of their own religion has increased since the *umat* stopped cultivating Islam, and since Islam's ability to address real life issues has diminished. As a result, many Muslims do not even subscribe to an Islamic way of life, struggle for Islamic cause, or comprehend the reality of their Islamic creed in both detail and substance. Even though he is a Muslim, he is no different from a non-Muslim – no defining Islamic characters appear in or influence his daily life. There are many people who practise only some parts of Islamic teachings. Some only care about their private relationship with God, but neglect the importance of their relationship with fellow Muslims. It is obvious that the *umat* has been largely influenced by secularism.

What is secularism, then? According to Muhammad Qutb's *Ancaman Sekularisme: Threat of Secularism* (1986), secularism is meant to build a structure of life on top of a foundation other than Islam (*iqomatu al-hayati 'ala asasin ghayru mina al-dini*). When Islam is no longer adopted as the foundation of life, an alternative principle will appear that addresses the daily routine of the *umat*. Thus, instead of Islam, Capitalism rules the sphere of economy; permissive attitude reigns in the entertainment industry, fashion world, and social norms; nationalism dominates political discourses; and syncretic ideas influence religious practices. The capitalist economy undeniably produces materialistic benefits. However, capitalism creates serious problems, such as social inequality and dehumanization, reducing humanity to the endless pursuit of wealth and materialism. This capitalistic mode of life is not in harmony with human nature and its sense of vision and life mission. Meanwhile, nationalism has succeeded in dividing the *umat,* which used to be united, into about 50 countries, emphasizing the importance of national interest and pride instead of Islam and brotherhood. As a result, the *umat* has failed to become a recognized and respected global player. It has fallen prey to the imperialistic infidel.

Needless to say, all the problems faced by the *umat* are due to just one factor, that is, the absence of *syariat* Islam in life. In other words, the fall of caliphate system resulted in *ummul jara'min* (the mother of all kinds of disasters and damages) which has been felt across the entire Islamic community. To reconstruct the caliphate in order that Muslims may resume an Islamic way of life has become a vital issue (*qadhiyatu al-muslimin al-mashiriah*) which must be resolved. The challenge is how to establish the law of *Allah* (*I'adatu al-hukmi bi ma anzalallah*) in a comprehensive manner. The problems faced by the *umat* today will only be overcome by reinstating *syariat* and the caliphate; this is the only way to restore the honour of Islam and to regain the respect which the *umat* deserves (*izzu al-Islam wa al-muslimin*).

The need for a Caliph

What ought to be done? The only way out of this crisis is to revive the Islamic *umat*. It has been declared that fifteenth century of the Islamic calendar is a century of revival. However, "revival" can be interpreted in various ways. Sheikh Taqiyyudin an-Nabhani states in his book *Nidzamu al-Islam (Islamic system)* that revival must begin with changes in our way of thinking (*taghyiru al-afkar*) that are both profound (*asasiyan*) and complete (*syamilan*) and which critically address the relationship between humans, life, and nature, and the relationship between life in this world and the hereafter. Thoughts that promote comprehension (*mafahim*) of life will influence the behaviour of human beings. Therefore, Islamic behaviour will only be manifested when people comprehend Islam correctly. Thus, the revival of Islamic *umat* means the return of a wholesome comprehension of Islamic teachings and the resumption of an Islamic way of life which covers every aspect of human activity.

A summons (*dakwah*) to achieve this task is needed. Amid a general decline of the *umat* following on the absence of Islam from daily life, *dakwah* activities must "call for the resumption of Islamic way of Life (*da'wah li isti'nafi al-hayati al-islamiyyah*)", according to Syekh Abdul Qadim Zallum in his book *Manhaj (Methodology towards change of Hizbut Tahrir)*, who also argues that the aim of *dakwah* is to encourage comprehensive application of Islamic laws in matters of faith, acts of devotion, compliance with dietary restriction, clothing, morals, penal codes, socio-cultural issues, education, politics, and economices *'audatu al-muslimin ila al-'amal bi jami'I ahkami al-Islam min aqaidin, ibadatin...)* by establishing an Islamic Caliphate (*...bi thariqi iqomati al-khilafah*).

Dakwah should be carried out collectively (*jamaiyyan*), since no individual (*fardiyan*), regardless of his or her degree of knowledge and ability, can complete this task alone. Morever, the collective effort, which must be an organized entity, is by nature political (*kutlah siyasiy*), since the movement to resume Islamic way of life in comprehensively is essentially a political movement. Naturally, entities or groups that fail to concentrate their efforts on political activism will not realize the goal of *dakwah* as here defined.

In relation to personality building, the purpose of *dakwah* is to create an "Islamic personality" (*syakhsiyyah Islamiyyah*) in the minds of Muslims who think and act in accordance to Islamic teachings. The *umat* must understand the Islamic creed precisely and profoundly in all of its consequences in order to follow *syariat* Islam conscientiously (thus the Quranic *ss. al-Nisa'/*4:65; *al-Ahzab/* 33:33 and *al-Hasyr/*59:7). A proper understanding of Islamic *syariat* enables Muslims to understand the purpose of their lives and the right way of living it. For example, Muslims have to be devout and choose the correct apparel for covering their bodies properly, observe dietary restriction, interact with others, and deal with worldly matters in the way prescribed by Islam. Muslims must behave in accordance with Islamic teachings in mosques, offices, markets, and streets. They have to be "Muslims" when they pray, do business, and socialize with others. Furthermore, *dakwah* will create a profound awareness among the *umat* as to the society should be organized under Islam.

In relation to community building, the purpose of *dakwah* is to bring about Islamic society of which members are Muslims with Islamic personality. This Islamic community building-process should be guided by a Caliph. Raising Muslim awareness (*al-wa'yu al-Islamy*) is critical in order for them to realize that only under the Caliphate leadership will all laws be applied properly and the *umat* united. *Syariat* is the only way to solve the many kinds of problems faced by the *umat*, and the mercy of *Allah* will be bestowed not only upon Muslims but also upon non-Muslims as surely as Islam brings mercy to the whole world.

Conversely, the *umat* must realize that there can be no Islamic unity or proper implementation of *syariat* Islam without the caliphate system. Without *syariat*, problems cannot be overcome and the *umat* cannot regain its respect. Can we expect to obtain goodness and mercy from Islam? If not, why do we insist on living in an uncivilized and chaotic society like the present? On the one hand, we complain that life is getting more difficult and unsafe; prices are rising; violation of God's law is ubiquitous; pornography is everywhere; the youth has become more violent; bureaucracy is unreliable; and Muslims are being slaughtered, etc. On the other hand, why are we silent when we know that Islam is able to solve problems and make the best of society? One may draw an analogy to people who feel physical pain and complain about it yet, instead of consuming the medicine prescribed, keep staring at the medicine that they have procured at such expense. Do they expect to recover?

In a battle, people take up arms. However, we do not face a physical war (although wars are taking places in many parts of the world) at the moment, but rather an ideological war. We Muslim fighters must "shoot" the sharp bullets of solid Islamic thoughts at the enemies who promote wrong ideas. Our mouths and minds are our weapons, and we carry as ammunition the right understanding of Islam based on the solid and authentic revelations of the Prophet Muhammad. This was how our Prophet Muhammad used his mouth to transform uncivilized society into the civilized Islamic society. In this war, the enemies of Islam, using every means at their disposal, attack Islam, including bureaucratic networks and the mass media. Thus, it is necessary for Muslims, as members of Islamic movement, to be more active within their community to rouse fellow Muslims from their long and deep sleep. Once the *umat* realizes its responsibility, true revival can ensue. At the end of the day, the modern Islamic community blessed by the Almighty *Allah* will rise again.

But can this really happen? At an early stage of *dakwah*, Prophet Muhammad entered the barbaric society of Mecca alone. He was not powerful compared to the other established powers of the Persians or the Romans. However, he dedicated himself to propagating the call for Islam zealously under the guidance of revelations from *Allah*. Islam kept expanding. After the thirteen years of struggle, Prophet Muhammad succeeded in establishing the first stable Islamic society in Medina, which he led, ruled, and organized for ten years. He administered the city under *syariat* Islam, and Islam spread beyond the borders of Medina. Finally, the Prophet Muhammad subjugated the powerful city of Mecca, which had served as a center of opposition to the Prophet's leadership in Medina. Thereafter, Syria and Egypt were liberated and came into the fold of Islam. By that time Prophet Muhammad had already set out the basic principles of Islamic foreign policy of expansion, which included *dakwah* and *jihad*. The Prophet Muhammad said to the leaders of the region that he would not force them to embrace the Islamic faith, but that if they refused to submit to Islamic rules, a special tax called *jizyah* would be imposed on them, although their religious freedom would be assured. If non-Muslims rejected this offer and prepared to fight, war would be waged against them.

Several verses in the *al-Quran* treat the will to dominate and the means to assume global leadership. In *Allah*'s own words:

> Fight them, till there is no persecution (*fitnah*) and the religion is God's entirely. (*al-Anfal*/8:38)

According to Ibnu Katsir, *fitnah* (persecution/slander) means all kinds of deviation from *syariat* Islam, i.e., *maksiyat,* and the deviation from Islamic creed, such as rejection (*kufr*) and polytheism (*shirk*). The *umat* must struggle until there is no deviation from the creed and *syariat*, and people bear witness and submit to the faith of Islam. As this Quranic verse and other instances from the *Hadiths* clearly show, Islam should be brought to the rest of the world by means of *dakwah* and *jihad*. True Islam will be realized only when a Caliph properly leads his fellow Muslims with a unified ideology (*mabda'iy*) and system of organization (*nidzam*).

In fact, only through its unification can *umat* Islam be fully developed. If they fail to unite, 1.5 billion Muslims will be scattered like foam on the sea. Without unity, Muslims will be unable to expoit natural resources properly. As a result, Islam will contract; the scattered *umat* will be targeted for exploitation by powerful countries. This is what is happening today. What can we do for our brothers in Palestine, Chechnya, Iraq, and Afghanistan, for instance? The Arab League, COI (Council of Islamic Organizations), *Rabithah Alam Islamy* (The Unity of Islam), and other Islamic organizations have been unable to stop brutality and oppression by Israel, Russia, the U.S., and their allies. This situation has lasted for a long time. It is obvious that these Islamic organizations are wholly able to solve the problem or to bring about solidarity of the *umat* as a whole. Islamic countries can certainly be members of these Islamic organizations. However, the members of these organizations prioritize their own interests and care less about Islam. Thus, we are not able to resist a small country like Israel whose population is less than that of Jakarta. Why is the whole *umat*, with 1.5 billion people, unable to resist so small country? It is absolutely vital for *umat* Islam to be united systematically under one leadership for the whole community.

Islam will be much stronger if the *umat* is united. Sheikh Muhammad Ismail states in his book titled *al-Fikru al-Islamy (Islamic thoughts)*, that there are three strengths that Muslims should possess: material strength (*al-quwwah al-madiyah*); intellectual strength (*al-quwwah al-ma'nawiyah*); and spiritual strength (*al-quwwah al-ruhiyah*). Regarding material strength, we all know that the potential of the *umat* is huge since it commands a significant amount of human and natural resources across Muslim countries.

In the era of globalization, the unification of *umat* looks increasingly relevant as information technology progresses, bringing faster communication to people all over the world. The geographical boundaries among countries seem to be less significant these days. No country can be prosperous and survive without the cooperation of other countries. The formation of trade blocks such as AFTA, NAFTA, and APEC proves that mutual cooperation between countries is necessary. Fourteen countries in the Western Europe took an important step in Maastricht in 1992 when they agreed to extend the European Union not only to trade but political and military operations. The "European Caliphate" has been already formed. Why not form the Islamic Caliphate needed for implementing *syariat* Islam?

Closing Remarks

Does this sound utopian? Maybe. But if Muslims are serious and maintain the spiritual strength needed to carry out their task, it will be a utopia no longer. Spiritual strength comes from deep awareness or conviction that the commands of *Allah* must be carried out even when the chance of success is slight. The Prophet Muhammad and his companions prayed for victory over the Persians and Romans, though it seemed improbable at that time. When members of the the Quraysh tribe, who were infidels, heard about the ambitions of Mohammad, they thought that the Prophet was insane. They even went so far as to say that Prophet was merely a magician. We can wonder what kind of encouragement made the Prophet and his companions remain committed to answer their call? It was the strength of spirit. Strength of spirit is something extraordinarily amazing and it will not diminish. The Prophet Muhammad spoke with conviction about the future of Islam:

> You fought against Arabs and, Allah subjugated them. Then, You fought against Byzantiums, and Allah subjugated them (*Hadith* narrated by Muslim).

Egypt was also subdued. This is the land that contains wealth and being said that it is good to the people (Narrated by Muslim).

Surely Constantinople will be taken. The best troops are to conquer the city, and the best commander is the one who conquer the city. People asked Prophet which city will be subjugated before that, Constantinople or Rome? The Prophet answered: Heraclea will be subjugated even before that (Narrated by Ahmad).

The Prophet Muhammad and his noble companions struggled with the help of their spiritual strength, refusing to accept that reality that was not in their favour as an excuse for not working to achieve their aspirations. They realized that it was reality that must be changed for another state to come about, one ruled and organized by Islam. They did it and they succeeded. With the unwavering will to fulfil the commands of *Allah*, the Prophet worked to change the world. Since then, Islam has expanded to every corner of the world and brought mercy and justice to various parts of the world. This is what we need to do, so that mercy and justice will return.

Finally, it should be emphasized that there is an inherent mechanism to correct or to control political authority within the caliphate system. The misapplications of Islamic *syariat* under previous implementations of the caliphate system reveal the caliphate to be a human system that is prone to error and deviation. Therefore, it is unreasonable to judge the nature of the caliphate system from past experience. What is necessary to bear in mind is *al-Quran* and *al-Sunna* are sources of ideas and laws which oblige Muslims to establish a Caliphate as a system of Islamic governance. Any political system controlled by humans always faces the possibility of deviation, and the caliphate system is no different. Unless there is an ulterior motive to destroy Islam, one cannot and should not focus solely on the past mistakes of the caliphate. God willing!

Wallahu'alam bi al-shawab

References

Abu Yusuf, *Mafahim Siyasiyah*, Jakarta: Hizbut Tahrir, n.d. [2000s].

Abdul Qadim Zallum, *Manhaj Hizb at-Tahrîr fi Tagyîr (Metode Hizbut Tahrir dalam Melakukun Perubahn Total)*, Jakarta: Hizbut Tahrir, n.d. [2000s].

Muhammad Ismail, *Al-Fikru al-Islamy*, Beirut: Maktad al-Wa'ie, 1958.

Muhammad Qutb, *Ancaman Sekularisme: Threat of Secularism*, Yogjakarta: Shalahuddin Press, 1986.

Saidi Zaim, *Soeharto menjaring matahari: talik ulur reformasi ekonomi Orde Baru pasca-1980*, Jakarta, Mizan, 1998.

Snyder, Jack, *Dari Pemugutan Suara ke Pertumpahan Darah*, Jakarta, Gramedia, 2003.

Syakib Arsalan, *Our Decline, its Causes and Remedies*, Kuala Lumpur: Islamic Book Trust, 2004 edn. *Forum* (5 March, 2002).

Taqiyyudin an-Nabhani, *Nidhamul hukmi fi al Islam*, Bogor: Pustaka Tharaqul Izzah, 2003.

__________, *Nidzamu al-Islam*, London: Al-Khilafah Publications, 2002.

9

Ethnic Identity, Nationalism, and Islam

— Eka Jaya

Islam is a universal religion, which was revealed by the almighty and omnipotent Allah through the first prophet Adam to the last prophet Muhammad. Islam is a religion of mercy given to the whole world (*rahmatan lil' alamiin*). Indeed, Islam encourages Muslims to bring about safety, health, happiness and peace to their present life as well as to the life after this world through their dedication to Allah. Islam, as a compass (*hudan*), gives people guidance in this world and the next.

By the period of Dutch colonization, Islam had already been embraced by the people of Betawi (an ethnic group originating in Jakarta). Islam has offered an ideal form of the life of people and has always helped people to maintain calmness in times of both happiness and hardship. The faith of Betawi people towards Islam has never wavered in 350 years. The Dutch colonizers never succeeded in "conquering" Betawi, and two parties existed as "oil and water" in the society of the time, which means that Betawi were never under the full Dutch control. Prof Dr Hamka, the former Chairperson of Indonesia Ulama Council (MUI), who used to live in a Betawi village, once praised the Betawi for their impressive commitment to the Islamic faith.

Many formerly agricultural areas of Jakarta have now been turned into "concrete jungles." Yet, we can still hear the sound of *azam* (the calls for prayer) that penetrate skyscrapers built on the soil of Betawi. It is an undeniable truth that we, the Betawi, feel Islam is always with us. Ridwan Saidi, who heads the Betawi Culture Centre (LKB), has declared that "if you are Betawi, you are Muslim. They are two sides of the same coin," about which he is absolutely correct. In this paper, we will examine the ways in which Betawi, as very devout Muslims, can play a role in the nation-building process in Indonesia, while at the same time focusing upon the social realities in this, the most populous Muslim nation in the world.

Betawi Tradition and Islam

As a capital city, Jakarta, formerly known as Batavia or Betavi, has been the centre of political as well as economic activity since colonial times. Jakarta has experienced relatively swift development compared to other parts of Indonesia. In other words, over time rice paddies, plantations, and the residential areas of Betawi in Jakarta have become housing complexes, office buildings, shops, and recreation sites. It is not surprising, therefore, that large numbers of people have moved to Jakarta. Even though these newcomers to Jakarta have brought their own religious orientations and cultures, Betawi have never felt inferior to or intimidated by them. In fact, Betawi have existed with them fairly harmoniously. Betawi acceptance of newcomers is evinced by the fact that there are quite a few cases of intermarriage between Betawi and non-Betawi. Again, to borrow the words of Ridwan Saidi, Betawi is one of the most mature ethnic groups to support the concept of the national motto, *Bhinneka Tunggal Ika* or Unity in Diversity. For Betawi, modernization and acceptance of different religions have been a matter of everyday life throughout history.

However, it is also true that Betawi have been pushed to the edge of the society as rapid development and the growth of non-Betawi population have become more and more visible in Jakarta. In general, Betawi feel marginalized in the place of their birth,

Jakarta. Consequently, Betawi people have tried to maintain a decent position as native inhabitants of Jakarta by establishing several organizations, such as the Betawi Rempug Forum (FBR), the Communication Forum of Betawi Youths (FORKABI), the Union of Tanah Abang Community (IKBT), the Unity of Betawi Citizens (PERWABI), the Association of Betawi Society (IKBT),the Unity of Betawi People (POB), and the Committee of Betawi Society Conference (BAMUS), etc. One of the largest Betawi organizations is BAMUS, which is headed by the Governor of Jakarta, Fauzi Bowo. BAMUS fights for the preservation of traditional Betawi culture and expresses the aspirations of Betawi people. This organization also deals with social issues related to the improvement of Betawi condition, and, in so doing, even criticizes government policies.

We also should remember that Betawi culture, which is identical with the values of Islam, has been influenced by Chinese and Arab cultures. These syncretic features of Betawi culture and tradition can be seen in *marawis Hadroh* (traditional drum), *shalawat* (the recitation that praises Prophet Muhammad), *gambang kromong tanjidor* (Betawi traditional musical instruments), *lenong Betawi* (Betawi opera plays), wedding processions, and the ceremony of circumcision.

Social Problems and Islam

Not only Betawi people face serious social problems but Indonesians in general are exposed to a number of major challenges. One of the most serious problems in Indonesia today is the decline of morality. We know that if this problem persists in Indonesia, the country will face further downfall. Corruption, which may lead to economic collapse, is clear evidence of the decadence of society. Moreover, if corruption continues, the gap between the rich and the poor will widen, unemployment will grow, and criminal activities will become more ubiquitous in our country. Needless to say, it is our shared understanding that all corrupt action should be rejected. Unfortunately, however, it is also a fact that both high- and low-ranking officials in the governement are secretly involved in corruption. Sad to say, many people put money above all else and have no scruples about taking bribes, something which is also a breach of their religious duties.

Furthermore, Indonesia faces various social problems, such as the widespread use of drugs, prostitution, the circulation of pornography, gambling, and the distribution of alcohol. Although we have already passed regulations and created organizations to prevent and eradicate such illegal activities, it is still difficult for us to find the origin of and the solution for these problems. It is like a tangled thread, which cannot easily be untied.

The question we have to ask is why these social problems prevail in a country where Muslims make up the majority of the population. It is obvious that this predicament has come about because the teaching of Islam *(iman)* is not correctly understood by Muslims. In other words, *iman* and *ihsan* (right actions as Muslims) have not been made into central pillars of the nation or the life of Muslims.

Iman, which is the highest form of belief, is an essential canon to which Muslims must hold fast in order to stand firm, whatever happens. *Iman* makes Muslims understand that they are creations of Allah. If they do, Muslims will always take the right actions *(ihsan)* as Muslims. Both *iman* and *ihsan* can be achieved when the five pillars of Islam *(rukun* Islam) are observed correctly by its followers.

Five Pillars or *Rukun* in Islam

The mission of Islam is not only to provide personal identity to its followers but to set out the way to foster decency as human beings. In order to achieve this, Muslims should discipline themselves as guided by Prophet Muhammad, the messenger of Allah. There are five pillars of Islam *(rukun* Islam) that Muslims should follow, namely, *syahadat* (confession of the faith), *sholat* (prayer), *puasa* (fasting), *zakat* (alms), and *haji* (pilgrimage). All Muslims are supposed to fulfil these obligations, although *haji* is applicable only for those who are affluent enough to travel to Mecca.

Syahadat is a sacred contract between Allah and His servants, i.e., Muslims. *Syahadat* consists of two statements: there is no God but Allah; and Muhammad is a messenger of Allah. Stating these confirms one's loyalty and obedience towards Allah, and allegiance to the guidance provided by the Prophet Muhammad. This *syahadat*, in fact, serves to maintain a "vertical relationship" between Allah and human beings.

However, it is important to note that the five doctrines in Islam, including *syahadat*, are also beneficial for sustaining a harmonious relationship between all human beings, which one might call a "horizontal relationship." Muslims who perform their religious rituals rightly can therefore create amicable relationships within families, schools, and any other social community. In this regard, Betawi people have a strong determination and commitment to creating a better community in Jakarta by working with other members of community, including non-Muslims.

On the subject of of *sholat* or prayer, we should understand the difference between "praying" and "commitment to prayer." The first is a physical move with the statement of *Allah akbar*, which means Allah is great. This also helps Muslims be more disciplined and improve the sense of togetherness with other Muslims. On the other hand, commitment to prayer means that Muslims feel the existence of Allah and reflect upon their lives. Muslims can thereby grow and avoid behaviour inappropriate for followers of Islam.

Puasa or fasting is not merely an annual abstention of food, beverages, and sexual intercourse during daylight hours. Rather, the month of *puasa* or *Ramadhan* is a time of reaffirming the supreme values of Islam that Muslims should always cherish, such as honesty, patience, humility, purity of spirit, compassion, solidarity, and self-restraint. By the end of *Ramadhan*, we have gained new perspectives that lead us towards a better life. We appeal sincerely to non-Muslims to understand the holiness and importance of the month of *Ramadhan*.

Zakat is a social practice relating to wealth distribution in the Islamic community. This doctrine contributes to the strengthening of social welfare. By donating part of their wealth to the less fortunate, people learn the importance of mutual help in this world. In addition, almsgiving functions to narrow the gap between the haves and have-nots. As Muslims, we believe that one person's wealth should be shared with other people in the community. Furthermore, the circulation of wealth unquestionably stimulates economic activity in a way that increases the income of the entire community.

The fifth pillar of Islamic doctrine is pilgrimage to Mecca or *haji*. The visit to Mecca is required only once in a lifetime. It is a time for Muslims to show their absolute submission and obedience to Allah, and to overcome selfishness. However, those who are not financially able to visit Mecca are not required to perform *haji*.

Iman: Responsibility of Muslims

Iman is related to various aspects of Islamic life, such as how Muslims maintain righteousness, how Muslims should confess the faith, and how Muslims should behave in a society. These important norms for believers can be deprived both from scriptures such as *al-Quran* and the *Hadith*s, and from human reasoning. If believers utilize these resources of *iman*, their beliefs will be so deep and strong that they will never stray from the path of Islam. In other words, Muslims cannot take the right course of action (*ihsan*) without having *iman*. The right *iman* is sustained by true knowledge, obedience towards Allah, and willingness to embrace the path of Allah.

The Prophet Muhammad said that there were about 70 levels within *iman*. The highest *iman* is the statement (*zikr*) that "there is no God but Allah" (*Laa ilaaha illa Allah*). Meanwhile, the lowest *iman* is that you pull a thorn from someone else's finger, which means that you help others when they face misfortunes. It is this lowest *iman* that encourages Muslims to behave in a positive manner. We know that even people who hold *iman* can be both strong and weak. Muslims become weak when they violate the law of Allah. Conversely, Muslims are very strong when they overcome desires and temptations. If all believers of *iman* remain firm in their belief, then they will show honesty, sincerity, and responsibility in their own community, and their position in the society will be elevated.

A true Muslim does not feel desperate when something unexpected or unwelcomed happens in his or her life. We should know that almighty Allah is responsible for everything that happens in our lives. There is no need to worry about things in your life that may seem negative. What is more important, here, is that we should know that life is not only for this moment. Rather, we will have a life hereafter, one that is truer and everlasting. True Muslims should believe in the existence of *akhirat* or a life after this one. In other words, the actions and attitudes of Muslims should be determined by what is regarded as virtue in Islamic teaching. They include the love for Allah, sincerity, and the attitude without arrogance. As importantly, Muslims should not lose hope in the face of hardships and should always be willing to work with other people. Regardless of one's faith, whoever follows this path can be a follower of Islam.

Ihsan: how Muslims should Strive for Perfection in the Eyes of Allah

As mentioned, there are various problems in our society, such as corruption, collusion, drugs, and circulation of pornographic materials. This situation has created selfish people who prioritize materialistic achievement without any vision for the future. As a result, many Indonesians, including the young, have fallen into a valley of shame. For this reason I feel strongly as a Muslim that I am responsible for liberating these 'contaminated people' from their evil situation.

If you, as a Muslim, believe in the truth of Islam as given by Allah and behave as instructed by Allah, you will not engage in any act that violates the teachings of Allah. In this sense, your belief or *iman* will be your 'weapon' to annihilate wrongdoing in society.

Holders of *iman* are responsible for the social problems seen in Indonesia today, including those in Jakarta. This means that we, as good Muslims, are obliged to take a concrete measures to improve the condition of the society, namely, *ihsan*. The Islamic Defenders' Front (FPI) works hard to eradicate social problems that would, in the long run, ruin the whole society.

For example, I myself had to "stop" the operation of one of the cafés in Jakarta by force during the month of *Ramadhan* in 2004. Before that action was taken, we sent warning letters to the owner of the café telling him to respect our tradition and religion, but our request was ignored. It is also true that we received several complaints regarding disrespectful operation of the café from the residents in the area. My physical tactics was the last option, and I had no choice but fulfil my duty of *ihsan* as a Muslim who holds *iman*. It was not an anarchic action, as is often perceived, but the sacred action of a Muslim.

Needless to say, rituals, including prayer and fasting, are the opportunities for Muslims to make contact with Allah. Yet, it is important to remember that social actions of Muslims only count if Muslims truly wish to make a sacred concord with Allah, which means that Muslims should watch what they say and do in their everyday life. The encounter with Allah can be possible only when they behave properly as Muslims. Again, my physical action, directed to infidel behaviour, was an 'unavoidable' step to build a more solid and righteous society. Remember, Allah is almighty. One of the verses in *al-Quran* reads:

> We created man. We know the promptings of his soul, and are closer to him than his jugular vein (s. *Qaaf*/50:15)

This verse suggests that true Muslims realize that they are always being watched and cared about by Allah wherever they are and whatever they do. Therefore, even though Muslims are exposed to seduction and temptation, they can reject them. This is what we call good deeds of Muslims or *ihsan*. We can find an explanation of *ihsan* in one of the *Hadith*s.

> *Ihsan* means you worship Allah as if you virtually see Him. But if you cannot see Him, you should know that it is Allah who truly sees you (HR. Bukhari and Muslim).[1]

As you can see, *ihsan* is a very positive value for everyone. Once Muslims understand the meaning of *ihsan* correctly, they can eliminate all kinds of negative actions. If *ihsan* prevails in this earth, the world we live in will surely be as beautiful and glorious, as the *Quran* reveals:

> But seek, by means of that which God has given you, to attain the abode of the hereafter. Do not forget your share in this world. Be good to others as God has been good to you, and do not strive for evil in the land, for God does not love the evil-doers (*s. Al- Qasas*/28:77).

This verse suggests us that Allah always makes Muslims have a balance between social life and spiritual life. It also tells us that several values, that is, equality, justice, brotherhood, discussion, mutual appreciation, and support, are essential elements in the life of Muslims. If Muslims follow and realize what Allah tells them, both Muslims and Indonesia will receive the blessings of Allah.

Fundamentalism and Life of Humans

It is quite true that fundamentalism, which exists in Indonesia today, has a negative image, and is often equated with extremism, radicalism and conservativism. Many people think that fundamentalists reject any sort of development. However, fundamentalism, in fact, leads Muslims to the true Islamic way of life, which is defined by *syariat* or Islamic law and which enlightens Muslims. In the process of realizing the true Islamic way of life, both *ibadah* (rituals) and *iman* (belief) are essential factors, and Muslims who disregard them will gain nothing in their lives.

Muslims' duty to follow *syariat* Islam is explained in *al-Quran*:

---

[1] B. Hussein, *Himpunan Hadits Shahih Bukhari*, Surabaya, 1981, p. 379.

Believers, submit all of you to God and do not walk in Satan's
footsteps (*s. Al-Baqarah*/2:208).

In keeping with this verse, Muslims should make every effort to
match the orientation of the nation and their life with *syariat* Islam.
However, this harmonization should be executed in a complete
manner and should take place with all possible haste. Muslims
will know a perfect model for the Islamic life only when *syariat*
Islam is implemented correctly.

It is our urgent task to apply *syariat* Islam to our life as soon
as possible because a so-called "Islam Liberal Network" (JIL),
created by young Muslims intellectuals, has emerged in Indonesia
today. Unlike us, they firmly reject the implementation of *syariat*
Islam. One of the advocates of JIL, Prof. Dr Nurcholish Madjid's
opinion is cited by Hassan, and reads:

> ...it is clear that *fiqih* (understanding of laws regarding rituals
> and obligations in Islam), whatever might have been said by
> reformist groups, is no longer relevant to the reality of modern
> days. In order to adjust our mindset with the modern way of
> life, what is necessary is knowledge on all aspects of modernity.
> Then, competence and importance obtained through this process
> are not only for Islamic communities but also for other religious
> communities.[2]

The implication of this statement is that JIL and other liberals
disagree with the opinions of *ulamas* who exercized their *ijtihad*
when referring to *al-Quran* and *Hadiths* on the question of *syariat*
Islam and matters such as rituals, the treatment of criminals, *jihad*,
war, and so on.

However, no matter how society changes and regardless of
the orientation of the state, that is, being Islamic or being secular,
the *fiqih* understanding and practice as drawn by *ulamas* on *syariat*
Islam, which urges the complete implementation of Islamic law

---

[2] This passage can be found in the writing of Hasan Mukmin Mabruk,
Bahaya Islam Liberal, which is available at http//:groups.google.co.id/
group/soc.culture.indonesia. Cf. Madjid, *Islam, Kemodernan, dan
Keindonesiaan,* Bandung, 1987 edn.

in all aspects of life, is still important and relevant. Imagine what would happen if Muslims did not rely on *fiqih* in their performance of rituals such as prayer, fasting, alms-giving, marriage, and distributing inheritance. We should not forget that the details of these rituals can only be found in *fiqih*.

It is obvious that liberal groups such as JIL are seeking to spread notions of secularism and pluralism. Secularism involves ideas and practices that reject the teachings of religion. The separation of religion and state is another characteristic of secularism. Pluralism is the idea that all religions are equal and the same. We should not regard someone else's religion as our religion.

Are not liberals' ideas in complete opposition to the teachings of Islam, which could, in fact, enrich Indonesia as a nation? Unlike liberal groups, we, the true members of the Islamic community in Indonesia, should properly address and acknowledge the difference between Islam and other religions. This attitude will never be the cause of the frictions between religions.

The Unity of Indonesia and Muslims

Once they appreciate the differences between religions, Muslims are able to decide properly how to live. This is the process that gives Muslims a mature understanding of religion. I strongly believe that as the difference among religions becomes more obvious, the unity of the Republic of Indonesia will be enhanced. Rather than paying lip-service to non-Muslims, it is more practical to acknowledge the difference among religions in order to create a greater "oneness" of Indonesia, because honesty will bind the people.

As the majority religion, Islam has always given Indonesia the strength and the will to resist colonialism, something that we can call *jihad fii sabil allah* (the holy struggle in the way of Allah). Islam has also played an important role in instilling Indonesians the decent attitudes which we Muslims call *amar ma'ruf nahi munkar* (command good deeds and forbid bad deeds). In Indonesian history, Islam has been one of the most important elements in eradicating of Western colonialism. It should be remembered that the formation of the Republic of Indonesia, as the Constitution of the Republic of Indonesia states, would not have been possible without the mercy of Allah.

We have seen the historical sacrifices made by many Indonesians for the sake of their country. The nationalism shown by our patriotic ancestors should be remembered and respected. All Indonesians, regardless of our religion and race, should love our great nation. At the same time, loving your nation or nationalism is one of the elements of Islamic belief.

Colonialism and imperialism do not always take a physical form, but prefer convert control of people's minds and culture. It is no exaggeration to say that liberal movements in Indonesia today seem to be working with a "colonial power" that seeks to regain control of our nation by non-military means. This is the reason why true Muslims like us disagree with JIL and other secularly-oriented Muslims. Our so-called fundamentalist movements, such as FPI, seek to protect the sovereignty of Indonesian people. Is it not obvious which movement is more beneficial for our country?

References

Bahreisj, Hussein, *Himpunan Hadits Shahih Bukhari*, Surabaya: Al Ikhlas, 1981.

Hasan Mukmin Mabruk, *Bahaya Islam Liberal*, statements available at *http//:groups.google.co.id/group/soc.culture.indonesia*

Madjid, Nurcholis, *Islam, Kemodernan, dan Keindonesiaan*, Bandung: Mizan, 1987 edn.

10

Life from Muslim Women's Point of View

— Qothrun Nadaa

L ife is *Ibadah* (Worship):

Allah, *subhanahu wa ta'ala*, stated in His Book *Al Qur'an*: *"And I have not created Jinn and Man except to worship Me"* (s. Adz-Dzariyat/51:56).

The literal meaning of *Ibadah* in Arabic is *"to lower oneself."* According to the dictionary edited by Al-Fayrooz Abaadi, *Al-Qamoos Al-MuHeet, "Al-Ibadah means obedience."* Therefore, *Ibadah*, with its vast and comprehensive implications, means: obedience with submission, lowering oneself, embracing any existence led by *Allah (subhanahu wa ta'ala)*, and accepting everything that He has permitted and forbidden (*Shari'ah* commandments). *Ibadah* is not limited to a small section of Islam, such as personal rituals, including prayer (*salat*), fasting (*saum*), alms giving (*zakat*), and pilgrimage *(hajj)*; rather *ibadah* of *Allah* means comprehensive implementation of Islam, without neglecting even a single ruling and without differentiating between one command and another.

Muslim women, just as Muslim men, should believe that human beings do not know what is best for them in this secular world. Then, they realize that men's intelligence is very limited.

They often find that something they thought bad in the past becomes something very good today. Muslim women should believe that *Allah*, who created them, knows every kind of knowledge, everything good for humans, and everything that humans do not know. That is the very reason why Muslim women obey *Shari'ah* willingly.

Every commandment in *Shari'ah* originates in *Al Qur'an* and the *Hadiths*. It is the address of *Allah*, the Legislator, who owns every power over men's action. There is no human action without Allah's rule (*hukm sharii*). *Hukm sharii* can be divided into five categories:

> *Fard* (compulsory), for example performing routine *salat*; paying *zakah*, fasting in the month of *Ramadhan*, studying to obtain knowledge, being ruled by Islam, wearing *jilbab* (women), obeying parents or husband as long as they order something that is in no contradiction with *hukm syarii*, working to support his family for basic necessities (men), etc. A person who complies with *fard* will be rewarded in the next eternal world while one who disregards *fard* will be punished.

> *Haram* (prohibited), for example: earning benefit from interest, gambling, drinking alcohol, cheating, being corrupt, eating pork, etc.

> *Mandub/sunnh/nafilah* (recommended), for example: attending the sick, giving alms to the poor, smiling to other persons, etc. The one who performs these will be praised and rewarded while the one who does not perform recommended actions will be neither punished nor blamed, but will lose a chance to be rewarded.

> *Makruh* (disliked), for example: eating garlic before visiting *masjid* for *salat*. The one who abstains from this will be praised and rewarded while the one who does this will be neither punished nor blamed.

> *Mubah* (permissible), for example: women working to gain money, eating lamb or chicken, watching television etc. One will be neither rewarded nor punished for an action in this category.

Muslim women should live their lives with every action of *fard*. If possible, they should perform things that are defined as *mandub* and *mubah* as well. They should feel satisfied and be themselves in the frame of *ibadah*, and should not feel satisfied or being themselves while appreciating freedom of behaviour, freedom of opinion and so on. Muslim women should only care about whether *Allah* can praise them. As long as rules come from *Al Qur'an* and *Hadith*, they know that commands come from Allah the Creator. Then they will obey the rules because they know *Allah* will ask them about what they did in this world on the Day of Judgment.

Muslim Women's Lives as Part of Men's and Women's Community

Muslim women should see life from a communal point of view, not from an individual one. This means that they should care about not only their individual interests but also communal ones. Muslim women should consider their individual problems as part of a communal problem. They should understand that Islam has established its social system on a firm basis which ensures communal and societal cohesion and elevation. It offers true happiness for both men and women, and humans can receive the dignity and honour of *Allah*, as in His saying:

> And indeed We have honoured the children of Adam (*s. Al-Isra*/17:70).

The *sharia'ah* commandment covers all aspects of social life and encourages all Muslims to take part in any activities that would bring about communal advancement. For this purpose, in some cases, men and women are given the same rights and obligations, but in some other cases, different rights and obligations are given to men and women. This difference should not be considered as discrimination or subordination. The Creator has disposed women and men properly in the community. He placed the right men in the right places. People will be honoured because of their good deeds, not because of their position arranged by *Allah*. The following discusses the arrangement of the Islamic community.

Each man and woman has to reach a standard quality of being a human. There is no difference between men and women for this requirement. Thus, it is *fard* (compulsory) for each Muslim to study (get knowledge); to eat proper food (*halal* and *thoyib* food) which is gained in a *halal* way (not by stealing, corruption, or any other improper way); to have a good spiritual life by fulfilling duties, such as *salat*, fasting, *zakat*, and *hajj*; and to have *ahlaq* or moral attitudes.

Islam puts great emphasis on having a family, viewing it as the cornerstone of society. The family unit produces decent citizens and is responsible for providing proper education to the younger generation that can contribute to constructing a better society in the future. The well-functioning and stable family is essential in a successful society. From the very outset, men and women have been encouraged to stay together to benefit mankind, that is, marry and procreate. Marriage is the foundation of every relationship, and thus it is crucial for both men and women to choose their partner rightly. Marriage should provide companionship, security, and stability for both the wife and husband and should ensure certain rights that both parties are entitled to have. Both men and women are encouraged to look for their partner with piety. Men should look for a potentially good mother for their future children. Once married, the respective roles, rights, and duties are clearly defined as to how the men and women should form a family. It is incumbent upon both partners to maintain a peaceful relationship. They should strive for intimacy and love. Divorce should be considered as a last option. The objective of the marriage is that the men and women live together harmoniously in order to build a family that is full of peacefulness and cooperation. Therefore, *Allah* has given both men and women distinct roles to balance one another, and to prevent friction and conflicts.

Men have a duty to protect women. A man, as a head of the family, is responsible for his wife's well being and has the final say in any matters related to the marital life in order to avoid discord in a family. A man should treat his wife with justice and take counsel from her. The wife in turn accepts these Islamic marital arrangements and must show obedience to her husband.

Men are the protectors and guardians over women (*s. Nisa*/4:34).

Meanwhile, women have a duty as a mother and housewife. *Sharia'ah* elucidates matters that are related to pregnancy, childbirth, nursing, custodianship and *iddah* or a suspension period of remarriage for divorced a woman or widow. We find that *shari'ah* allows women not to fast in the month of *Ramadhan* if they are pregnant or need to nurse a baby. In addition, *shari'ah* exempts women from the duty of daily prayer if they are menstruating or pregnant. In the case of divorce or any disputes over a child, *shari'ah* prohibits a man from taking his child from the place where the mother resides, as long as she still has custody over the child. A man has no rights to take a child from its mother as women are supposed to execute their duty as mothers. A mother has full responsibility for pregnancy, delivery, nursing and custody. Muslim women should nurture children who bear an Islamic orientation and are physically and psychologically healthy. Muhammad (saw) said: "Honour your children and bring them up well." As it is obligatory (*fard*) for men to earn money for the family, women are supposed to concentrate on raising children at home. Women also should be in charge of house work for they stay at home longer than men.

It is true, according to the teachings of Islam, that the primary role of women is to be both mother and housewife. These two roles are crucially important to make women distinctive and differ from men. Women, in a way, have the responsibility to prosper the human race as a whole. At any rate, women are important in terms of creating a better society.

Women and men should work cooperatively in society. The woman's primary role as mother and housewife does not necessarily mean she is prevented from pursuing other activities. In the frame of worship of *Allah* in life, Muslim women may undertake recommended activities or *sunnah/mandub* as long as they execute things that are *fard*. Considering every teaching of Islam, women can contribute to the public without neglecting their prime responsibility as mothers and housewives.

Allah allows women to work in the agricultural industry and any other fields that are related with trading. He also gives them the rights to own all types of property; to invest in property; to start businesses with other people; to run businesses by themselves; to lease property; to undertake any matters related to trade and business transactions (*Mu'amalat*).

However, women are not permitted to take up the leadership of political society, such as being the head of state who owns legal authority. This is due to what has been narrated by Abu Bakrah. When the news reached the Messenger of *Allah* that the people of Persia appointed the daughter of Chosroes (Kisra) as a queen over them, Abu Bakrah said: "People who appoint a woman to run their affairs shall never succeed." It is clear that women should not be given any positions that provide power to lead the people. In an Islamic governmental system, these governmental positions include *Khaleefah* (the head of state), his *Mu'awin* (assistant), *Wali* (governor), *'Amil* (Mayor) or *Qodli Mazollim* (a special judge who has the authority to repudiate any decisions of the leader that are regarded as injustice), and are not meant for women. In a non-Islamic governmental system, according to Islamic creed, political positions, such as President, Prime Minister, King, or Governor, also should not be taken by women.

Although the "authority of ruling" should be held by men, women are permitted to take other "leadership" positions, such as division head of a governmental office, headmistress of a school, executive manager at a factory, etc.

Women are given the right to choose the person who rules the community that they belong to. *Shari'ah* assures the legal right of women to approve or disapprove a ruler because women are allowed to give *Bay'a*[1] to the *Khaleefah* (Caliph). It is narrated from Umm Atiyya: "We gave our *Bay'a* to the Messenger of *Allah*, so He recited to us 'they should associate none with *Allah* and he forbade

---

[1] *Bay'a(h)* is a sort of contract given to Caliph from members of the community to accept his leadership.

us from wailing (upon the dead)…" Giving the *Bay'a* to the Prophet was a sign to show obedience to the ruler. This *hadith* shows that women can give *Bay'a* to the *Khaleefah* and approve his leadership.

Women have the right to voice their political, economic, legal or any other opinions. They also have the right to appoint anyone as their representative to let him/her express his/her opinion. A woman also can be a representative of someone. Islam has given women the right to articulate their opinion in the same manner as men. Men and women are treated equally when consultation (*shura*) takes place. Two of the verses in *Al Qu'ran* read:

> And consult them in the affair [*s. Al- Imran/*3:159]; and conduct their affairs by mutual consultation [*Ash-Shura/*42:38]

Both men and women must conduct something good (*Amr bil al-ma'ruf*) and refrain from any evil actions (*Nahi 'an al-munkar*). He said:

> Let there arise out of you a group of people inviting to all that is good (Islam), commanding *al-Ma'ruf* (good) and forbidding *al-Munkar* (evil) (*Al- Imran/*3:104).

And the Prophet said: "Whoever of you sees a *munkar* (evil) let him change it." Correcting their leader is obligatory for both men and women Muslims. Both men and women are entitled to give advice (*Al-nasiha*) to their leader. The Prophet said: "The *deen* (way of life) is to give advice (*nasiha*)." It was asked "to whom O Messenger of *Allah*"? He replied "To *Allah*, His Messenger, to the rulers of the Muslims, and the Muslims at large." He did not limit the right to offer advice only to men. Rather, all Muslims, including women, have the right to give advice to the leaders of their community.

Allah has granted the same rights and obligations to both men and women when their biological capability and nature are adequate for these. However, Allah has granted different rights and obligations respectively to men and women when their biological capability and nature require different treatment. This "different treatment" of men and women should not be regarded as an inequality between sexes. The difference between men and women is not a matter of equality or inequality. In Islam, one of the most important matters is to maintain the Muslims' community at its best possible manner, which means that Islam appreciates all human beings. Therefore, Muslim women should not ask for the same rights and obligations as men unless they wish to ruin the Muslim community to which they belong.

11

Islam as Life's Solution

– Cecep Firdaus

Happiness is mankind's purpose in life, and to achieve this purpose, Man is constantly fulfilling his daily needs, because he thinks that happiness is in worldly prosperity. Consequently, to realize happiness, Man is willing to sacrifice his fellow men, his brothers, even himself by making himself a slave to worldliness, enslaved by his own life and always seeing everything in material terms.

The greatest concern is, in realizing this aim, Man sacrifices real wealth, that is, religion. The reality is, that with Islam, Man can achieve true happiness because Islam works in such a way that he is not deceived by a dazzling superficial happiness. Thus it is quite natural that, if man abandons his religion, then what he finds is not happiness but rather entry to eternal destruction, both in this world and in the hereafter. In this world, he will be beset by a life of torment. Allah SWT decreed in the Koran:

> Whomsoever Allah decides to guide He opens his heart to Islam will give advice. And whomsoever Allah misguides He constricts his heart as if he is forever climbing, and verily Allah punishes those who choose not believe (s. *Al-An'am*/6:125).

And in the hereafter they will be punished by being eternally damned to hell, as Allah SWT decreed in *s[ura] Al-Mulk*/67:6; and those who deny Allah are punished in the hellfire and what a disgraceful place of return it is.

The *Tablig Jamaat* is an Islamic movement with a mission to urge mankind to return to a totally pure Islam that leads to true happiness. The *Jamaat*, which was founded by Sheikh Muhammad Ilyas, grew rapidly in India, Pakistan and Bangladesh and spread throughout the world.[1] The *Jamaat*, which has made the mosque the centre for education, has experienced rapid growth in Indonesia, although in some places it has met obstacles and scandal. This paper reflects the vision of the Indonesian *Tablig Jamaat* and presents the ideal life for the Muslim.

Mankind and Happiness

A Look at the Theory of Man

Man is Allah's creation to whom he has given various abilities and potential, and these can generally be located in three cavities: (1) the stomach cavity which contains Man's various digestive organs which have the function of taking in all kinds of food and drink; (2) The head cavity which contains the human brain to take in all kinds of knowledge and experiences; (3) The chest cavity which contains the heart as the place where faith and conviction resides.

If Man cultivates his stomach well, then it will produce strength and good health. And if Man cultivates his head or mind well, then this will give rise to intellectuals of a higher degree that those in the previous group. A factory owner, for instance, is of a higher status and income than his workers who only rely on their strength. But if Man cultivates the contents of his chest, in other words, his heart, then this will give rise to men of the highest

---

[1] [For background, J. Ali, *Islamic Revivalism Encounters the Modern World: A Study of the Tabligh Jama'at* (Studies in World Religions, 2), Delhi, 2011. Eds.]

quality compared to the other two groups. This is the object of the mission of the prophets – to bring Man to the height of civility and towards a real happiness.

Because the outlook from the heart is based on Islam it will never fail to recognize something and will arrive at the authentic truth, but if the outlook is only based on the mind or the "stomach" then it will always meet obstacles and barriers, so it can never arrive authentic truth. For example: if we investigate something using science and technology with their foundation in concrete facts, because it is only based on the brain, we will arrive at a wrong analysis. Take fire- it has the power to burn, but we do not think about who gave fire that power nor do we think about who created fire, and we reach this truth only via the heart, that is, with a guiding faith in Allah.

In fact, science and technology, which Man so eagerly desires, are the results of thinking and experience that are relative, that over time continue to undergo change. The theory of John Dalton, to illustrate, that stated that the atom is the smallest particle and cannot be split, was proven at the time. However, after some years the theory was disproved by another theory which was also able to be scientifically proven, i.e., that the atom itself can be split into three parts – into proton, electron and neutron. This is the science that Man so eagerly desires, a science that has no certainty because it is only based on Man's very limited brain. Compared to science, Ialam, which is taught by the prophets and apostles, will never be wrong and will never ever undergo change because it comes from the Real Truth, Allah SWT.

If science and technology only show what the power of creatures together with Man is like, it is faith or Islam filling man's heart that shows what the power of Allah together with mankind is like. Consequently no matter how far we develop science and technology, we will never be able to exceed the power of faith. Even if non-Muslims were to attack Muslims with nuclear weapons, for example, although such weapons are the result of the highest science and technology, clearly Muslims would not tremble before them, despite being armed only with simple equipment.

Happiness

Happiness and prosperity are two words very familiar to Man's intellect, because Man has already formed the opinion that with riches, he will be happy. Consequently, Man thinks and strives day and night with all his might, to achieve worldly prosperity, because he is convinced that people who have great wealth will achieve happiness. With this conviction, Man becomes greedy and feels that what he has is not enough, and it makes men be suspicious of each other, thinking that happiness is what other people have. An employee, for instance, can come to think that happiness is what the businessman has because he is not constrained by time.

On the other hand, the businessman thinks that the employee has happiness because he has a fixed wage every month. With this attitude, that is the desire to achieve worldly prosperity, many people are sacrificed. Actually they themselves become victims, by being slaves to the transitory world; and if such is the case, we would always feel Allah SWT's hatred, because we no longer care about His law. This is the beginning of the real destruction of mankind and what Man greatly fears, but because of his stupidity in desiring happiness he even immerses himself into the depths of destruction. The is amply shown by the number of people who work hard day and night for prosperity so they can achieve happiness, but in doing so, they become stressed and many have even been driven mad or been struck down by other illnesses.

However, in regard to this concept of prosperity or what we often call wealth, we have to know that there are two different types of prosperity, i.e., that prosperity as material wealth is what makes Man lose his way with only superficial happiness resulting; and that prosperity as riches of the heart is the true wealth that will bring authentic happiness when the heart is filled with faith. When the heart is rich in faith, although life may be totally lacking in material wealth, Man will feel true happiness which is not measured by how much or how little wealth he has.

For example: there was once a king who was extremely rich. He had a vault of riches beneath his throne, but one day he locked himself in his vault and no one knew where he was. With the kingdom experiencing a power vacuum, his son was crowned king and given the key to the vault where his father kept his wealth. One day when he unlocked it and looked inside he was surprised to find his father lying stiff in the vault and in his hand a letter saying, "I am dying of thirst and hunger in the midst of abundant riches."

This parable is proof that abundant riches cannot guarantee someone's life will be happy. How many people are there who are enormously wealthy but do not sleep soundly in their grand homes, even those who sleep in hotels or in nice hospitals, because they are always nervous. This is a sign that happiness is not the same thing as prosperity or riches. Wealthy people are, of course, able to buy a luxurious and comfortable place to sleep but they can't buy the enjoyment of sleep. And for the rich, it is easy to buy expensive medicines of guaranteed quality and even afford to go overseas for expensive treatment, but clearly they cannot buy health. This is proof that prosperity cannot provide true happiness.

The Relationship between Islam and Happiness

The Scope of Islam

Islam is the set of regulations revealed by Allah SWT to govern Man's life, because, in his life, there are his own rights (and duties for himself) and the rights of others. The most fitting example of this is in domestic life, because indeed marriage fulfils the religious command in which there are the rights of the wife and also the rights of the husband. It is a husband's right to receive service from the wife (meaning the duty of the wife) and there is the wife's right to receive service from the husband (meaning the duty of the husband), such as the provision of living expenses, the educating of her to be a devout wife, etc. Consequently, if each is aware of the fulfilment of these rights, then a peaceful, loving and affectionate family will be formed.

And in the fulfilment of these rights we do not demand our rights from other people, but we fulfil our rights (our duty) as well as possible to create a secure atmosphere of life, this will give rise to tranquillity for the whole of Man's life, as well as his acquiring of real happiness, because tranquillity based on Islam (authentic tranquillity) will be a source of a happiness that is true.

So the function of Islam is to regulate the fulfilment of Man's rights (and duties) in life, both between each other as shown above and between Man and the Creator, as in the fulfilment of our duty as servants of Allah SWT in obeying His laws (or what is called worship.)

Absolute Obedience to Allah SWT

The security, comfort and happiness that man desires actually exists in Allah's laws. He decreed:

> Only in the remembrance of Allah do the hearts find contentment.

The meaning of remembrance here is obedience to Him. Only through obedience to Allah SWT will our hearts become calm, i.e., by following His commands sincerely because Allah is the one and only. And such an attitude will receive help from Allah SWT. He decreed:

> Verily, Allah is with those who are believers.

This means His strength, His greatness and His help will always be with "those who are believers" in Him. And so, because of this, the attitude of believers will always be independent – they are not in need of other human beings, they only need Allah. Therefore it is quite natural that the prophet Abraham AS said, "It is sufficient to have Allah SWR as my Helper" when he was about to be thrown into the blazing flames; and Allah made the fire go cold. This was brought about by his obedience to Allah SWT, and his great faith in Him. And the prophet Abraham fully understood the meaning of "*Laa ilaha illallah,*" that there is no one worthy of worship but Allah SWT. And we must reach an understanding ourselves that we deny what is apparent and believe in the unseen. We might say by way of examples: we can deny that fire is hot or can burn you, but it is Allah SWT who causes the burning. We deny that medicine can cure you, but it is Allah SWT who cures. We deny that a knife can cut, but it is Allah who cuts.

This is the highest understanding of the interpretation of the above statement of faith so we sever our hopes in the creations and only ask for help from Allah SWT. So, if Allah SWT wants to raise or lower the price of goods, as in the case of the rise in the price of basic commodities, and the government is unwilling to lower them, we do not really need to hold demonstrations against the government (as they are creations of limited power), but rather demonstrate by getting up in the middle of the night and direct our pleas and complaints and prayers to Allah SWT.

For example: in India there was a man who had to go to court regarding an important matter. On that particular day, however, the river which separated his town from the town he was going to was in full flood and impassable. In his confusion someone suggested he go to the home of a man who could pray to Allah SWT for the floodwaters to recede and he was surprised when the river really did recede and he was able to cross. When asked what his secret was, the man replied that he had never slept with his wife nor ever eaten any thing. And when his wife heard him say that, she said, "You are lying, my husband. So who then do all these children belong to?" Obviously the husband meant that he never ate or slept with his wife except when Allah willed it. This is true belief, the belief in Allah alone.

There are two kinds of convictions. First, true conviction that is the belief only in Allah SWT. This is what will bring about happiness and success and the obtaining of help from Allah SWT. Second, incorrect conviction, i.e., the belief in others apart from Allah SWT, or belief in His creations, as if believing that idols can bring benefits or misfortunes to men, or believing that the source of happiness is in wealth, or holding other beliefs founded only in His creations. This is the source of disaster and of losing the way for mankind because it will make all Man's actions harmful, both in this world and in the hereafter (when he comes to face Allah SWT).

Denying Allah: the Reality in Indonesia

Man greatly fears regression or destruction, but because of the limitations in his thinking, he often leads himself to destruction – by getting involved with those things that cause it. And the most important cause is the denial of Allah SWT, or having incorrect convictions

Therefore confusion and problems always arise in our everyday lives, and in our nations these occur not because of poverty, or a lack of material goods, but because there is no belief in our hearts and because of how far away from the law of Allah our life is. And clearly Indonesia is not the poorest, because there are still many people with vast wealth and there are still natural resources that are unexploited or badly managed. The problems that occur among us are due to a lack of belief in our hearts, but because so many officials of our country misuse our wealth for their own interests, and due to their actions many Indonesian people are victims of neglect.

Rosululloh[2] SAW once said, "The hand above is better than the hand below" (i.e., giving is better than receiving). We should not think that giving is something only the rich can do, for clearly many rich people are unable to give because of their meanness. Actually, giving can be done by anyone, rich or poor, as long as they have belief. It has been shown that the generosity of the companions of the Prophet (SAW) who reached the highest level of mercy were able to give something to others, although they had to sacrifice much (because they too, were needy), yet these friends did not feel oppressed. They even felt happy and achieved complete success.

---

[2] [The Prophet Muhammad, the Messenger (*Rasûl, Rasol*). Ed.]

Therefore, it is no longer in doubt that obedience to Allah SWT leads to happiness, and denial of Allah SWT leads to destruction, such as happened to the people of Madiun, destroyed because they refused the invitation by their brother who was appointed by Allah SWT to be his prophet (i.e., the Prophet Syuaib AS), despite the fact they were prosperous and were involved in a flourishing trade. And also notice how Allah SWT destroyed the people of Saba and the people of Tsamud who denied Allah SWT. Happiness which we find by denying the laws of Allah SWT is transitory and relative, and later we will be continuously tormented throughout our lives.

For example: Pharoah was a very rich king, but because he dreamed that his kingdom would be destroyed by a baby boy, one of the Children of Israel, his life from then on was filled with nervousness and anxiety. So he issued a command that all the Israelite baby boys be killed to save his kingdom from destruction. This was an irrational command, a sign that his ruling came from a king with a tormented soul. If a king were to order the capture of all criminal thugs with the aim of making his kingdom safe, this would be a natural command. But if a king were to order the death of all male babies with the aim of making his kingdom safe, this is hardly natural.

This is proof that denial will not bring happiness; meaning it is blatantly obvious that, through denial of the law of Allah SWT, you may obtain great wealth, because the many methods of getting rich are not blocked for you, both those that are permitted and those are forbidden. However, in fact, great wealth will not bring calm and happiness into your life; and certainly riches which result from corruption, for instance, is wealth without blessing. However, if we obtain riches by obeying Him (by following his laws) this is wealth with blessing. Even if it is a small amount it will be sufficient for our needs, and if it is a large amount, the important thing is, it will bring us happiness.

The biggest disaster for Man is when he denies Allah SWT and does not follow His laws, that is, when his heart is empty of belief. The trials that beset us and our country in everyday life, such as accidents, fires, hunger, poverty, floods and the like are not great trials, need not leave us confused. But if belief is lost from our hearts then we must weep and beg for His mercy, because these trials will bring torment both in this world and the next.

Propagation

Man's body is made up of several important parts, such as eyes for seeing, ears for hearing, feet for walking, hands for holding things, etc. However, most important of all for sustaining life is the heart, which can never rest. Other parts of the body can rest: our eyes are an organ that can rest some of the time, that is, when we are asleep; and our feet can rest some of the time, that is, when we are sitting. It is different for the heart, which is a part of the body that can never rest, even when we are asleep or sitting, because the only rest for this organ is death, which eventually will befall all our bodies.

And it is the same for the religious effort of propagation, which invites others to the path of Allah SWT and to know Him. This effort may never cease because when it ceases death will befall us; propagation is thus similar to our heart not being able to stop working in our bodies. And death for a Muslim is the place for rest where there is no longer any effort to earn reward, so when Man is still in this world he must always strive to earn his reward from Allah SWT and never cease before death comes. The most important effort, and one that may never cease, is the religious effort of propagation. As Allah decreed:

> Verily, there is for you by day prolonged occupation with ordinary duties, but praise him wholeheartedly (s. *Al-Muzzamuil* /73:7-8).

In Arabic the word "praise" that is used here is *sabaha*, which also means to swim. Here we find the example of praising Allah is like swimming which, when we see the word swim, it is used in an interesting way. To simplify things, we take the example of swimming in mid-ocean, where if we stop we will inevitably sink and drown. So praising Allah is like swimming whereby we cannot stop throughout our lives because so ceasing will bring misfortune upon us. And to invite other people to know Allah SWT and praise him is a religious effort which has great reward from Allah SWT.

This religious effort was the effort of all the prophets of the past, and it is what made them strong in their belief and well known among their communities, although being famous was not the aim of the missionaries (but rather inviting others to know Allah SWT). They achieved fame nonetheless because they were always going from one place to another. And what they had to guard against was not being well known in the circles of their communities, but how their efforts would be accepted by Allah SWT. Those who carry out propagation with the desire to become famous are not accepted by Allah SWT. Those who immerse themselves in the effort of the prophets will never again be troubled by earthly concerns such as riches, wellbeing, or even daily necessities. He decreed:

> And whoever fears Allah, he ever prepares a way out (of their problems) and He provides for him from sources he could never have imagined, and if anyone puts his trust in God, sufficient is Allah for him (s. *Ath-Tholak*/65:2-3).

The prophets did nothing but work at this religious effort, and clearly they lacked nothing in life and always lived contentedly, because they were given their 'wages' by Allah SWT, who has control over the whole universe. And so it is normal for Man to join in these efforts and immerse himself in propagation, and in doing so one will never lack anything in their life nor need to do any other work.

A university student once asked, "How is it possible that carrying out His commands such as prayers and propagation may bring great wealth?" And the sheikh (a teacher) answered by giving an analogy: there was a policeman whose job it was to oversee the flow of traffic at a crossroads. He did his job with the highest degree of professionalism. And why did he do this? The student could not provide an answer. The sheikh continued, saying it was all due to the policemen having the steady knowledge that at the end of every month he would get his wages in return for doing his job, which was to ensure the smooth flow of traffic. So too, it is with Allah SWT that, when we carry out His commands such as prayers or propagation we will have a comfortable life, on the condition we have full conviction in this promise. And behind Allah's commands there really is success, because when the prophets strictly followed these religious efforts they were successful. Likewise, when we follow the efforts of the prophets we will achieve success.

This is the promise of Allah SWT which is true for all mankind who constantly believe in Him, and indeed as creations, we ought to obey the God who has created us, for everything we have, even including our own selves, belongs to Allah SWT. The object of the effort of propagation is to fill the heart of Man with belief in Allah SWT so he that becomes someone who always obeys God, his Creator. And the prophets were only concerned with the way that belief could be acquired by the heart of Man, so they would bring Man to success.

Rosululloh SAW, to illustrate, taught his companions and implanted belief in their hearts so that these companions became chosen men who were willing to defend the Prophets and bring the Islamic community to the pinnacle of civility in those times, as it was in the time of the Caliphs. Also the companions were no longer influenced by worldly attractions, as evinced by Salman Al Farsi, who left his wealthy parents to seek the Prophet Muhammad SAW and live as a poor man.

Islamic Life – Life based on Islam

Man is said to be alive when the soul is in the body, and is said to be dead when the soul has left the body. When the soul is not in the body, then the body is no longer of any use and gradually decomposes and will be buried in the ground and eaten by earthworms.

Unlike the body, the soul does not decompose and will not be eaten by earthworms, but will live forever, whether in happiness or in everlasting torment. From the moment we pass through the doorway of death, there begins a change from the physical world to the afterlife, where Man will bear responsibility for all his actions. If he gains bounties then this is true happiness and if he gains torment this is misfortune or true destruction. Therefore Islam has been revealed to save mankind from true destruction, that is, torment by Allah SWT.

When Man follows Islam and practises it obediently he will not just acquire happiness in the afterlife but in this world too. He will acquire the advancement and success that Man desires. Just as was the case with the success of the companions, particularly at the time of the Caliphs (the leaders who received directions from Allah SWT), who were able to achieve control over more than half the world. Clearly, with power such as this, Man can permit all means to obtain such power, even doing so without conscience, and can thus be crueller than a wild animal.

However, when Man abandons Islam and rebels against Allah, he will not just receive torment in the hereafter, but he will also be struck by all kinds of disasters in this world. It will bring him to true destruction and the loss of his powers. Although he may achieve outward success and have the most sophisticated weapons, he will still not make the enemy tremble.

This is what is happening to Muslims today. Despite the fact Muslims in Indonesia are in the majority, non-Muslims see them from a biased point of view only. They do not fear Muslims and possibly the factor behind this is that Muslims in Indonesia are nominal Muslims only, and do not follow true Islamic law. They only practise the outward symbols (such as the head scarf, and other rituals of worship) and they do not understand the real meaning (thereby causing incorrect understanding).

A student at the London School of Economics carried out research into happiness, to ascertain which society is the happiest in the world. The findings were that Bangladeshi society was ranked number one, as the happiest society in the world, while English society came in only at 36th and American at 42nd place.

Bangladeshi society is obviously the poorest society compared to the other two, with their very high level of prosperity, and yet the latter have lost out to a society way below their level of material prosperity. What makes Bangladeshi society the happiest in the world is the strength of their belief that flourishes in their lives. They are very devout in practising the religion revealed by Allah SWT and consequently they have achieved what Allah SWT has promised – true happiness. But it is different for societies which deny the laws of Allah SWT. Despite their high level of prosperity, they suffer in this world; their lives are beset by confusion, anxiety, stress and situations in life that are full of chaos.

The Development of Islam

As mentioned before, when Islam is visible in Man's life then he will achieve success and real happiness. Therefore, Islam must be developed and introduced to all mankind and all situations in the world. There is the example of a Muslim working as crew aboard a ship and, while the ship was at sea, he had problems practising the commands of Islam, such as the five daily prayers, Friday prayers and finding *halal* food, because none of the others on the ship were Muslims. Later, this man asked his sheikh (a teacher) whether he should leave his job. The sheikh forbad him from doing so, however, and told him to be patient because if he left no one would know about Islam and there would not be any Muslim who knew about the situation on the ship. The sheikh advised him that when it was time for the compulsory prayers, both the five daily prayers and the Friday prayers, he should make the call to prayer beforehand, and the prayers should be communal. And if there was no *halal* food he should get provisions before embarking on a journey, even if it was just eggs. He should be strict in carrying out this advice which later would gradually be known by the whole ship because he was doing something different and he was doing it commendably. After a time, some of the others would become interested, followed in his footsteps and embraced Islam.

And eventually people aboard other ships would be living according to the laws of Islam. This is the proof that Islam has to enter into all situations, no matter how bad, but with patience and trust in God (being active in carrying out the commands of Allah SWT and surrendering our affairs to Him). Surely Allah will provide us with the best way out. And Islam will develop in communities that have these two characteristics: a simple life, and self-sacrifice (or sincerely carrying out religious commands).

Therefore, at the beginning of the emergence of Islam, it was welcomed and developed among Arabs of the middle and lower classes, because clearly, apart from its complete teachings, the community had these two characteristics, i.e., they lived simply and practised self-sacrifice. For, when Man has a contrary attitude to these two, by living in luxury and taking it easy, then Islam will not develop because a life of luxury which tends to be wasteful, is specifically forbidden by Islam and will cause the destruction of unity because we cannot feel the suffering of others, especially the poor. As He decreed:

> And render to the kindred their due rights, as (also) to those in want, and to the wayfarer: but squander not (your wealth) in the manner of a spendthrift. Verily spendthrifts are brothers of the Evil Ones: and the Evil One is to his Lord Himself ungrateful (*s. Al-Isro*/17:26-27).

And the process of self sacrifice is the beginning of Man becoming accustomed to carrying out the regulations of Allah SWT, which are imprinted in this religion, although in fact these regulations are not opposed to Man's true nature and Man is really willing to carry them out. Consequently, when Man has become accustomed to these regulations then God's grace will appear here, that is, the feeling of pleasure when we follow the laws of Allah SWT. Therefore, when life of mankind is far from self-sacrifice in practising religion, then forever the opinion will arise that Islam is very controlling and does not suit these modern times (orthodoxy or the old religion is only for the past). Such an impression that Islam is very controlling is really caused by Man himself who contravenes Allah's laws, and when Man himself is honest, clearly he will not go outside of his deepest natural inclination.

Eternal Life

Lukman, the Wise, said that man can be divided into three parts: one third is the part that will come back to Allah SWT, that is, the soul; one third is the part that we keep for ourselves, that is, our deeds; and the other third is that part that will return to the ground and become food for worms, that is, our body.

Our bodies are created by Allah SWT from earth, because our food comes from the earth, such as fruit and rice. And at times the body becomes ill and cannot take food, although it needs it, such as when the body is very hungry but we are unable to eat and, if forced to do so, we will vomit. And if the illness becomes serious, then the body will die and decompose and be buried in the earth and become food for worms.

It is different for the soul, which Allah SWT created on His direct command; and so too was food for the soul created on His command. And just like the body, there are times when the soul falls ill too, when it too cannot take its food and does not take pleasure in carrying out the commands of Allah SWT. However, when the soul is healthy it is a different matter, and it will happily carry out His Commands. If the soul is ill it will bring misfortune to us, because the soul is accounts for all of our deeds. If our deeds are good, then we will be happy, that is, we will dwell forever in heaven and this is true happiness. However, if our deeds are bad, then we will receive the utmost severe torment, and we will dwell forever in it, and this is true misfortune.

These are the two places we could end up, that is, heaven or hell, where we will dwell forever. Can we truly guess where we will one day dwell forever? We can, by looking at our deeds in this world or, in other words, the extent to which we make sacrifices (by sacrificing our desires) to fulfil the commands of Allah SWT. And verily, these sacrifices of ours will be repaid by Allah SWT, not only in the hereafter but in this word we will also be rewarded. Take the example of Ummu Habibah who fled to Abyssinia, and her husband converted to Christianity in that land. Later her husband tried to get her to convert to Christianity, too, but she refused and they divorced. And by this sacrifice, that is maintaining her beliefs, Allah SWT repaid her in this world by giving her the best husband in the entire world – Rosululloh SAW.

What we Should Know: Closing Remarks

The purpose in life is to know Allah SWT and to worship Him. And in order to encourage mankind to know him, Allah SWT has created two signs, i.e., the verbal signs which are the verses found in the Koran, and the physical signs which are the signs found in the physical world. These two signs are the same and are not contradictory, indeed the physical signs prove the truth of the verbal signs and explain or prove the Greatness of Allah SWT.

Rosul SAW spoke thus: "Think about His creations and do not think about Him." This means we have to think about the creations of Allah SWT so we know His greatness, because if we think about Him, then clearly our minds will never be able to achieve knowing Him. Consider, for example, the heat and the revolving of the sun and the moon; who is it causing them to revolve? All these signs of greatness prove and bring mankind to the essence of the Almighty and the Coordinator. However, the existence of the world also represents a test for mankind. For example, the grapes we often eat, are they produced by the grape vine alone; and the workers who receive their wages from the factory, is it the factory owner who provides their income? Yet in these cases the grapes and the owner are all only means or intermediaries, proving the Omnipotence of Allah SWT in coordinating everything.

Islam is the only life solution for mankind, because only through Islam can the whole of man's life be regulated in an orderly way. Also through Islam, man can know the purpose of life and how he must live, and through religion he can know his place in the physical world. Islam can reveal all the deceptions of life in this world, so that the one who follows Islam obediently will not be deceived by false happiness, and will forever be aware of the death that awaits him without prior warning, which will one day bring him to the gateway of eternal life where all our deeds are accounted for. The Tablig Jamaat is a group which wants to bring back the purpose of life to mankind and the true purpose (the function) of Islam, and to return the beliefs of Man to the true beliefs to find authentic happiness.

Reference

Ali, Jan, *Islamic Revivalism Encounters the Modern World: A Study of the Tabligh Jama'at* (Studies in World Religion, 2), Delhi: New Dawn Press, 2011.

12

Islam and *Pancasila*
The Message of a Former Judge

— Bismar Siregar

Pancasila **and Tolerance**

As there are many tribes and religions in Indonesia, it is difficult for us to maintain national solidarity. It is my strong conviction, however, that *Pancasila*[1] greatly contributes to the maintenance of the unity and the development of Indonesia, as I believe that *Pancasila* is sacred and is being blessed by Allah. Some might not agree with me, saying that the first principle of *Pancasila* does not clearly state that the one and only God is Allah. However, it is true that, for Muslims like me, the one and only God always means Allah. Why should we care about other people's faiths? We should remember one of the verses in *al-Quran*, which reads:

There shall be no compulsion in religion (*s. al-Baqarah*/2:256)

---

[1] The five state principles, these are: Belief in the One and Only God; Just and Civilized Humanity; The Unity of Indonesia; Democracy Guided by the Representatives; Social Justice for the Whole of the People of Indonesia. *Pancasila* consist of two Sanskrit words, namely, *panca* which means five; and *sila*, meaing principle.

For me, *Pancasila* truly realizes the principle that each faith should be respected. In other words, anyone who denies *Pancasila* does not live in accordance with the basic principle of Islam. We humans are not supposed to accuse each other of false beliefs. Such matters will be taken care of by Allah. Let Allah punish infidels, if there be any.

Understandably, many people fear the the trend of atheism or *jahiliah* (secularism, as I prefer to translate it)[2] emerging Indonesian culture since the Communist uprising of the 1960s. We need to ask here what *jahiliah* truly means. *Jahiliah* does not necessarily mean having a secular state. *Jahiliah*, in fact, means a state of moral and social decadence. In other words, there could be a religious state (theocracy) without morality and decency. At the same time, there might be a secular state which supports morality and decency. This suggests that the political character of the state is unimportant in the process of creating a morally sound state. *Pancasila*, which embraces both theocratic and secular values, seems to be the most suitable state philosophy in Indonesia where there exists great socio-cultural diversity. Differences among people, including the differences of religion, should be respected. Moreover, the 'differences' are merely relative, which means that all human beings, regardless of their religion, are blessed by Allah. This fact should be always remembered, so that we can show tolerance towards others.

Pancasila and Values

Modern global society values physical and worldly happiness. The capitalist and liberalist versions of happiness are just temporary and do not bring real satisfaction. This Western-oriented culture often prioritizes the right of individuals and undervalues the importance of collective obligation. *Pancasila*, by contrast, promises comprehensive happiness, including spiritual happiness and meaningful co-existence. The struggle for Indonesian independence

---

[2] *Jahiliah*, in fact, referred to the social condition of Arabian Peninsula before Islam was revealed, and the word means unenlightened.

was, of course, based on the values of *Pancasila* insofar as Indonesians hoped to create a state in which all ethnic groups and followers of different religions might co-exist harmoniously and lead full lives. Knowing this fundamental fact about the independent struggle in Indonesia, it is obvious that the values of *Pancasila* should be applied not only at the national level but at the individual level as well.

Some say that *Pancasila* is outdated in this global and modern society. However, such attitudes reinforce the *jahiliah* culture that creates a society filled with egoism. What we as Indonesians should do is re-examine our deeds and reaffirm the morals and the tolerance that *Pancasila* upholds. We should all remember the fundamental principle of *Pancasila*: "Love others as you love yourself."

The values of Pancasila do not clash with the values of *syariat* Islam. It is very clear that anyone who professes faith in Islam (*syahadat*) is automatically obliged to follow the path of Islam under the guidance of *syariat* Islam. However, how a Muslim follows *syariat* Islam depends entirely on the depth of his or her faith. Again, only omnipotent Allah has the right to determine the fate of the followers of Islam. What we should bear in mind is that the humans cannot force others to follow *syariat* Islam through the force of law.

Values of Pancasila *Realised in a Legal System*

The values of *Pancasila* have been already implemented in actual laws, that is, Law No. 19. 1964. It reads:

Article 2 (1):

FOR JUSTICE BASED ON BELIEF IN THE ONE AND ONLY GOD

Elucidation of article 14, paragraph (1)

As an officer of the court, a judge is deemed to understand the law. Plantiffs come to him to receive justice. Should he not find the answer in statute law, he is obliged to turn to non-statute

> laws for his verdict. The judge should be wise and respect the
> truth of the One and Only God, himself, society, and the nation.

This is indeed a reflection of the values of *Pancasila*. However, unfortunately people seem to have little faith in Indonesian legal institutions. Much sarcasm has been directed at the legal system in Indonesia. For example, people often use several abbreviations to mock the legal system as well as legal experts, such as SUMUT (*Sumua Urusan Musti Dengan Uang Tunai*: all affairs must be settled in cash), KUHP (*Kasih Uang Habis Perkara* (hand over money and the case will be closed), or HAKIM *Hubungi Aku Kalau Ingin Menang* (contact me if you wish to win).[3]

It is a great pity that the principles of *Pancasila* have been abandoned by the Indonesian legal system. The source of the trouble perhaps lies in the system of legal education in Indonesia, which draws on two traditions, namely, European Continental legal education; and commercial legal education. The first tends to focus on the mastery of laws, regulations, and legal doctrines; while the second emphasizes commerce or market-related issues. These two orientations tend to overlook the importance of morality, which I believe is the origin of corruption in Indonesia. It is now time for us to liberate Indonesia from the legacy of colonial legal system and to build a new system in accordance with the values of *Pancasila*. What is needed is a legal education based on *Pancasila*, which emphasizes tolerance, social justice, and morality as important values for legal experts.

Changing the current system poses a major challenge. However, the process of the "*Pancasila-ization*" of the legal system, in a way, is tantamount to the creation of a new legal culture, one that just and free of corruption. No matter what people think, it is our duty to establish and maintain this new culture. In my opinion, the individual effort to be a decent person is the key to a brighter future for all mankind. Some will say that this is too

---

[3] In Indonesian, SUMUT means north Sumatra; KUHP means criminal code; and HAKIM means judge.

naïve. Yet, we should remember that all of us are blessed by Allah, and each of us is capable of responding to Allah.

Epilogue

Every morning I wake up and think about the future of Indonesia. It is sad to say that we often hear horrifying and pathetic news stories about our countrymen. Cases of corruption, murder, deception, and moral decadence are frequently reported in the news. Should I be sad? Angry? Or abandon hope?

We have committed so many sins before Allah. We have wrongly cited Your words in the Book. We have deceived each other, using words such as justice and faith in the one and only God. Please forgive us. We believe in Your message. Now we should repent and begin our new life. There is no point in accusing someone who has acted wrongly in the past. Remember, only Almighty Allah has the power to punish them. Let us not waste time by hating each other. *Pancasila* is the only principle that unites all believers of all religions. Mutual understanding and tolerance will prevail if all members of society truly become followers of *Pancasila*.

13

Progress of the Country with Justice and Prosperity

— Zulkieflimansyah and Yon Machmudi

In 1995, Douglas E. Ramage stated in his book *Politics in Indonesia: Democracy, Islam, and the Ideology of Tolerance* that *Pancasila*[1] is an ideology to protect all ideologies and religions that exist in Indonesia. The purpose of *Pancasila*, then, is to offer the middle ground between secularism and Islam. Ramage gives us a more complete explanation, referring to the words of the first President of the Republic of Indonesia, Sukarno: "If the new state was based on 'belief in God' then it would be neither an Islamic nor secular state but a religious state."[2] It is very true that Islam is an important element in social and political life in Indonesia. Although Indonesia does not take the form of an Islamic state, the aspiration of the *umat* Islam (Islamic community) has been always well accommodated in the Republic of Indonesia.

---

[1] Five state philosophy of the Republic of Indonesia: Belief in the one and only God: a Just and civilized society; the Unity of Indonesia; Democracy led by the wisdom of deliberations among representatives; Social justice for the Indonesian people.

[2] D. Ramage, *Politics in Indonesia, etc.*, New York, 1995, p. 16.

It is an historical fact that Indonesia has embraced an idea of belief in one God, which orientates a "religious state," and simultaneously has assured religious freedom for any religion, including Islam. This is an obvious reflection of the first principle of *Pancasila*, which was formulated by the founding fathers of the Republic, including Muslim leaders. If you think that *umat* Islam in Indonesia has no commitment to *Pancasila* as an ideology of the country, you are wrong. You cannot deny the fact in history that *umat* Islam has already contributed to the development of Indonesia, including the state ideology.

What is important for *umat* Islam in Indonesia for the future is that Islam continues to play an important role in the process of national character building. National character reflects the reality of local culture, religion, and tradition. We should never overturn our Indonesian ideals, which were set by our great fighters and thinkers at the beginning of the foundation of this country. History has shown us that Indonesia has never been ruled either by Muslim fundamentalists or by radical secularists. Thus, Indonesia is not divided by religious values today. Indonesia should maintain its strong yet moderate religious orientation in the country. Moreover, it should be remembered that Indonesia is the most populous Muslim country in the world, which surpasses the countries in the Middle East. What is unfortunate is that Islam is always represented by the countries of the Arab world, not by the ones in Southeast Asia. The image of Islam as inflexible, intolerant, and revolutionary is more widely spread rather than the image of Islam as peaceful, moderate and reformist. This is one of the important reasons why the Justice and Welfare Party, or PKS, was founded. PKS originally started as the Justice Party (PK), which was founded on 9 August 1998, and changed its name to PKS on 20 April 2003.

Islam and Politics

According to Islamic teachings, participation in politics is one of the important duties for Muslims. This means that religion is inseparable from social, cultural, economic and political activities. In other words, religion should impinge upon all human activities that take place in this world. Then, religion can offer the solution to the problems which human beings face, including political ones. In Islam, politics should not be oppressive, oligarchic, or authoritarian.

Politics should coincide with "values." The teachings of Islam that feature universalism and appreciate humanism are so important in practical politics; they can create decency in politics without any of those wrong deeds that bear no morality. Islam indeed offers "values," such as equality, justice, and welfare, and puts much positive influence on practical politics. However, politics is currently only manipulated by politicians for their own personal interests, ignoring the aspirations of the common people. Islam, in fact, is able to give a direction that every decision, attitude, and Islamic behaviour in politics is based on a strong sense of morality and responsibility. Politics is one of the major factors that parallel all activities of humans in society and the intention of *Allah*, who is a creator and guardian of peace, uniformity and eternity of nature. Thus, the role of Islam in practical politics in Indonesia is to provide moral awareness and guidance for creating "values." Politics should comprise moral and spiritual values, which you might call "spiritualization of politics." Such values correspond to the purpose of religion (*maqasid al-syariah*), that is, to protect soul, knowledge, property, family, and the freedom of faith.

Syariat Islam

All aspects of human beings are regulated by Islamic law or *syariat* Islam. *Syariat* is not only understood as laws that give punishment to criminals, but is also feared by various groups in society. *Syariat* Islam is only comprehended as cruel punishment, such as the cutting off of hands and stoning (criminals to death). Muslims who wish to apply *syariat* Islam to their lives are sometimes regarded as harsh, and people believe that these Muslims criticize women who do not wear the headscarf (*jilbab*), attack night spots, and destroy the places of other religions. This view is totally wrong in the truth of Islam. If you simply emphasize the part of cutting off hands, stoning, and the enforcement of the wearing of the headscarf in *syariat* Islam, the genuine purpose of *syariat* Islam will be lost.

In fact, the purpose of *syariat* Islam is to provide protection and freedom of belief for all religions, and to make sure that the followers of any religion are safe to practice their own faith. Any citizen in the country should be treated equally without any discrimination originated in race, ethnicity, personal background, or religion. The fact that *syariat* Islam emphasizes the aspect of daily life and the protection of any human existence regardless of one's orientation is often disregarded by the people who promote the application and formalization of this Islamic law. We can see various social problems in Indonesia today, with many people still living under the poverty line; education not well provided; human rights not valued; and, above all, with no one who protects these rights. The struggle to eradicate poverty, obtain a decent education, and protect human rights is tantamount to what *syariat* Islam aims to realize. This is what *syariat* Islam underlines and practises based on its core element, and we know that it was already demonstrated by Prophet Muhammad. This factuality of *syariat* Islam should be promoted so that all groups in the society will support it. However, we should remember that only concrete actions will bring about the goodness of *syariat* Islam. Thus, we need to have institutions or even political organizations that constantly work for the betterment of the people.

In this regard, you understand why the Justice and Prosperity Party (PKS) works hard to satisfy the basic needs of the people. For PKS, the application of *syariat* Islam is twofold. First, it is related to the individuals that the rights of the citizens at all levels should be protected without any violation. People should have full access to education as well as to politics, and economic opportunities also should be given to the people. It is crucially important to maintain equality of the people and to eradicate any sort of discrimination in Indonesia. Second, it is related to the government and nationhood in that good governance and the best public services for the people should be realized. The culture of corruption spread among politicians and bureaucrats should be eradicated. The collected tax should be efficiently utilized for the people of Indonesia, and the way of spending the tax should be transparent. All leaders of the country are expected to work professionally and trustworthily. We can now see many examples of what *syariat* Islam can bring about and what Indonesia longs for. PKS itself also intends to restore decency to the Islamic community or the *umat*. The followers of PKS should be able to carry out these duties and be a generator of a reformation movement to improve the standards of the people and the country.

Prosperity and Justice

What counts in implementing *syariat* Islam is to materialize prosperity and justice. These two issues are fundamental principles in Islam: the ideals that *umat* Islam always struggles for is the realization of prosperity and obtaining protection from the almighty God. This is clearly mentioned in *al-Quran*:

> For the natives of Sheba there was indeed a sign in their dwelling-place: a garden on their right and a garden on their left. We said to them: "Eat of what your Lord has given you and render thanks to Him. Pleasant is your land and forgiving is your Lord" (s. *Saba'*/34:15).

Prosperity and happiness exist not only for the sake of a certain religious group but also for all members of Indonesian society without any exception. Leaders must always respect justice and protect the interests of all Indonesian citizens. This attitude is one of the most important qualities of a leader. Justice is a universal concept, and it is explained by *Allah* in *al-Quran*:

> Believers, fulfil your duties to God and bear true witness. Do not allow your hatred of other men to turn you away from justice. Deal justly; that is nearer to true piety. Have fear of God; God is cognizant of all your actions (s. *al-Maidah*/5:8)

Generally speaking, the issue of prosperity often draws little attention in the dynamism of politics in Islam. Some politically-oriented Muslim groups tend to prioritize formalization of the teachings of Islam, but they disregard the matter of prosperity.

Consequently, some economically successful Islamic countries that have already implemented *syariat* Islam manipulate political power and fail to balance its economic success and Islamic law. It is ironic that the image of Islamic countries is sometimes full of poverty and unbalanced, damaged economy. The countries that are rich in natural resources, such as oil and natural gas, face political problems. These countries tend to be authoritarian and restrict the freedom of the people. What is happening in these countries is that political elites only try to maintain their authority and protect their own interests. Then, the gap between the political authorities and the people grows so wide. Political elites enjoy their extravagant lifestyles and exercize their unlimited power, while ordinary people do not receive anything beneficial from the economic development in their own country, and their lives are so restrained as their political aspirations are never heeded. Having known the reality as mentioned above, the concept of prosperity, indeed, has to be transformed into the economic development for the people in Islamic countries.

The matter of justice also necessitates a complicated discourse in order to be realized. When the position of ordinary people is weak and their political rights and the freedom of expression are restricted, people loudly talk about the need for justice. However, once they obtain power, and their position becomes stable, they seldom talk about justice anymore. Although people have already obtained their "power," which brings justice to them, they have not realized that the power they have gained is a potential threat to the realization of justice for other people. In an Islamic context, justice is essential for both citizens and political authorities. We know that justice does not exist when a minority group is denied access to basic needs in their lives. This is an indication of the degree of justice in a society. On the other hand, when a minority group holds every power and monopolizes all assets in the country, oppressing a majority group, you live in a society where justice does not exist.

Both discrimination and apartheid bear no tolerance for and contradict the concept of justice. Thus, the equity between the origin of the value of justice and religious belief has to be developed as a guide within the Islamic community. To realize this, it is necessary to have a commitment to building democracy. Democracy that is valid for all, in fact, has much resonance with the teachings of Islam. According to Islam, political oppression should be eradicated, and authorities should be obliged to be non-partisan. Social and political entities that bear the potential to realize this can be found in the *umat* or the Islamic community. The *Umat* is expected to contribute to characterizing Indonesia as the most populous Muslim nation in the world. The teachings of Islam and democracy should be well coordinated and should offer an alternative political model for Islam to the other Islamic countries, including those in the Middle East.

You can find the meaning of PKS in that this political party offers an alternative political practice in Indonesia. Generally speaking, politics that gives opportunity to the ones who only have personal interest and ambition destroys politics itself. PKS came into existence with the support of the people, and its history is long enough to ensure its being one of the influential political forces in civil society with the intention of leading Indonesia to a better future.

As the people of Indonesia had to live under the authoritarian New Order government for a few decades, a system that is open and appreciates humanity had been very much longed for. PKS makes every effort to develop the values of Islam and internalize Islam in the minds of the followers as a base of morality in politics. The implementation of *syariat* Islam is also comprehended more widely in order to meet the demands of the people of Indonesia. Historical and cultural reality and social politics in Indonesia are very unique, and these are the important elements in the political expression of the Islamic community. The accommodation and effort to harmonize different groups in Indonesia will give the characteristics of Indonesian politics. How Islamic political parties relate Islamic teachings to secular issues is the key to success for obtaining greater constituency. Therefore, you can say that the slogan "Lead and Serve," held up by PKS, is a true manifestation of *syariat* Islam, which is practical, close to the lives of people, and promotes Islam as a carrier of peace, justice, and prosperity.

Reference

Ramage, D.E., *Politics in Indonesia: Democracy, Islam, and the Ideology of Tolerance*, New York: Routledge, 1995.

14

The Role of Islam in Politics: Struggling for Political Peace, Justice, and Mercy of Islam

— Andi M. Ramly

This article explores the role of Islam in the thick forest of politics. The author mainly tries to show several basic ideas about how Islam plays its role in contemporary politics, while paying attention to the original doctrines and the history of the relationship between Islam and politics in the early times. It relates Islamic history to a reflective context treats the Islamic role being played in the world of politics; and, most important, analyses the Islamic stance towards global politics.

We need to understand the literal meaning of Islam, that is, the religion of peace or *aslama-yuslimu-waislaman*. Islam, indeed, is a way of peace or safety for anyone who believes in oneness of Allah and Muhammad as the last prophet. Therefore, anyone who claims to be a Muslim should confess the faith (*syahadah*) and struggle to create peace as Allah and Prophet Muhammad already taught. It is important to note that the task of creating peace as a Muslim is not only for oneself but also for others (*rahmatan lial-alamin*). It is an ideal of Islam that all of the followers believe in the path of peace and the promises given by Allah and Prophet Muhammad.

The problem, however, and the irony of religion, is that although the ideal of Islam regarding everyday matters is clearly visible in the words of Allah found in the Holy Scripture, the rightfulness in Islam can be realized only when Muslims themselves take action. On the occasion of Friday prayers in Mosques, Muslim politicians deliver their speeches, and Muslim scholars preach to their fellow Muslims in high-pitched voices. Yet, the ideal of Islam can only be heard physically but never truly be understood.

In the reality of everyday life, the teaching of Islam, which was glorious before, has been trapped with the phenomenon of war and violence. And this is the very reason why Islamic communities almost everywhere in the world now have been dragged into the cycle of violence. The violence and the suicide bombings recently executed by several Islamic groups have shown how Islam has been wrongly identified as an agent of terror and violence despite the true teaching of Islam, that is, peace and compassion, which we can clearly find in the holy *al-Quran*, in the *Hadith*s (the tradition of the Prophet), and in the statements of respected *ulamas* (Islamic scholars) based by their *ijtihad* (human reasoning), and *ijma* (consensus). One of the most conspicuous examples of present-day violence is the bombing of the 200-metre tall twin towers of the World Trade Center, a symbol of American prosperity, on 11 September 2001. This tragedy resulted in the complete collapse of the buildings, 5,000 deaths and a few thousand injuries.[1]

This bombing, which took place in the beginning of the twenty-first century, truly made people of the world horrified. And President George W. Bush who, is a Protestant politician, right away accused Yemen-born Muslim Osama bin Laden as a

---

[1] C.J. Masroer, "Bom dan Dilema Orang Beriman," *Journal Religiosa* 1, 1 (2006): 51.

mastermind of the attack. The government of the United States of America has officially declared that Osama bin Laden and his organization *al-Qaeda* were responsible for the bombing. In consequence, US troops with modern and sophisticated weapons bombarded Afghanistan where they thought Osama bin Laden was hiding.

The tragedy is that the bombardment by US troops also caused a considerable number of casualties among those who are totally innocent. The bombing by the US killed thousands of Afghans, the majority of them women and children. In a very short time, Afghanistan, which was once world famous for carpet trading, has turned into something like a monument of collapse of Islamic civilization. Having caused chaos and misery, the frequent bombing by the US is obviously a failure. Osama bin Laden, who was the target of the bombing, has never been found.

A year after the tragedy of "Black September," Indonesia also had to face a series of bombings. Imam Samudra and Amrozi were very keen to be martyrs and bombed a night spot packed with tourists in Kuta beach in Bali. Hundreds of Hindus, Muslims and Christians were shattered. The whole world condemned this bombing, and international media branded Indonesia, which used to be known as a peaceful Islamic country, as a nest of terrorists, commenting that Indonesia would jeopardize the peace of the world. The Indonesian government searched for the mastermind of the bombing. Imam Samudera was captured and tried. He now faces capital punishment as he committed such an inhumane crime. Yet, bombings in Indonesia did not stop, as several other places in the country became the target of the bomb attacks, such as the Hotel Marriot and the Australian Embassy in Jakarta, and Tenena Pasar in Central Sulawesi. The casualties of these bombings were about a hundred innocent Muslims and Christians.[2]

Looking overseas, one of the most horrifying bombings was perpetrated in a famous tourist spot in Shram el-Syaikh in Egypt,

---

[2] *Ibid.*

which claimed 82 deaths. London, which is one of the most prosperous cosmopolitan cities in the world, was also the target of bombs. Four English-Pakistanis carried bombs to the subway stations and buses and exploded themselves, killing 59 people and injuring more than 700 people.[3] Ever since the US invasion of Iraq, there have been suicide bombers from both Sunni and Shiia groups, killing one another in the markets and mosques. A few thousand people have already lost their lives because of bombings in Iraq. These suicide bombers and violent acts of Muslims only create an image of Islam as a politicized and belligerent religion, bringing about murders, intolerance, and destruction of this world. Conversely, however, *al-Quran*, in fact, forbids extremist attitudes that destroy this world. It reads:

> ... whoever killed a human being, except as punishment for murder or other villainy in the land, shall be deemed as though he had killed all mankind; and that whoever saved a human life shall be deemed as though he had saved all mankind (*s. Al-Maidah*/5:32).

The question now is whether a recent phenomenon related to Islam is contradictory to that verse in *al-Quran* mentioned above. It is true that the teaching of peace in Islam can be related to world politics. With regard to politics, Muslims might think that peace will be materialized only when the justice of God exists in this world. Therefore, as some Muslims believe, Islam should be the central political authority in order to realize the justice of God as it was the case during the time of Caliphate rulings in the past. In the past, this conviction of Muslims truly substantiated the ideas that Islam should be engaged in politics and that they ought to be interacting strenuously. And this integration of politics and Islam is based not only on the history of Islam but also on the doctrinal argumentation in relation to the practice of Prophet Muhammad and his followers in the early history of Islam.[4]

---

[3] *Ibid.*

[4] J.T. Johnson, *Perang Suci Atas Nama Tuhan dalam Tradisi Barat dan Islam* (The Holy War Idea in Western and Islamic Traditions), Bandung, 2002, p.37.

For the above-mentioned reasons, Islam can be regarded as a religion of politics, or *al-din wa al-siyasah*, in that there is no distinction between sacredness and profanity unlike in the Christian-oriented Western tradition. This inseparable connection between Islam and politics has been a religious duty for Muslims since the emergence of Islam. The move of Prophet Muhammad from Mecca to Medina (known as *Hijrah*) exemplifies how Islam historically expedites its political strategy: seizing power in a peaceful region, Medina; subjugating Mecca; and expanding its structural as well as religious influence over the whole Arabian Peninsula.[5] In Medina, the Prophet Muhammad was respected not only as a spiritual leader but also as a political leader who successfully united several groups in the region hitherto separated. This unification of the people of Medina that Prophet realized was based on the first political contract among races in world history, known as the Medina Charter or *mitsaqu al-Madinah*.[6] In fact, Prophet Muhammad was not a mere head of the nation who maintained the integration of the country, but he also became a commander of the country. All sorts of political struggles of Muslims at the time, indeed, show how Prophet Muhammad commanded the army of Muslims and his followers in order to maintain their sovereignty in Medina.

However, the problem is that fundamentalists nowadays just exploit the political history of Islam, creating a religious ideology in order to justify their violent behaviour. This distorted interpretation of Islam could be the ideological base of Muslims in order to oppose Western ideology and, thus, can be usefully adopted by fundamentalist Muslims. Religious ideology that justifies the action of bombing or violence can be taken as the means of self-defence, which Prophet Muhammad used to adopt.

---

[5] Fachri Ali, *Islam Pacasila dan Pergulatan Politik*, Jakarta, 1984, p. 3.

[6] Abu Ridha, *Saat Dakwah Memasuki Wilayah Politik*, Bandung, 2003, p. 2; B. Ahmad Sukarjda *Piagam Madinah Dan Undang-Undang Dasar 1945*, Jakarta, pp. 2-3.

In the process of the implementation of *syariat* Islam, the real message of politics of peace and justice, which truly existed in the early history of Islam, has been already abandoned and lost. The action of *jihad* for the implementation of *syariat* Islam crystallizes the notion of exclusive religion, and fundamentalists only heed the glorious history of Islam and wish to bring back their religion to that time without any reflection on the problems of global politics today.

More or less, it is true that ideology embraced by fundamentalists pertains to violent actions and terror because of their narrow-mindedness and intolerance. A long-time conflict between Palestine and Israel has already proved that Islam – and it is the same with the Zionist movement of the Jews – is being influenced by an intolerant ideology. As a consequence, conflicts and violence have been spread, and the value of peace and justice is less appreciated. What exactly has emerged here is the enthusiasm for starting war in the name of a holy religion. Several Muslim groups in the world perpetrated a series of suicide bomb attacks and engaged in violent actions in the name of Islam, and, according to them, they are the warriors of Islam (*mujahidin*). This is how Islam is now readily associated with violence and bloodshed.

In fact, Islam, as a politically-oriented religion, strives for the realization of justice and peace. In the same manner, the understanding of the origin and the doctrine of Islam should be contextualized in accordance with contemporary global politics. Democracy, human rights, pluralism, and the freedom of religion are so important for Islam that Islam itself plays a transformative role in contemporary politics. The realization of justice and peace should coincide, and the universality of Islam should be maintained in order to create a civilization with the idea of pluralism.

Islamic scholars (*ulama*) from boarding schools (*pesantren*) in Indonesia have strategically contextualized the teaching of the peaceful realization of justice in world politics. All *ulamas* gathered under *Nahdlatul Ulama* (NU) have been actively playing their political roles for that.[7] Issues such as democracy, nationalism, pluralism, human rights, and religious freedom have become main topics of discourse for NU, which is the largest Islamic mass organization in Indonesia (perhaps the world), and NU regards these issues as the core of the faith (*beruf*) and *jihad*. Needless to say, when NU struggles with global politics, it does not unconditionally adopt the ideas and values of the West. Rather, NU takes local wisdom and value into consideration that have been written in the holy *al-Quran*. Basic teachings in *al-Quran*, such as tolerance (*al-tasamuh*), discussion/deliberation (*al-syura*), and a neutral stance in politics *(al-tawasuth wa al-adalah)*, should be the primary values of NU in the contemporary world.

Therefore, it is true that all *ulamas* struggle for the realization of democracy, not only for the sake of the word "democracy," but also for the sake of the perpetuation of law and ethics. Human rights also should be appreciated by the global society, and *ulamas* should present their views on five important human-right issues for the sake of stabilizing 'basic life' or *al-ushul al-khamsah*. The five basic human rights are: the right to have a faith (*hifzh al-din*); the right to live (*hifzh al-nafs*); the right to protect reason (*hfzh al-aqal*); the right to protect property (*hifzh al-amal*); and the right to create offspring (*hfzh al-irdl wa al-nasal*).[8] NU also views both social pluralism and religious pluralism as gifts of Allah, and Muslims should receive and transform these gifts into the three principles of brotherhood in the theology of pluralism, that is: the brotherhood of all religions (*al-ukhuwah al-Islamiyah*); the

---

[7] P.L. Berger (ed.), *Kebangkitan Agama Menantang Politik Dunia* (*The Desecularization of the World: Resurgent Religion and World Politics*), Yogyakarta, 2003, p. 26.

[8] Endang Turmudzi (ed.), *Nahdlatul Ulama; Ideology Politics and the Formation of Khaira Ummah*, Jakarta, 2003, p. 58.

brotherhood of all nations *(al-ukhuwah al-wathaniyah)*; and brotherhood of the universe *(al-ukhuwah al-basyariyah)*.[9]

The NU, as an organization representing the moderate Islamic movement, here provides an example of how the Islamic world *(dar al-Islam)* should transform the basic principles into the context of global politics. Only when Muslims uphold the above-mentioned principles will pluralism be enriched. In addition, Islam as a religion of civilization, a religion of justice, and a religion of the conveyance of compassion will develop in the process of creating pluralism in the contemporary world.

References

Abu Ridha, *Saat Dakwah Memasuki Wilayah Politik*, Bandung: Syamil Cipta Media, 2003.

Ahmad Sukarjda, *Piagam Madinah Dan Undang-Undang Dasar 1945; Kajian Perbandingan Tentang Dasar Hidup Bersama Dalam Masyarakat Yang Majemuk*, Jakarta: UI Press, 1995.

Berger, Peter L. (ed.), *Kebangkitan Agama Menantang Politik Dunia* (The Desecularization of the World Resurgent Religion and World Politics), Yogyakarta: Arruzz, 2003.

Endang Turmudzi (ed), *Nahdlatul Ulama; Ideology Politics and the Formation of Khaira Ummah*, Jakarta: PP Lembaga Pendidikan Ma'arif NU, 2003.

Fachri Ali, *Islam Pancasila dan Pergulatan Politik*, Jakarta: Pustaka Antara, 1984.

Fealy, Greg[ory], and Barton, Greg[ory] (eds.), *Tradisionalisme Radikal; Persinggungan Nahdlatul Ulama-Negara* (Nahdlatul Ulama, Traditional Islam and Modernity in Indonesia), Yogyakarta: LKiS, 1997.

---

[9] Pengurus Besar Nahdlatul Ulama, *Hasil-hasil Muktamar Ke-29 Nahdlatul Ulama*, Jakarta, 1996, pp. 27-29; G. Fealy and G. Barton (eds.), *Tradisionalisme Radikal; Persinggungan Nahdlatul Ulama-Negara* (Nadhlatul Ulama, Traditional Islam and Modernity in Indonesia), Yogyakarta, 1997, p.160.

Hinson, David F., *Sejarah Israel Pada Zaman Alkitab diterjemahkan oleh Mawene dari buku* (History of Israel), Jakarta: BPK Gunung Mulia, 2000.

Johnson, James T., *Perang Suci Atas Nama Tuhan dalam Tradisi Barat dan Islam* (Holy War Idea in Western and Islamic Traditions), Bandung: Pustaka Hidayah, 2002.

Masroer, Ch. Jb., "Bom dan Dilema Orang Beriman," *Journal Religiosa* (Fakultas Ushuluddin UIN Sunan Kalijaga Yogyakart), 1, 1 (2006): 51ff.

Pengurus Besar Nahdlatul Ulama, *Hasil-hasil Muktamar Ke-29 Nahdlatul Ulama*, Jakarta: Lajnah Ta'lif Wan Nasyr PBNU, 1996.

Roy, Olivier, *The Failure of Political Islam*, Cambridge-Mass.,: Harvard University Press, 1994.

15

Islamic Politics and Political Islam: A Standoff between Islam and the State

— Andi M. Fatwa

Islam is a well-spring that continues to be discussed, interpreted and actualized. This is also why Islam has become a multifaceted religion, something that has strengthened the existence of Islam itself. Indeed, since the beginning of its history, Islam has presented itself as a religion which addresses social conditions. The success of the Rasulullah [Muhammad] lies in his ability to put the divine teachings (revelations) into dialogue with the social realities of his time.

Dialogue is the process of acculturation or the transforming of the holy verses of God into cultural languages that can be understood by human beings of every kind. Success in translating Islam into a cultural medium or language at every level of society will increasingly make Islam the most alive, down-to- earth and authentic religion. It is in this process of transformation that various expressions of religious practice have been manifested by religious groups in different aspects of their lives – economically, politically, socially, and culturally. Economic and political systems start by forming a territory which is free of religion. This territory is celebrated by the nation's children, religious and non-religious alike. This territory is also a value-free area which could be ruled by anyone. The place of Muslims there is to introduce values which accord with the teachings of Islam. Efforts to construct such a system could be undertaken in various ways, depending on the paradigm used.

Islam's entry into Indonesia has strengthened the assumption that Islam is a religion which has always been able to put its teachings into dialogue in a continuing social-cultural context. As history shows, the acculturation effected by Islamic missionaries has shown that Islam is extremely culture-friendly. This historical fact should form a foundation for building the struggle of Muslims in the future. Islam itself teaches that goals can be reached through various doors (*min abwabin mutafarriqah*). This means that many strategies of struggle could be used by Muslims to create a life full of peace and care (*rahmatan lil 'alamin*), the main foundation behind the birth of Islam.

It is also from history that we learn that during the struggles of this current reformation era, the freedom in which to express diversity has increased. Ideally, this could generate momentum for the constructive actualization of Islamic teachings in the interests of Muslims. On the other hand, this reformation era, which has opened such wide rooms of public space, could also turn into a reaction against the freedom of public space itself, if it is not managed in accordance with the national politicies currently being developed.

In the context of state life, different sets of attitudes and behaviour currently exist in three groupings among mainstream Muslims. First, there are groups that strive to make Islam an ideology of the state to be applied in the form of Islamic *syariah*. Such groups believe that religion contains the most sacred and universal teachings capable of regulating the lives of citizens of the state. Second, there is a set of groups seeking to separate religious affairs from those of the state. Here, religion is deemed to be an area which cannot be intertwined with the state, and vice versa. Third, there are those who regard religion and the state as two interdependent conditions for the welfare of all of the nation's children. While the state plays the role of protecting and facilitating all existing religions, religion supports and strengthens the foundation of the state.

These three main approaches are rooted in differing perspectives on the mechanisms of the state, thus giving birth to divergent political attitudes and struggles. The first group emphasizes the importance of enforcing Islamic *syariah* by means of legislation carried out by the state for the sake of all its citizens. This legal enforcement of Islamic *syariah* is seen as able to provide a solution for all of the nation's problems. The second group treats the existence of a pluralistic nation as its main consideration in building such a nation. Its protagonists perceive the state as a worldly arena whose problems can be solved through a mechanism which is also worldly. God (religion) belongs to a divine territory which addresses the personal, not public, space, while the state has the authority to regulate public matters. Religion, therefore, only plays a role in strengthening relationships between individuals and God. The third group, meanwhile, puts more emphasis on the principle of mutual symbiosis, presenting both religion and the state as forces which could cooperate for the common good.

Political Reformation of the People

Until now, Islamic politics have often been identified with efforts to enforce Islamic *syariah*. This perception has arisen due to a distorted understanding and historical facts that do not always run in conformity with the universal values of Islam. This perception has not only arisen from the opinion of the groups that struggle for Islamic *syariah*, who tend to be "exclusive" insofar as they do not admit alternatives, but comes above all from anti-Islamic *syariah* groups projecting Islamic *syariah* as a "threat." Such distorted apprehensions of Islamic *syariah* have ultimately harmed efforts to enforce Islamic *syariah* itself.

The second group, on the other hand, has from the very beginning closed off any possibility for religious involvement in the state, regardless of the fact that all of its citizens have a religion, which is Islam for the majority. Seen from a democratic perspective, the perspective of the second group actually disregards the freedom and rights of citizens to realize their aspirations, including in matters of religion.

These two first groups have, at certain points, been trapped in extremism, or tendencies that prevent the emergence of a civil society (*masyarakat madani*). Neither group allows for constructive alternatives, which are much needed for the future development of democracy. Participation has only developed fragmentarily, with no common thread or synergy between each civil and religious 'social components.' As participation has been in part, no strategic ties currently exist for the empowerment of politics for those Muslims who, quantitatively speaking, form a majority in Indonesia.

Reformation: A Space for Actualizing Aspirations

Although reformation provides a public space which has become increasingly open to all strata of society, including the Muslim majority of this country, this does not automatically mean that all the wishes and aspirations of Muslims can be realized. This is evinced by the still undecided nature of various issues relating to Islamic politics, including efforts to enforce Islamic *syariah*, which has only been occasionally debated, as during elections or other key moments when opinion-holders are mobilized.

Ideally, in an increasingly more open society and with the greater possibility of socio-political participation, the struggle of the majority Muslim group becomes a very strategic matter. The struggle to enforce Islamic *syariah*, indeed, should be quite easy given the present opportunities.

In a democratic system, many factors determine the realization of aspirations. The intensity of interactions, socializations, and communications between existing social communities largely determine the level of realization of developing aspirations, since sovereignty is vested in society. The government is merely a mediator which can process and manage developing aspirations (input) and turn them into policies (output).

So far, many aspirations have been realized, particularly those related to the desire to apply Islamic *syariah*, a quite normal aspiration in a democratic society whose citizens are overwhelmingly Muslim. In a pluralistic nation with diverse cultural values, however, the majority is not an absolute factor to determine the fate of all, as if the fact of plural interests can be overlooked. Democracy must appreciate the interests and welfare of all members of the society, and this is truly accordance with the will of God. Everyone's aspirations have equal dignity and meaning irrespective of whether they come from a minority or majority group. We will, therefore, reject dictatorial, authoritarian, or tyrannical systems of power. Here, democracy must guarantee two things: recognition of aspirations; and pluralism. The struggle for aspirations, therefore, must take place in a fashion that respects the procedural framework of democracy.

In the teachings of Islam, diversity and plurality form part of *sunnatullah*, which must be respected. From this diversity, a process of interaction will develop which can only strengthen the mission of Islam as the spreader of blessings in the universe (*rahmatan lil 'alamin*), as described in the Quranic *s. Al-Anbiya*/21:107. This mission explicitly acknowledges the existence of diversity: one is expected to be inclusive, tolerant, and appreciative of all beings in the universe without prejudice against certain groups. Implicitly, this verse urges us to create a harmonious living structure by fostering interactions among different tribes, cultures, and even religions as proof of our good deeds. This is confirmed in *s. Al-Maidah*/5:48: "If God so willed, He will group men into one group (only), but as God seeks to test you with His blessings, do compete against one another in doing good..."

Strategy of Struggle

The goal of applying Islamic *syariah* law in Indonesia is based on a number of factors, among them the view that religion ought to regulate all dimensions of life. In addition, there is also a demand for an alternative ideology to replace the current modern system which has failed, and Islam is seen as just such an alternative. Given this, Islamic *syariah* should advisedly be pursued by means of two approaches.

The first approach is cultural. Here, the core of Islamic *syariah* lies in the values reflected by the attitudes and behaviour of its followers. *Syariah* forms a part of culture and mutual interaction. This process can only take place through an understanding of Islamic values which are directly reflected in everyday life. The second approach is a legal one. Here, Islamic *syariah* is to be integrated into national laws and regulations. This could be achieved through political struggle within the legislative bodies. This needs not to be considered taboo since our national laws have been derived *de facto* from four components, namely customary law, Islamic law, colonial law, and newly developed law.

These two approaches are not separate. Enforcement of Islamic *syariah* could be done synthetically, namely through sowing and realizing Islamic ideas at a cultural level and through the adoption of Islamic teachings into laws, regulations, etc. that influence the lives of the nation's children as a whole. In essence, the effort to actualize the teachings of Islam require a process that is continuous, consistent (*istiqomah*), and democratic in nature so as to operate at more than just a symbolic level.

The ideologization and doctrination of Islamic *syariah*, which disregard the cultural aspect of everyday life, would distort the rightness of Islamic *syariah*. Cases of corruption, which completely contradicts the teachings of Islam, have been rampant in Indonesia. Ironically, if the commitment to enforce Islamic *syariah* were real, corruption would be the first thing to be eradicated: it is the main enemy of a nation that has been labelled as the most corrupt in Asia. Corruption has been a driving force. Corruption has also greatly exacerbated the people's suffering. It is highly ironic that corruption should remain in society when Islam offers a set of solid rules and regulations.

The above illustrates the importance of internalizing religious values through attitudes and behaviour (culture) in place of meaningless symbolic gestures that only serve to cast religious teachings in a poor light. This process of internalization will, in turn, give rise to role models which can be used as reference point for everyone's behaviour.

Learning from History

The struggle to enforce Islamic *syariah* has not only been taking place in Indonesia, a country whose population is predominantly Muslim. In other countries with similar situations, such as in Malaysia, Pakistan, Afghanistan, Egypt, Sudan and Nigeria, the same struggle has been fought. This shows that the majority is not always identical with or does not automatically become the sole determiner of state and national policies. In addition to polarization by the majority, which perceives and places Islam as a set of teachings, the interests of political authorities count in the decision-making process. People who live in countries where Muslims are a majority must therefore struggle for the enforcing of Islamic *syariah*.

The independence of the Republic of Indonesia has ensured that pluralism and heterogeneity, cultural and religious alike, be placed within the framework of *Pancacila* and the 1945 Constitution, which also bear the imprint of strong religious values. Differences and varieties in religion have been strongly tolerated in the State of the Republic of Indonesia. Under such conditions, there is no room at all for the enforcement of religion as a state ideology, but rather the possibility of religious influences being exerted upon laws applied by the state. And this is currently the most feasible possibility in the context of religion and state relations. Three models of relationships between the state and religious laws currently exist. The first, communalization, is a relational model which sees religion as being separate from state laws. The second is nationalization, or the process of transforming religious laws into state laws. The third is theocratization, when the national laws are based on specific religious laws.

Of the above three models, nationalization represents the most strategic approach to transform Islamic *syariah* into national law. As a result, it is through this much celebrated democratic procedure that we see momentum today for Muslim aspirations.

Islamic Values in our Constitution

In truth, various Islamic values have already been instituted in our constitution. The values of Islam have for the most part been adopted in the carrying out of state life. Although it is hard to deny the fact that Western (Dutch) law is still dominant, it would be a challenge for us all to adopt Islamic laws in our state laws through strategic and democratic political steps. Several Islamic laws, which have been recognized as state laws, include the Law of Marriage, the Law of the Conduct of the Hajj Pilgrimage, the Law of Tithe (*Zakat*), the Law of Religious Foundations (*Wakaf*), and the Presidential Decree on the Compilation of Islamic Law. This indicates that the state has given us room to pursue our goal of implementing Islamic teachings.

Even the preamble of the 1945 Constitution contains clearly Islamic nuances, as in the sentence "Due to the blessings of Allah the Almighty." Unfortunately, however, such acknowledgment has stopped short, without any concrete effort being made to express our gratefulness for independence. Independent Indonesians, possessed of a vast and fertile territory, should have been able to lead their nation to a richer and more prosperous life. Abundant natural resources and vast swathes of forestry have, instead, turned into arenas of greed and voraciousness, in turn damaging the environment.

Even during the swearing of inaugural oaths, the name of God (Allah) has become meaningless because it is merely recited rather than realized practically. Corruption has plagued every level of government at both central and regional levels, as well as in the bureaucracy and political parties. We are not yet in a position to guarantee that Islamic *syariah* could indeed eradicate all of these moral failings. Throughout its history, the formalization of Islam has often stopped short at the level of formality and symbols far distant from the attitudes and behaviour patterns of its followers. States which profess an Islamic ideology are not any better and at times even worse than those which are secular in nature.

These facts prove that ideologies or other forms of doctrines do not always guarantee a better life, even though *syariah* itself has been made for the common good, for both Muslims and others. Islamic law, as several *fiqh* texts record, emphasizes the protection of life, possessions, future generations, properties, and honour. These five elements are, of course, universal in nature and not rights that are exclusive to Muslims. It is here that work of transforming supreme and universal Islamic values into culture in the form of attitudes and behaviour plays so important a role.

On the Affiliations of the Indonesian Authors

(in order of appearance)

Luthfi Assyaukanie is Co-founder of Liberal Islam Network, and Lecturer at Paramadina University.

Lily Zakiyah Munir is Director of Centre for Pesantren and Democracy Studies*

The late **Abdurrahman Wahid** was the Fourth President of the Republic of Indonesia and former Chairman of Nahdlatul Ulama

Zakiyuddin Baidhawy is on the Presidium of the Muhammadiyah Youth Intellectual Network and Lecturer at State Institute of Islamic Studies, Salatiga.

Siti Musdah Mulia is Senior Researcher of the Ministry of Religious Affairs in Indonesia*

Soffa Ihsan is Manging Editor of Islamic Magazine *MataAir*

Abu Bakar Ba'asyir is a founder and former Chairperson of *Majelis Mujahidin Indonesia* (and has been accused of being connection with Jaama Islamiyah). He established new organization called Jaama Anshoru Tauhid in 2008, and is currently on trial for allegedly funding terrorist activities.

Ismail Yusanto is on the Presidium of Hizbut Tahrir Indonesia.

Eka Jaya is an activist of the Islam Defenders' Front known as FPI

Qothrun Nadaa is an Activist of Hizbut Tahrir Indonesia*

Cecep Firdaus is Chairperson of Majelis Tabliq Indonesia

Bismar Siregar is former Supreme Court judge of Indonesia

Zulkieflimansyah is on the Executive of the Prosperity and Justice Party writing with **Yon Machmudi**, Lecturer at the University of Indonesia, with both being founding members of PKS

Andi Muarly Ramly is on the Executive of National Awakening Party

Andi M. Fatwa is fomer Vice-Speaker of Indonesian Parliament; and as a member (now Deputy Chairman) of the National Mandate Party, he was jailed for his involvement in Tanjung Priok incident (the clash between Muslims and Indonesian army) in 1984

---

* Women Muslim leaders in Indonesia.